The Time-Life Gardener's Guide

DESIGNING YOUR GARDEN

A

REDEFINITION
BOOK

Other Publications:

MYSTERIES OF THE UNKNOWN
TIME FRAME
FIX IT YOURSELF
FITNESS, HEALTH & NUTRITION
SUCCESSFUL PARENTING
HEALTHY HOME COOKING
UNDERSTANDING COMPUTERS
LIBRARY OF NATIONS
THE ENCHANTED WORLD
THE KODAK LIBRARY OF CREATIVE PHOTOGRAPHY
GREAT MEALS IN MINUTES
THE CIVIL WAR
PLANET EARTH
COLLECTOR'S LIBRARY OF THE CIVIL WAR
THE EPIC OF FLIGHT
THE GOOD COOK
WORLD WAR II
HOME REPAIR AND IMPROVEMENT
THE OLD WEST

For information on and a full description of any of
the Time-Life Books series listed above, please write:

Reader Information
Time-Life Customer Service
P.O. Box C-32068
Richmond, Virginia 23261-2068

Or call:

1-800-621-7026

This book is one of a series of guides to good gardening.

The Time-Life Gardener's Guide

DESIGNING YOUR GARDEN

TIME-LIFE BOOKS, ALEXANDRIA, VIRGINIA

CONTENTS

THE FRONT YARD

OUTDOOR LIVING SPACE

THE GARDEN FLOOR

arden design is largely a matter of organizing space. Each part of a garden serves a distinct purpose. The front yard must look attractive, but it also must provide access to the house. The backyard calls for a sense of seclusion; it is where a family spends private time. The lawn and beds are the foundations for plantings —grasses, ground covers, shrubs and flowers. Walls, arbors and pools are structural accents; they separate one part of the garden from another and provide background for the plantings.

Each of the how-to techniques contained in this volume is set in the context of such a unit of the garden. How to build a flagstone path, for instance, appears *(pages 14-15)* in a chapter about the front yard because some kind of pathway is sure to be needed there. But the same technique is applicable to laying a flagstone path in the backyard or anywhere else. Similarly, double digging—a technique for creating a deep, rich planting bed —is in a chapter entitled The Garden Floor, but double digging can be done when preparing the soil for any part of the garden.

For plant information, see the Dictionary of Plants; for assorted tips on design, maintenance and troubleshooting, see Making the Most of Nature.

4
ADDING DIMENSIONS

5
MAKING THE MOST OF NATURE

6
DICTIONARY OF PLANTS

1
THE FRONT YARD

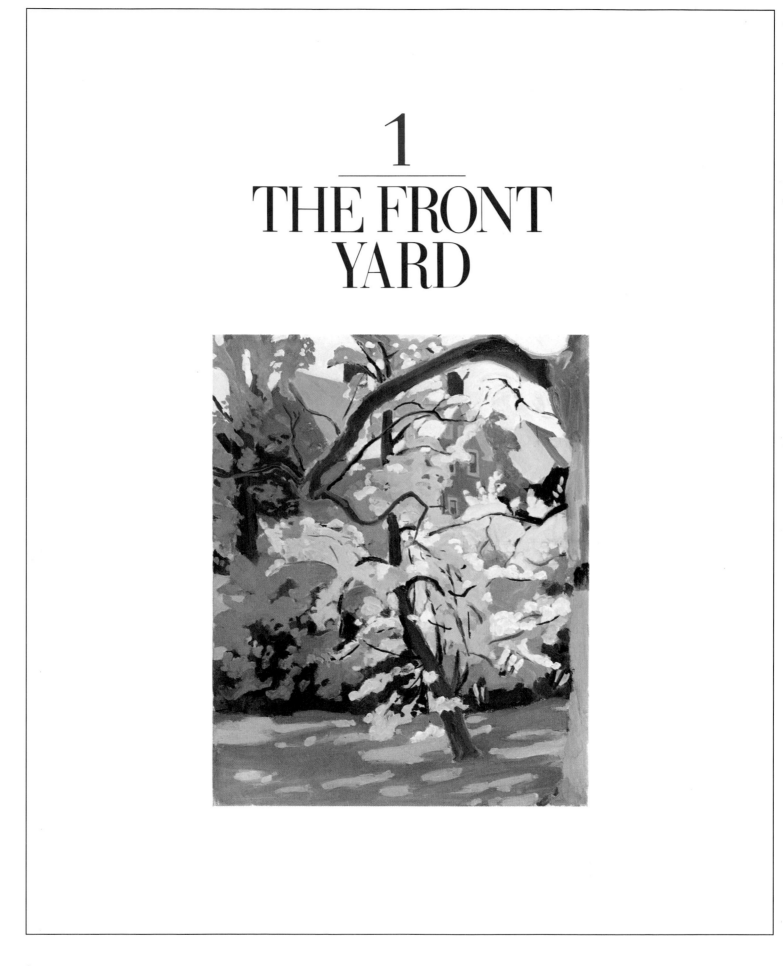

More than any other garden area, the one at the front of the house reflects the tastes of its owners. Probably this is because in the front yard alone, the garden is purely decorative. It does not have to function as a playground or an outdoor dining room; its sole purpose is to frame the house and to welcome guests.

In pursuit of this goal the design of the front yard can be serenely simple, composed of only a few well-chosen types of plants, artfully arranged. Or it can be exuberant and colorful, punctuated with unexpected combinations of textures and shapes. It can project the look of a tousled cottage garden or reflect the formality of a mirrored palace. The only stricture that applies to its design is that it must look good in all seasons; the front yard has no downtimes.

To achieve these year-round decorative ends, professional gardeners routinely rely on several basic plant types. Trees, sometimes even a single tree, will provide a visual point of focus; shrubs, often called the workhorses of the garden, establish line and shape and texture—and are sometimes a source of seasonal color. Azaleas, for instance, are synonymous with spring, and the familiar red berries of the pyracantha decorate the winter lawn. Rounding out the list are the bulbs and herbaceous annuals and perennials that come and go, enlivening the scene with flashes of color.

On the pages that follow, you will find ideas for creating this ornamental setting and ways of handling some of the common tasks required: how to plant a tree and a shrub, how to choose and plant spring-flowering bulbs for optimum effect, how to propagate your own flowers from seeds. Because the walkway from street to house is an important component of the front yard, you may want to lay one, as shown. And finally, to save you from having to correct a gardening mistake, the chapter tells how to plan the design for your front yard with paper and pencil—before you actually set shovel to soil.

PLANTING SHRUBS FOR GREEN AND GROWING DECOR

The white and pink flowers of low-lying azaleas accent the entrance to this fieldstone and shingle house. Azaleas bloom best when shielded from excessive sun and wind, so they make ideal additions to yards dominated by large shade trees.

Shrubs are among the most versatile elements in garden design. A single shrub can become a focal point that draws the eye; a row of shrubs can form a backdrop for colorful flowering plants. Shrubs can be shaped to give either a formal or an informal feel to your yard and can add line, color and texture to a plan.

Designing with shrubs poses a challenge, since seasonal changes and continual growth alter a shrub's appearance. The front-yard forsythia that exhibits a flare of springtime yellow will summer in green anonymity before stripping to a wintry skeleton of bare branches. The young shrub you plant today will grow taller and fuller, taking on new shape in a few years' time.

Shrubs that will enhance your yard season after season, year after year, are available in three categories: deciduous shrubs, such as forsythia and lilac, which lose their leaves in the fall; broad-leaved evergreens, such as rhododendron and holly; and needle-leaved evergreens, such as juniper and yew.

Plant shrubs in cool weather to avoid subjecting them to high temperatures and intense sunlight. Early spring and fall are ideal planting times, since the roots can get established before the shrub blossoms or before the ground freezes. The shorter the branches, the better the shrub can expend its energy establishing roots. If you buy a new shrub at a garden center, ask if it has already been pruned. If not, prune off one-third to one-half the branches' length before planting.

Shrubs less than 3½ feet high can be set in the ground by hand. A bigger shrub should be rolled onto its side and eased into place with the aid of its burlap wrapping *(opposite);* do not handle a shrub by its branches or they may break. The root balls of most shrubs come wrapped in natural-fiber burlap, which will decompose quickly in the soil. When you buy shrubs, ask if they are wrapped in chemically treated or synthetic burlap; if so, request specific planting instructions.

1 With a shovel, mark a circle twice the width of the plant. Dig a straight-sided hole to a depth 1 to 2 inches less than the height of the root ball; save the soil. Sprinkle fertilizer into the hole; adjust the amount according to the variety of plant and type of soil. Roll the shrub onto its side and ease it into the hole. Hold the shrub by its root ball; avoid handling the branches.

2 To position a shrub so its most attractive side faces a desired direction, grip the wrapper in two places and twist. If the burlap is pinned to the root ball, unpin two corners to get a firm grasp. With rope-tied burlap, grip any two loose areas. Settle the shrub so the root ball's top sits 1 to 2 inches above the ground.

3 Mix the remaining soil with organic amendment and shovel it into the hole until the root ball is half-covered. With the shovel handle, tamp the soil to eliminate air pockets *(above)*. Continue adding soil, leaving ½ to 1 inch of root ball aboveground.

4 Sprinkle fertilizer over the area covering the root ball, then grade the soil in a gentle slope away from the trunk. At the outer edge of the root area, build an earth dike 3 inches high to catch water. The dike will wash away with rain; maintain it for the first few months while the roots get established. Spread 2 to 3 inches of mulch around the shrub with a spading fork and a rake; leave a small space between mulch and trunk so the mulch will not draw moisture to the trunk, away from the roots. Soak well. □

TREES TO GIVE STRUCTURE TO A LANDSCAPE

A young sycamore maple rises past the roof of a low-lying suburban house, its rounded shape contrasting with the flat planes of house and lawn, its leafy branches providing shade. The sycamore maple is a fast-growing tree that reaches approximately 70 feet at maturity.

A tree can dramatically alter the character of your yard. It imposes structure on a landscape and creates a focal point of interest. Choosing the right tree for your yard—and planting it—is a simple matter if you know what result you want to accomplish and avoid a few common pitfalls.

First, select a shape that will suit your purposes. If you want strong vertical lines to frame a path, tall evergreens would make a good choice. If you want to shade a sunny patio, choose a rounded deciduous tree.

Next, consider scale: select a tree that will still fit its context when fully grown. Make sure you plant it where it has room to grow safely; branches overhanging a chimney can be a fire hazard, and spreading roots may interfere with buried pipes that pass through the yard. A tree too big for its site or in the wrong place may eventually have to be cut down. Your nursery can tell you how much space to allow for each species of tree.

Climate, soil, drainage, and exposure to sun and wind can spell the difference between a healthy tree and a wasted investment. See what kinds of trees flourish in your area and ask your nursery for advice on what to plant.

There are, of course, many more aspects to consider in choosing a tree. You may desire a bold splash of autumnal color, or a ready source of fruit, or shade for the warmer months. For each of these purposes, and more, there is a suitable tree. Consult the Dictionary of Plants *(pages 96-152)* for the characteristics of various trees.

Trees come from the nursery in three different ways: bare-rooted, in containers and with the root ball wrapped in burlap. If you buy a balled-and-burlapped tree, ask whether the wrapping is natural burlap. If it is not, ask for planting instructions.

A method for planting a flowering dogwood sapling wrapped in natural burlap is shown at right and on the following pages. One caution: handle a tree by its root ball, not by its trunk; if it is held by the trunk, the weight of the soil in the root ball might break off some of the roots.

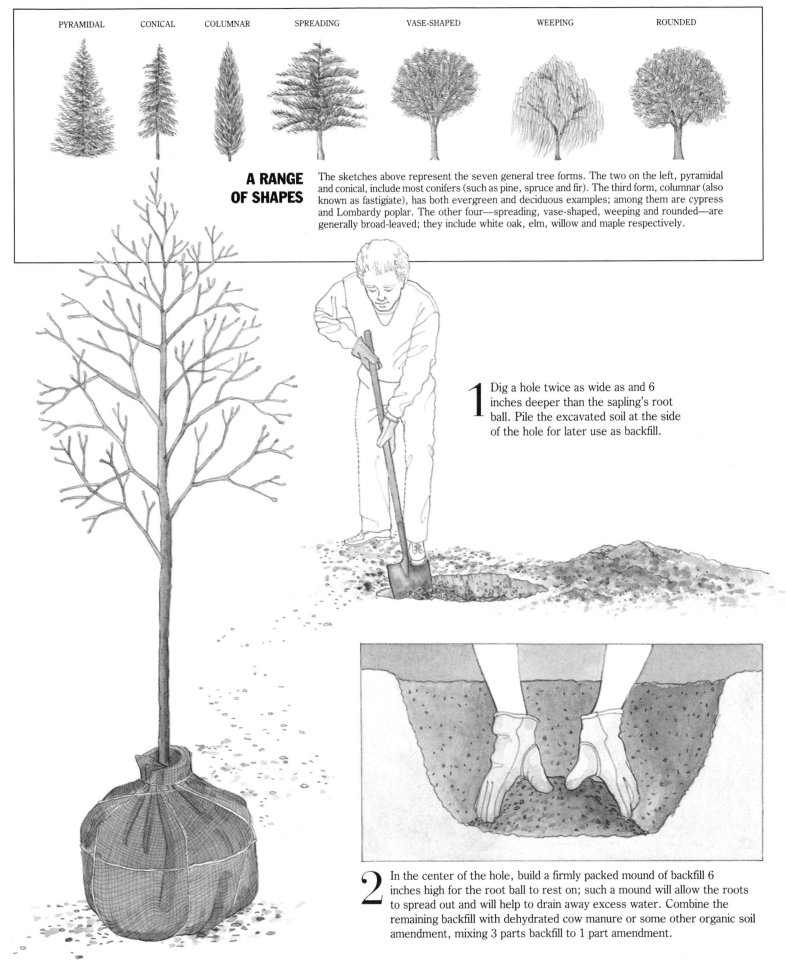

A RANGE OF SHAPES

PYRAMIDAL CONICAL COLUMNAR SPREADING VASE-SHAPED WEEPING ROUNDED

The sketches above represent the seven general tree forms. The two on the left, pyramidal and conical, include most conifers (such as pine, spruce and fir). The third form, columnar (also known as fastigiate), has both evergreen and deciduous examples; among them are cypress and Lombardy poplar. The other four—spreading, vase-shaped, weeping and rounded—are generally broad-leaved; they include white oak, elm, willow and maple respectively.

1 Dig a hole twice as wide as and 6 inches deeper than the sapling's root ball. Pile the excavated soil at the side of the hole for later use as backfill.

2 In the center of the hole, build a firmly packed mound of backfill 6 inches high for the root ball to rest on; such a mound will allow the roots to spread out and will help to drain away excess water. Combine the remaining backfill with dehydrated cow manure or some other organic soil amendment, mixing 3 parts backfill to 1 part amendment.

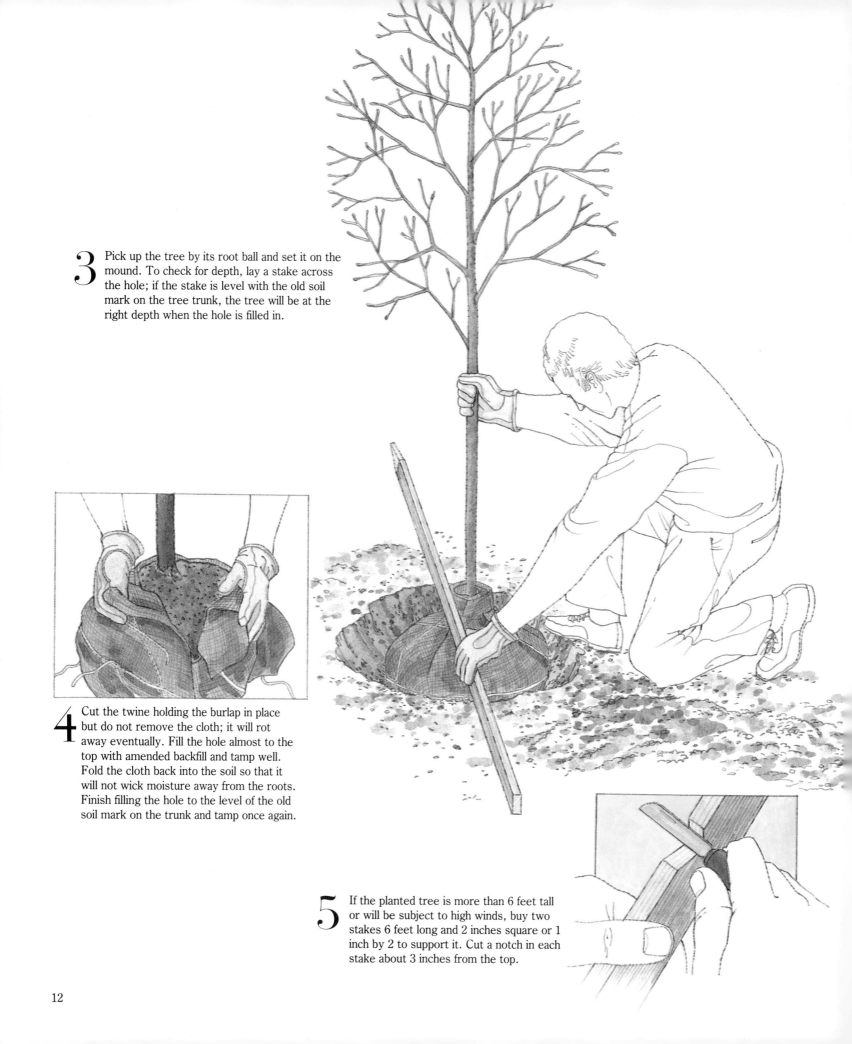

3 Pick up the tree by its root ball and set it on the mound. To check for depth, lay a stake across the hole; if the stake is level with the old soil mark on the tree trunk, the tree will be at the right depth when the hole is filled in.

4 Cut the twine holding the burlap in place but do not remove the cloth; it will rot away eventually. Fill the hole almost to the top with amended backfill and tamp well. Fold the cloth back into the soil so that it will not wick moisture away from the roots. Finish filling the hole to the level of the old soil mark on the trunk and tamp once again.

5 If the planted tree is more than 6 feet tall or will be subject to high winds, buy two stakes 6 feet long and 2 inches square or 1 inch by 2 to support it. Cut a notch in each stake about 3 inches from the top.

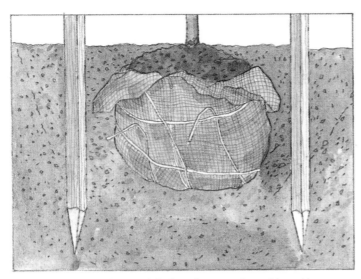

6 Drive the stakes straight into the ground on either side of the root ball; they must go deep enough to reach into the firm soil below the filled hole. Form a basin at the outer edge to concentrate water on the roots, where it is needed most. Spread mulch 2 to 3 inches deep around the tree, leaving a small space between the mulch and the trunk. Soak the root ball with water.

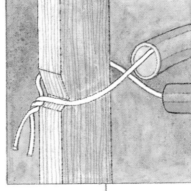

7 Cut two pieces of garden hose, each 1 foot long, and slip each one over a 3- or 4-foot length of wire; the hose will protect the tree trunk. Bend one hose-covered section of the wire around the trunk; loop the protruding wire ends into a figure eight and secure them in the notch of one stake. Repeat with the other piece of hose, wire and stake. Leave the wires loose enough for the tree to flex with the wind. The stakes may be removed after a year. □

PAVING THE WAY THROUGH THE YARD

A paved walkway is both practical and esthetically pleasing. It forms a transition from one part of the yard to another, and it helps direct foot traffic. Materials of various kinds can be used: brick, tile, masonry blocks or flagstone.

You can buy flagstones cut in rectangles; or, for a jigsaw effect, you can lay flags of random shapes and cut the edges to fit together. Use a circular saw, and wear goggles and a nose mask when cutting the stone. You may want a helper; flags are heavy to lift.

Lay out the path with string or garden hose. To accommodate two people walking abreast, a path should be about 3½ feet wide. Mark the outlines with lime. Figure the square footage of the path. The measure will be converted into weight at the quarry where you buy the flagstones.

In excavating the bed, dig from the outer edges toward the center to keep the sides sharply defined. Remove enough earth so the flags will be flush with the ground after they are laid over 4 inches of crushed stone. Spread the crushed stone; then make sure the surface slopes ¼ to ½ inch per foot from side to side for drainage. Wet the stone with a fine spray from a hose to settle the dust and wait a day before laying the flags.

Lay the flags with the smoother side up. Place smaller stones in the center and larger stones at the edges. The larger stones are more stable; they help preserve the edges of the path and hold the center in place. Think ahead about which stones will fit together well, so you have a minimum of cutting to do and won't be left with stones that don't fit together at the end of the walk.

Flagstones of various shapes fit together in a design that seems to unite with the pattern of shadows cast by nearby trees. The crevices are filled with crushed bluestone, which blends with the flags and helps hold them in place.

1 After excavating the path and spreading crushed stone, lay two flags. If the edges do not match, place the edge of one stone on top of the other. With a stonemason's chisel, scratch the outline of the upper edge onto the surface of the lower one.

2 With the masonry (or carbon) blade of a circular saw, cut about halfway through the flagstone along the traced line. Wear gloves, goggles and a nose mask to protect against flying chips and dust.

3 With the chisel, scratch a matching line on the underside of the flagstone; turn it on edge to check the cut on the opposite side as you go.

4 Place the chisel on the scratched line and strike it with a stone hammer. Move along the line, striking the chisel until the stone breaks; this may require two or three passes along the line. If the new edge is uneven, chip away the roughness with the chisel.

5 Put the flag in place alongside the first one —allowing ½ inch of space between them. As you lay the stones, check the slope from center to sides repeatedly; if necessary, adjust the crushed stone bedding with a trowel. Pound each flag with a rubber mallet to secure it. When you have finished, sweep crushed stone across the surface to fill the spaces between flags and wet the walk with a fine spray. □

COLORFUL BULBS
THAT HERALD SPRING

A broad swath of tulips forms a warm, welcoming curve leading to a front door. The red flowers border a broad expanse of green lawn, creating bold color contrast. The gray-green foliage softens the combination.

Flowers are the glory of the garden. They provide the color that gives it personality and character. They lift the spirit in spring, after the bleakness of winter; they perk up the dog days of summer and they brighten the lengthening shadows of fall.

You can change color from season to season against an established backdrop. To conduct a successful show, first develop a plan. Use colors singly or in combination to achieve special effects, and maintain color as long as possible by planting with the seasons in mind.

In selecting a color theme, consider some facts of color theory having to do with analogous and complementary colors *(opposite)*. Then plan for the spatial effects you want. Warm colors, such as red and orange, seem to advance, and are useful at the far end of a yard because they are visible from a distance. Cool colors, such as blue and violet, tend to recede and give an open feel to a small area.

White flowers stand out in the dark and are effective in a garden that you use at night. To give a finished look to your overall design, plants with gray-green foliage will unite different elements and soften the hard edges between colors.

Different types of flowering plants can be mixed to provide color throughout the growing season. Spring-blooming bulbs will come to life soon after all danger of freezing is past; other bulbs emerge with the first signs of fall. Annuals started indoors can be transplanted in early spring, and perennials will surface for late-spring and summer color.

To kick off a parade of color in the first rush of spring, create a bed of spring-flowering bulbs. Plant the bulbs in the fall, either singly in individual holes, or if you have a large area to be planted, in trenches, as shown here. Bulbs provide an inviting feast for rodents, so protect your investment by lining the trench with wire mesh. For continuing color when spring yields to summer, see the following pages.

COMPLEMENTARY AND ANALOGOUS COLORS

Complementary colors are pairs of contrasting hues—blue and orange, yellow and purple, red and green. In flowers, these color pairs can form bold combinations, such as blue hyacinths and orange tulips, yellow daffodils and purple iris, red tulips and green-leaved hosta *(above)*. Analogous colors adjoin on the spectrum and may share a basic pigment. Some examples are pink tulips with purple crocus and blue grape hyacinth; or red anemones, orange daffodils and yellow crocus *(right)*.

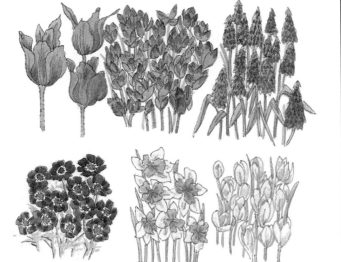

1 Dig a trench 2 to 8 inches deep, depending on the type of bulb and the instructions provided by the mail-order house or the garden center from which you buy them. Line the floor and the sides of the trench with wire mesh to protect against burrowing animals. Cover the flooring mesh with 1 to 2 inches of soil mixed with superphosphate or bone meal.

2 Arrange the bulbs in the trench. Check the bulb package for correct spacing. If you are not sure which end of the bulb is the top, lay it on its side; the stems will always grow upright. Cover with soil. Water well. □

BRIGHT HIGHLIGHTS FOR SUMMER: ANNUALS AND PERENNIALS

For garden color in summer and fall, consider the vast variety of annuals and perennials. Annuals sprout, mature, bloom, bear seed and die in one growing season. Perennials live for years, dying back in winter, then resurrecting to produce flowers summer after summer. The two types of plants work well in combination. Most annuals bloom longer than perennials, but perennials have varied leaf shape and texture.

Generally, annuals and perennials require little care after they have been planted, and both supply midsummer color without much effort on the gardener's part. Since perennials provide stable flower color and foliage each year, annuals offer greater flexibility. Their one-season life span allows the gardener to change color and, to some extent, design every summer.

Annuals are easily started from seed. Seeds can be sown directly into the garden, but insects and disease organisms in the soil may harm them and delay flowering. It is better to start seeds indoors and transplant the seedlings into the garden in early spring.

Seeds can be planted in nursery flats, low boxes or cut-down milk cartons. Be sure the containers have holes in the bottom for drainage. Fill each container to within 1 inch of the top with sterile potting soil and moisten. After planting, cover the container with a plastic bag to create a greenhouse effect. Water often enough to maintain a slight film of moisture on the inside surface of the bag.

Once transplanted, annuals need frequent watering to prevent wilting. Snip off old blossoms every few days to encourage new growth and to keep the garden looking fresh.

This brilliant multicolor border combines rows of three summer-blooming flowers. Tall cosmos plants form the backdrop for zinnias and marigolds. All three plants are annuals that bloom from late June to the first frost.

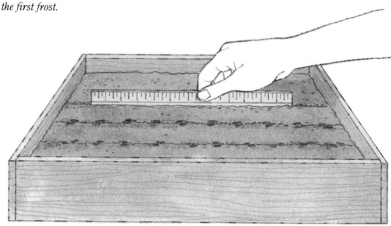

1 Fill a container with potting mix. With a ruler, make indentations for rows. Plant seeds as suggested on the packet. Not all seeds will germinate; the type and age of the seeds affect germination.

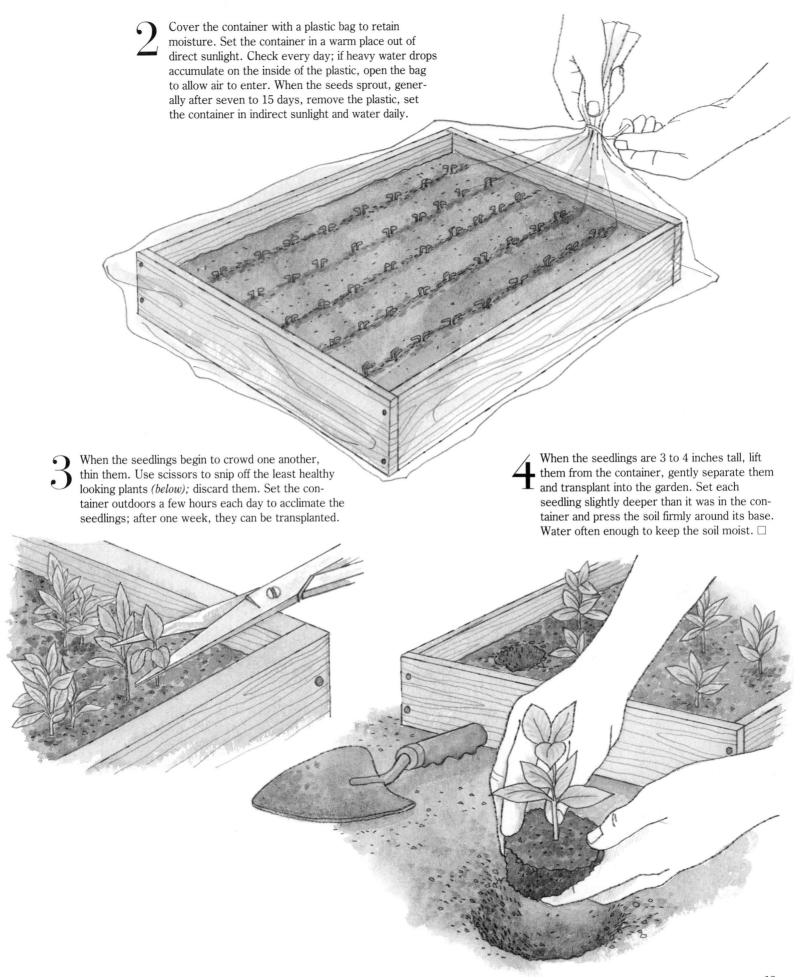

2 Cover the container with a plastic bag to retain moisture. Set the container in a warm place out of direct sunlight. Check every day; if heavy water drops accumulate on the inside of the plastic, open the bag to allow air to enter. When the seeds sprout, generally after seven to 15 days, remove the plastic, set the container in indirect sunlight and water daily.

3 When the seedlings begin to crowd one another, thin them. Use scissors to snip off the least healthy looking plants *(below)*; discard them. Set the container outdoors a few hours each day to acclimate the seedlings; after one week, they can be transplanted.

4 When the seedlings are 3 to 4 inches tall, lift them from the container, gently separate them and transplant into the garden. Set each seedling slightly deeper than it was in the container and press the soil firmly around its base. Water often enough to keep the soil moist. □

FOR SUCCESSFUL DESIGN: A PLAN ON PAPER

The foundation for a well-designed yard and a beautiful garden is a drawing that you make of your existing property. Such a drawing is called a base plan. One of its most important functions is to give a two-dimensional overview of the space you have to work with. A careful look at the base plan will reveal relationships between large plants and small ones, and between them and the spaces you have to fill. It will enable you to try out different arrangements—before you make costly mistakes with real plants.

To begin, draw the base plan on graph paper with eight squares to the inch. Let the length of each square equal 1 foot; if necessary, tape two sheets of paper together. To get the boundary and house measurements, you can use the plot survey of your property, or you can do the measuring yourself with a 50- or 100-foot carpenter's measuring tape.

To try out different designs, lay a piece of tracing paper over the base plan and sketch in the plants you want to add, allowing for their size at maturity. A colorful border will define an area; ground cover will unify several plantings. Give thought to what designers call focal points—places on which the eye focuses. An intersection of two lines (as in a corner) is a ready-made focal point and a good spot for an attractive planting. You can create a new focal point by placing a tree or any other conspicuous planting in the middle of an open expanse of lawn. Consider how various trees, shrubs and flowers will look from different angles—and how they will look in different seasons and at different times of day. Consider wind pattern. For example, if cold north winds blow through your yard, consider planting tall evergreens to block them. If one design doesn't work on paper, just take a fresh sheet and try another.

Lacy white alyssum and purple lobelia edge a curving border of pink and orange impatiens, leafy rhododendron and graceful juniper that combine to draw the eye to an inviting front door.

1 After determining the measurements, draw property boundaries and the outline of your house on graph paper. Draw in the driveway, walkways, and existing trees, shrubs and flower beds. Indicate the direction north and any other pertinent information—an unsightly view to be obscured, the location of a septic tank, a window from which you want to maintain or create a pleasing view, the prevailing wind direction.

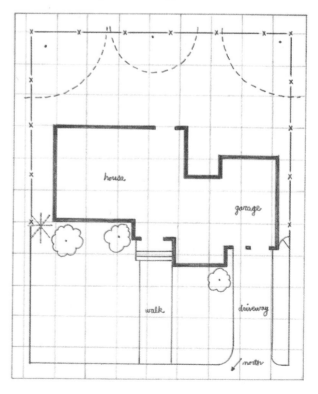

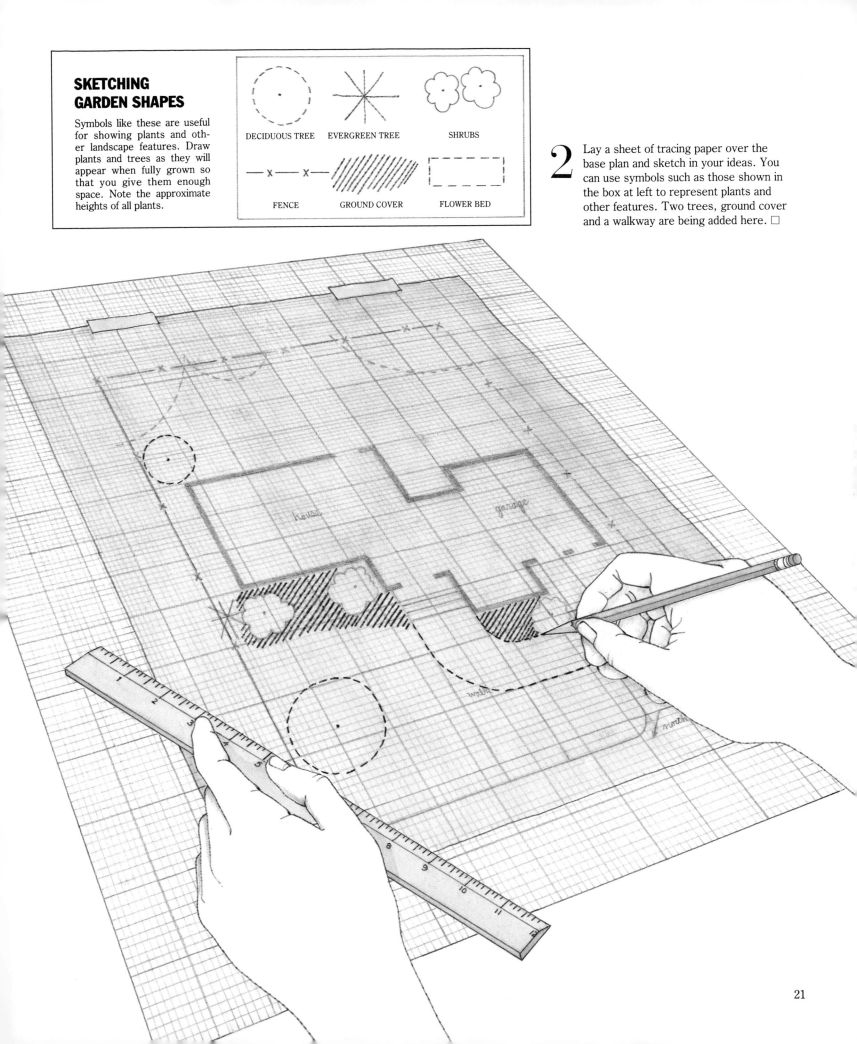

SKETCHING GARDEN SHAPES

Symbols like these are useful for showing plants and other landscape features. Draw plants and trees as they will appear when fully grown so that you give them enough space. Note the approximate heights of all plants.

DECIDUOUS TREE   EVERGREEN TREE   SHRUBS

FENCE   GROUND COVER   FLOWER BED

2 Lay a sheet of tracing paper over the base plan and sketch in your ideas. You can use symbols such as those shown in the box at left to represent plants and other features. Two trees, ground cover and a walkway are being added here. □

21

2
OUTDOOR LIVING SPACE

Behind the house, away from the street, is the garden that most passersby never see. But that garden is a constantly changing scene of family activity. It is a playground, an outdoor dining room, a peaceful, private place for reading, sunbathing or simply watching the progress of a bee as it flits from flower to flower in search of nectar. The garden may contain a jungle gym and a wading pool, a dog run and a kitchen garden, an assortment of outdoor furniture, a compost pile and a tool shed, and the ubiquitous barbecue.

With all those demands made on it, the garden is likely to pose some special design problems. To keep it looking tidy, the plantings must often function as screens or dividers without actually interrupting the sense of space and movement through the area. The following pages show you how to use flowering shrubs to create just such a screen.

Also of special concern in this outdoor living space are the disposition of sun and shade, conditions that vary in importance with season and personal predilection, and that in turn dictate the choice of plant materials. To help you plot the changing patterns of sun and shade across the garden, several pages of diagrams show you the angles of the sun's rays for two common latitudes in the United States at three times of day on the two days of the year, summer and winter solstice, when the rays are at their most extreme.

In other sections of this chapter you will learn how to build a simple brick terrace set on a bed of sand, how to light the garden at night for both safety and drama, how to start a maintenance-free wildflower meadow. And finally, because the changing needs of a growing family often alter the design of this garden area, you will find tips on how to move major plants from one place to another, using the ball-and-burlap technique of professional gardeners.

THE DECIDUOUS HEDGE: A BLOSSOMING GARDEN BORDER

The bright blossoms and gracefully sweeping foliage of hydrangea make a beautiful boundary marker. These fast-growing shrubs reach up to 25 feet, flower from June to September, tolerate sun or partial shade, and can be used in a freestanding hedge or as a screen against a wall.

The beauty of outdoor spaces is determined not only by what you see but by what you don't see. A hedge can hide an unsightly view, divide garden areas, increase privacy, and screen out noise and wind. Hedges vary from orderly green walls of privet to less formal plantings of shrubs such as forsythia and hydrangea, which are often left unpruned. Your choice will depend on local climate and soil and your taste in landscape design. Evergreen hedges make the best year-round screens, but many deciduous hedges are hardier and grow faster.

Plant a hedge in early spring, so the roots establish themselves before summer's heat, or in early fall, before the ground freezes. You can purchase shrubs by mail order or from garden centers. Since most deciduous shrubs come with bare roots, plant them right away to keep the roots from drying out.

Shrubs can be set either in individual holes or in a common trench. Check with your supplier for proper spacing; leave enough room between plants to allow them to grow together without crowding.

Whether you use holes or a trench, make the opening 6 inches wider than the spread of the roots. Dig to the same depth that the shrubs were accustomed to at the nursery. To determine this depth, look for a soil line on the bark near the base of each plant; bark that was underground will be lighter in color than bark that was exposed to sunlight.

If you can't plant the shrubs right away, protect them by a method called "heeling in." Unwrap the shrubs and lay them almost flat with their roots in a 6-inch trench in a shaded part of the yard. Cover them with loose, moist soil. Top with mulch. Under ideal conditions—wet weather, dormant plants (most mail-order shrubs arrive with neither leaves nor buds yet sprouted)—heeling in can safeguard shrubs for up to two weeks.

If the shrubs have not already been pruned, prune them when you plant; then let them grow undisturbed for one season. Trim in the spring of the second year. Taper the hedge from a wide bottom to a narrow top so low branches will receive adequate light.

1 Use string and stakes to mark the planting area. After digging, mix 2 parts of the removed soil to 1 part peat moss. Place enough of this soil mixture in the bottom of the hole so that, when the soil is tamped, the shrub will sit at its previous planting depth.

2 With pruning shears, clip any root ends that are damaged, dry or too long for the hole. Tamp soil into a compacted mound. Set the shrub on the mound, spreading its roots carefully *(right.)* Add more amended soil, then work the soil between the roots by hand. Tamp to eliminate air pockets. Fill the hole with water.

3 When the water drains away, fill the hole with soil. Surround the area with a 2- to 3-inch earth dike. Prune any branches that are dead, dry or touching other branches, and shorten new stems until you have cut the shrub back to half its original height. Make cuts at a 45-degree angle, just above the outside buds. A slanted cut dries faster after a rain, and new growth from the buds is directed outward and upward. □

MAKING USE OF SUNLIGHT AND SHADOW

As afternoon wanes, the lacy shadow of a tall shade tree lies across a sunny lawn, making a pleasing pattern on the otherwise unbroken expanse of green grass.

When seen by an observer in the Northern Hemisphere, the sun appears higher or lower in the sky at different seasons, and different times of day, and its position determines the angle at which its rays strike the earth. At greater angles, sunlight will pass through more of the earth's atmosphere before reaching the earth, losing both brightness and heat en route. The maps here and on the following page indicate the two latitudes—46° N and 34° N—between which most Americans live. The more northerly (46°) runs from Washington on the West Coast to Maine on the East; the southerly (34°) from California to Georgia. The farther north you live, the longer the shadows; the farther south, the shorter. You can approximate the length of the shadows in your area by reference to these two extremes—and use the information in designing your garden. Walls and hedges can be sited to block or trap the sun's heat; beds and shrubs can be placed so they receive some light each day. Sun-loving annuals like marigolds belong in beds that face south or west, where the sun is strongest. Broad-leaved evergreens like rhododendrons and holly do best in shady northern and eastern exposures because they cannot tolerate too much sun.

WEST

Shadows shown on this page are cast along the 34th parallel, which runs from California to South Carolina *(above, heavy line)*. South of this line, shadows cast by a house and plantings of the same size are shorter, north of it longer *(overleaf)*.

On June 22, the sun creates small shadows as it passes above a house located on the 34th parallel. The shadow cast by a two-story house extends 9 feet to the west at midmorning, shifts north and contracts to 5 feet by noon, and stretches 22 feet east at 3 p.m. The 18-foot-tall tree shades little more than its own roots at noon. To keep a west-facing patio (behind the house in this illustration) shady in the afternoon, plant a tree with large overlapping leaves, such as Southern magnolia. In the front yard, roses will benefit from intermittent shade. Plants for sunny southern and western exposures include hibiscus and bougainvillea.

10 A.M.

NOON

3 P.M.

On December 22, shadows cast by the same two-story house in the same latitude are much longer because the sun is much lower in the sky. The shadows range from a noontime minimum of 41 feet to a midafternoon maximum of 90 feet. A one-story house in the same location on the same day would cast shadows half the size. To keep sun-loving shrubs such as yucca and fire thorn warm in the winter, back them up with a heat-retaining brick wall.

SHADOWS OF THE NORTH

Shadows on these pages are cast along the 46th parallel, which runs across the northernmost United States from Washington to Maine *(above, heavy line)*.

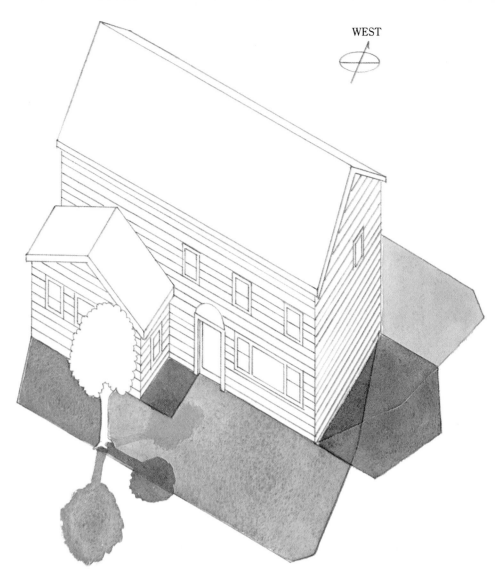

WEST

At 3 p.m. on June 22, a two-story house located along the 46th parallel casts a 12-foot shadow toward the east. Morning and noontime shadows are much smaller. The house and tree illustrated here are exactly the same size as those on the previous page. The shadow under the 18-foot tree varies from 12 feet at midmorning to 8 feet at noon to 14 feet at 3 p.m. Even partly shaded areas can have flowers all summer long if you plant shade-tolerant perennials like anemones, columbines, begonias, hostas and primroses.

10 A.M.

NOON

3 P.M.

At noon on December 22, the shadow cast by a house on the 46th parallel extends 68 feet to the north. By midafternoon a tongue of shade stretches 160 feet to the northeast. To get the best use of a patio in so northerly a latitude, plant a deciduous tree nearby to spread cooling foliage over it in summer and let warming sunlight through its branches in spring and fall. Dress up a fully shaded exposure on a north-facing wall with hostas, ferns and local woodland wildflowers that thrive on limited light. □

29

THE BRICK TERRACE: A HAVEN IN THE YARD

A brick terrace provides a platform for dining outdoors—in a tranquil setting that is surrounded by shrubs and ground cover, and partially shaded by trees.

A terrace is an outdoor room with a view. It is also an integral part of garden design because it serves to show off plantings. It may stand on a flooring of flagstone, tile, masonry blocks or virtually any other hard surface that weathers well, but a perennial favorite is brick.

Brick comes in any number of colors and textures and can be arranged in a variety of patterns *(box, lower left)*. These and other patterns can be laid inside perimeters of all sizes and shapes, from curved to rectangular. In addition to all that, brick is easy to install.

If you decide to install it yourself, make sure of the grade of your land. A terrace must be slightly sloped so that water will neither puddle on the terrace itself nor drain in the direction of your house. The chances are that the land was properly graded when the house was built—but check to be sure *(box, opposite)*. Once you have determined that the grade is adequate, dig away about 4½ inches of soil—enough to accommodate a 3-inch drainage bed underneath 2½-inch bricks. You can make the bed of sand, but crushed bluestone provides a firmer base. The finished brick surface should lie 1 inch above the surrounding ground.

Take care in choosing brick. Buy bricks made for the outdoors, ones that can stand up to severe weather. Do not use salvaged bricks, which may crack in the thaw that follows a winter freeze. Give some thought, too, to the pattern. Bricks designed to be laid with sand fill are twice as long as they are wide and can therefore be used with the running bond pattern. Bricks designed to be laid with mortar are made in different dimensions and may not work with some other patterns.

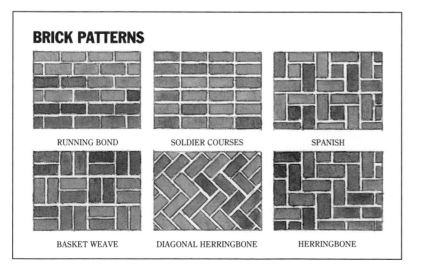

BRICK PATTERNS

RUNNING BOND   SOLDIER COURSES   SPANISH

BASKET WEAVE   DIAGONAL HERRINGBONE   HERRINGBONE

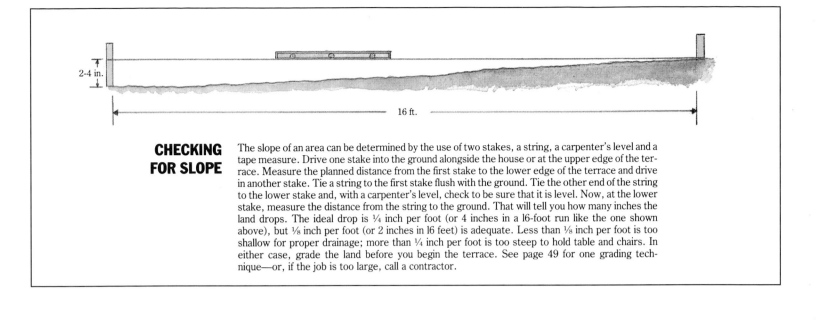

2-4 in.

16 ft.

CHECKING FOR SLOPE The slope of an area can be determined by the use of two stakes, a string, a carpenter's level and a tape measure. Drive one stake into the ground alongside the house or at the upper edge of the terrace. Measure the planned distance from the first stake to the lower edge of the terrace and drive in another stake. Tie a string to the first stake flush with the ground. Tie the other end of the string to the lower stake and, with a carpenter's level, check to be sure that it is level. Now, at the lower stake, measure the distance from the string to the ground. That will tell you how many inches the land drops. The ideal drop is ¼ inch per foot (or 4 inches in a 16-foot run like the one shown above), but ⅛ inch per foot (or 2 inches in 16 feet) is adequate. Less than ⅛ inch per foot is too shallow for proper drainage; more than ¼ inch per foot is too steep to hold table and chairs. In either case, grade the land before you begin the terrace. See page 49 for one grading technique—or, if the job is too large, call a contractor.

1 At the house wall, drive stakes at 4-foot intervals along the breadth of the terrace. From the first corner stake, come out from the house at a right angle and measure the planned distance from the house to the lower edge of the terrace and drive another stake. Tie a string 1 inch above the ground at the house stake and run it level to the stake at the far corner. At this stake, lower the string ⅛ to ¼ inch for every foot of the distance from the house. Do the same on the opposite side of the planned terrace. Tie strings connecting the four corner stakes to form the perimeter and add intermediate stakes every 4 feet. If the ground is irregular at the perimeter *(inset),* fill in or cut away soil to reach within 1 inch of the string. Inside the perimeter, irregularities will be corrected when you excavate.

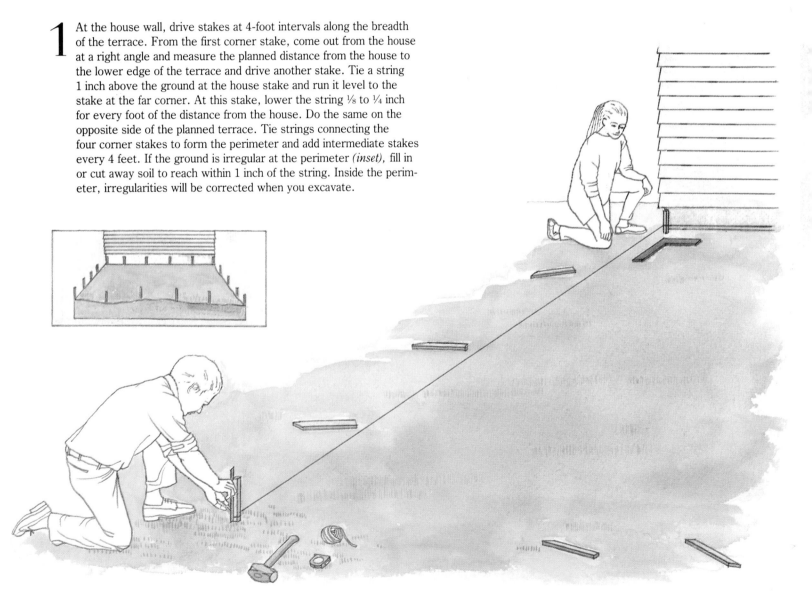

2 Dig out the soil within the perimeter of the terrace to a depth of 5½ inches below the string. Cart the excavated soil away in a wheelbarrow; save enough of it to use as fill for any smoothing needed along the perimeter and dispose of the rest.

3 Fill the excavated area with crushed bluestone, spreading it about 3 inches deep. With a tamper and a 4-foot board, tamp and level the bluestone so that it is about 2½ inches below the level of the perimeter strings. Where the perimeter string crosses the intermediate stakes, tie additional strings to make a grid *(inset)*.

4 Starting at a corner, lay perimeter bricks along the house wall, placing them side by side and snugly against one another. Make the tops level with the perimeter string; if necessary, adjust the bluestone underneath and pound the bricks into place with a rubber mallet. If the end brick does not fit in the far corner, cut into the soil, or fill in. Then turn the corner with a new line of bricks, laying them at a right angle to the first line. Go around the perimeter in this fashion.

5 To lay the running bond pattern, halve a brick; score it by tapping with a hammer and a mason's chisel around the middle. With the chisel on the scored line *(inset),* hit the brick sharply; it should split in half. Lay a half brick at the corner edge and then lay full bricks end to end across the first line, ending with a half brick. Lay a second line of full bricks; place half bricks at the start and end of alternate rows. Lay all bricks so the tops touch the grid of strings. When finished, spread sand over the surface and sweep it into the spaces between bricks. □

TRANSPLANTING SHRUBS: GETTING THEM OFF TO A GOOD START

Graceful juniper branches look feathery but are prickly to the touch; the needles are fine and grow close together but are sharply pointed at the ends. This coniferous evergreen prefers hot, dry, sunny conditions.

There are many reasons for transplanting a shrub. Its present site may be overcrowded; you may have an empty spot elsewhere you would like to fill; or you may simply want to change the look of your garden. Transplanting is easy to do—but it causes a shock even to healthy plants. To minimize the shock, prune the plant before moving it, because the less top growth it has to support, the better its roots can take hold. Cut off a third to a half of the branch growth. Then wrap the pruned plant in burlap *(opposite)* to protect its branches during transplanting.

When you dig into the soil, be careful not to cut into the fine "feeder" roots, the ones at the outer limits of the root system. They carry nutrients to the plant, and a shrub cannot afford to lose many of them. To safeguard them, keep a large ball of soil around the root system and wrap the root ball in two more pieces of burlap *(pages 37-39)*. The only expendable part of the root system is the taproot, which extends straight down into the ground and anchors the plant. It must be severed before the shrub can be removed from the ground. Slice through it with a sharp blow of a spade.

The best time to move a shrub is in the early spring, before the year's new growth has begun. Cool, moist weather is ideal. Carry small shrubs by hand, gripping them just above the root ball, where the branches are strongest. Transplanting a large shrub is a two-person job. You can use a wheelbarrow or a cart, but you may find it easier to slide the shrub onto a drop cloth and drag it along like a sled.

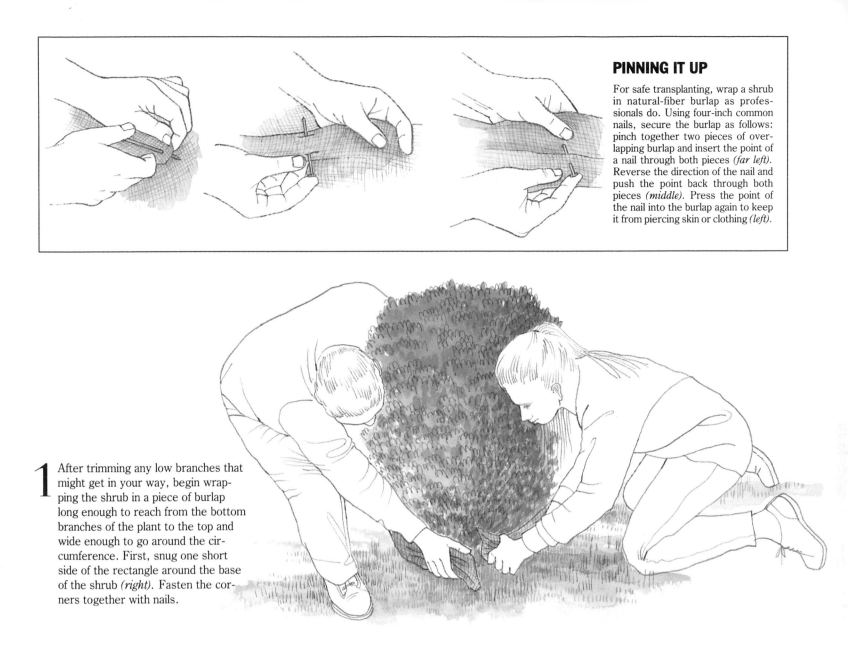

For safe transplanting, wrap a shrub in natural-fiber burlap as professionals do. Using four-inch common nails, secure the burlap as follows: pinch together two pieces of overlapping burlap and insert the point of a nail through both pieces *(far left)*. Reverse the direction of the nail and push the point back through both pieces *(middle)*. Press the point of the nail into the burlap again to keep it from piercing skin or clothing *(left)*.

1 After trimming any low branches that might get in your way, begin wrapping the shrub in a piece of burlap long enough to reach from the bottom branches of the plant to the top and wide enough to go around the circumference. First, snug one short side of the rectangle around the base of the shrub *(right)*. Fasten the corners together with nails.

2 Pull the other short side of the burlap rectangle over the top of the shrub so that it hangs in a flap *(left)*. Grasp the corners of the flap and pin them together to form a protective hood.

35

3 Pull firmly on the long sides of the burlap rectangle until they overlap in front. Pin the overlapping edges together *(left)*, using as many nails as you need; start from the base of the shrub and work toward the top.

4 Using a spade, mark a circle in the ground approximately one-third larger than the diameter of the shrub *(right)*. Keep the blade facing away from the plant. Dig a trench around the outside of the circle, always moving the soil away from the shrub.

5 Now turn the spade so that the blade faces the plant. Dig down deep, at a slight angle toward the roots, in order to loosen the soil around and under the plant's root system. Wherever you meet resistance, feel around with your fingers for the fibrous feeder roots and leave as many of them unharmed as possible.

6 To prevent loose soil from falling off the root ball when you move it, make a burlap skirt big enough to go around the root ball (a garden center can estimate the size if you give it the circumference of the shrub). To prepare the burlap for wrapping, find the midline by folding the long sides of the rectangle together. Then use a knife or pruning shears to cut along the midline; stop about three-quarters of the way down, leaving two long "tails."

7 Lay the burlap on the ground with a tail on each side of the shrub. Pull the tails toward you and snug them close to the top of the root ball. Pin the tails tightly around the root ball as follows *(diagram, below):* overlap and pin together corners 2 and 3. Bring corner 6 to the front of the shrub and pin it to the same spot. Fold over corner 4 and do the same. Repeat with corner 5. Then fold over corner 1 and pin it slightly to the right of the other pinned corners. Check for loose folds and secure with more nails.

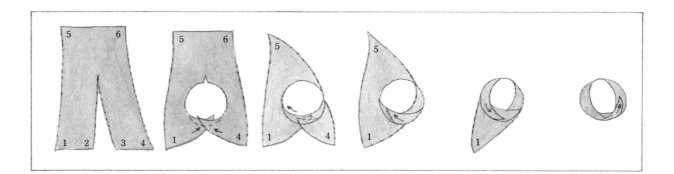

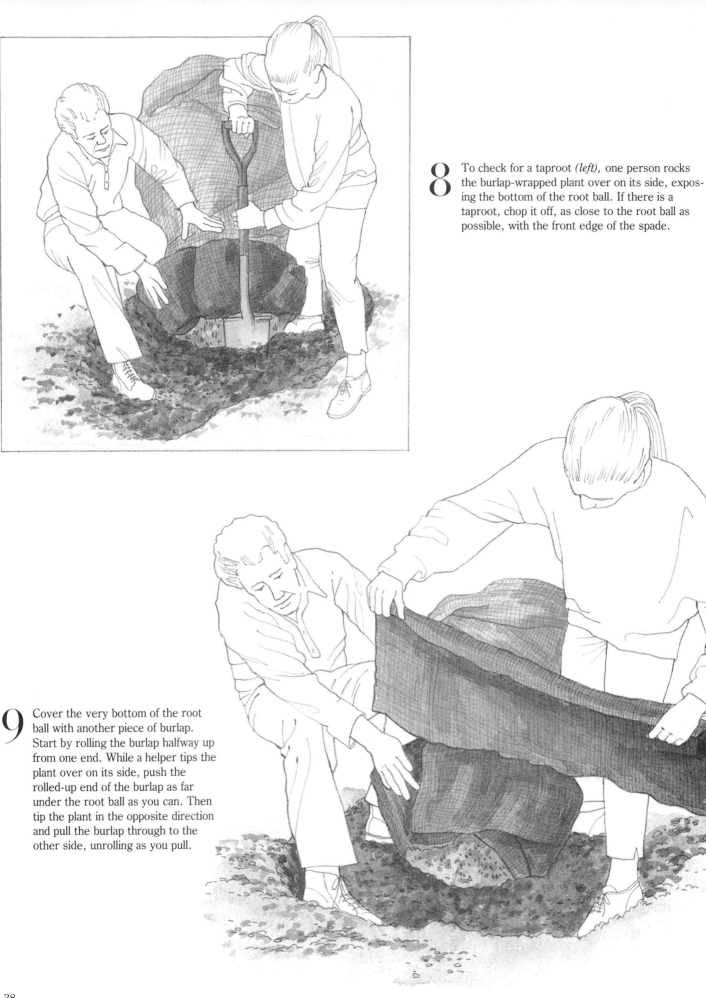

8 To check for a taproot *(left),* one person rocks the burlap-wrapped plant over on its side, exposing the bottom of the root ball. If there is a taproot, chop it off, as close to the root ball as possible, with the front edge of the spade.

9 Cover the very bottom of the root ball with another piece of burlap. Start by rolling the burlap halfway up from one end. While a helper tips the plant over on its side, push the rolled-up end of the burlap as far under the root ball as you can. Then tip the plant in the opposite direction and pull the burlap through to the other side, unrolling as you pull.

10 Taking hold of diagonally opposing corners of the burlap *(right)*, pin them together across the top of the root ball. Before pinning the last two free corners, pull up firmly and shake the root ball to make sure that it is as tightly packed as possible. Then pin together any remaining loose flaps and openings.

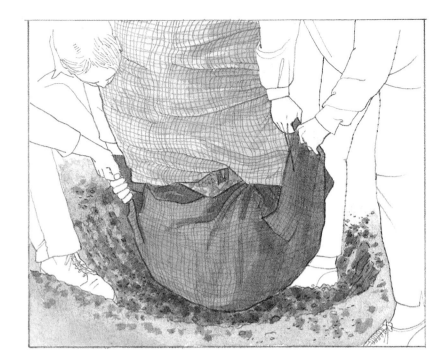

11 To lift the shrub, tip it to one side. Shovel some of the previously removed soil back into the hole *(above)*. Tip the shrub onto this backfill and shovel soil from the other side into the hole *(right)*. Tip the shrub again and add more soil from the first side. Continue alternately tipping the shrub and backfilling until the hole is full and the shrub has been raised to ground level. The shrub is now ready for planting somewhere else *(page 9)*. □

COLLABORATING WITH NATURE TO CREATE A WILDFLOWER MEADOW

A meadow vibrates with a showy blend of bluebonnet and orange Indian paintbrush, two colorful wildflowers native to the Southwest.

A wildflower meadow is one of the most pleasurable gardens to grow. You use plants native to your area, so you can create a field that seems to have sprung up naturally. It will do almost that. Wildflowers are so hardy and prolific that the gardener need only give the meadow a good start and an annual mowing to control weeds.

Most wildflower seed mixes are designed for specific conditions—for location, for kind of soil, for shade or for sun. The packet label will describe the growing conditions and the type of seeds the mix contains. Avoid mixes containing invasive species that will choke out the flowers you want. To find out what plants are invasive in your region, and to check the reliability of various commercial mixtures, consult a local wildflower society.

Some communities prohibit uncut fields on front lots; check your local ordinances or plant the meadow in your backyard. Do your annual meadow mowing in the fall, after the flowers have produced seed, or in the early spring, before growth starts.

HOLDING BACK THE FOREST PRIMEVAL

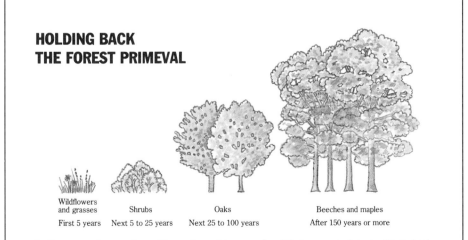

Wildflowers and grasses
First 5 years

Shrubs
Next 5 to 25 years

Oaks
Next 25 to 100 years

Beeches and maples
After 150 years or more

Left unmowed, a meadow will revert to wilderness. Land that was once forest will turn back to forest in precise stages. The outcome of this process varies by region. In the northeastern United States *(above)*, grasses and wildflowers will yield to shrubs after several years. Soil changes will then permit a succession of evergreen and deciduous trees to flourish. In time, oaks will grow; then maple and beech will dominate what is known as a climax forest, an environment that stays stable unless upset by catastrophe or human intervention.

1 To prepare for sowing, wet the soil and remove by hand any unwanted plants that can be easily yanked out. Then turn the soil with a rotary tiller *(above)* or with a heavy-duty garden fork to a depth of 2 inches.

2 Water the tilled area thoroughly to encourage all exposed weed seeds to germinate. After one to two weeks, remove weed sprouts with a hoe *(below)*. Remove rocks unearthed by tilling, break up large soil clods and smooth with a steel rake.

3 Soak the seedbed. Blend coarse sand with seed mix to add volume and aid in even distribution. Then sow by hand *(left)* or by spreader. Go from one end of the field to the other, then make a right-angle turn and walk back and forth again as shown in the diagram. You will need 5 to 6 pounds of seed per acre.

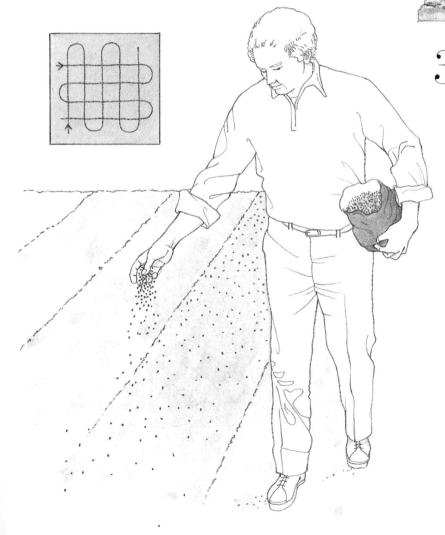

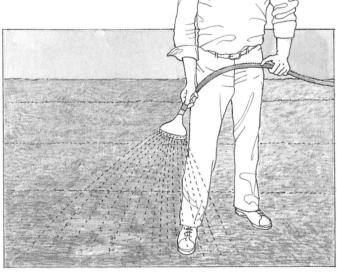

4 Cover the seedbed with hay to keep the seeds from blowing away. Spray daily *(above)* until the seedlings are established—usually about four to six weeks after seeding. Be careful not to step on the young seedlings. □

LIGHTING THE GARDEN AFTER NIGHTFALL

A circle of half-hidden flood lamps gives strong emphasis to the upward thrust of these California redwoods. Against the deeply shadowed background, the glowing bark and foliage suggest warmth and sanctuary.

Lighting a garden for nighttime activity and viewing offers a rare opportunity to combine the practical and the dramatic. Unobtrusive ankle-high lamps that guide visitors down a flight of garden steps after sunset may open the way to a spotlit stand of trees whose branches cast fantastic shadows on the wall behind them.

There was a time when the obvious benefits of outdoor lighting—enhanced access, security and beauty—were beyond the means of most gardeners. Equipment was costly and hazardous to install, and even the smallest job called for an electrician or a landscape architect. The advent of low-voltage lighting systems has changed all that.

Low-voltage wiring carries only 12 volts, the same as your car's electrical system, instead of the 120 volts that household fixtures use. You can buy do-it-yourself kits from hardware stores or garden centers for as little as $100. No permits or special skills are needed. A typical kit comes with a transformer box (for stepping down household current to 12 volts), a built-in timer, 100 feet of plastic-covered wire, a half-dozen weatherproof lighting fixtures and spikes to hold the fixtures in place.

Hang the transformer box on an outside wall near a three-pronged household outlet. Position the box at least 18 inches above the ground (you can mount it higher for more convenient access). If the wall is brick, hammer a masonry nail (with grooved sides to prevent slipping) into the mortar between bricks; leave ½ inch of nail projecting from the wall to support the transformer box.

Wire all lamps in daylight. Do not plug the transformer into the household outlet until the entire system is wired. Even a low-voltage electrical fixture can give you a small shock.

Lighting a garden is like painting with light and shadow. In general, less is better than more. Overlighting can make healthy plants appear sickly or artificial. Try for a natural look that brings out the drama inherent in the setting. This works best when the source of light is hidden from view. Mask fixtures behind trees, shrubs, branches and borders.

1 To try different lighting effects, move around your garden at night carrying a standard bulb (40 watts or less) in a clamp-on socket at the end of a grounded extension cord. Shield the bulb with cardboard. Drive a stake into the ground and clamp on the socket. Aim the light at plants and across steps. Leave a stake wherever you plan to place a lamp.

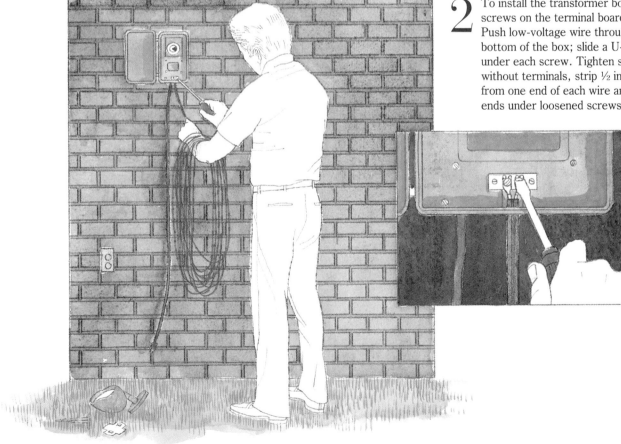

2 To install the transformer box, loosen both screws on the terminal board *(inset, below)*. Push low-voltage wire through the hole in the bottom of the box; slide a U-shaped terminal under each screw. Tighten screws. For wire without terminals, strip ½ inch of insulation from one end of each wire and wind the bare ends under loosened screws. Tighten.

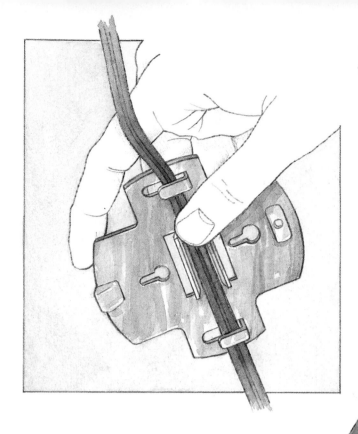

3 Unroll the low-voltage wire the full length of your predetermined layout to make sure you have enough for the project. Remove the screw from the base of the first lamp and detach the base plate. Slide the wire under the two metal clasps on the base plate—opening the clasps with pliers, if necessary—so that the wire lies in the trough between clasps *(left)*. Make sure that the lamp will face in the desired direction and slide the wire under the clasps from the proper side. Wire the rest of the lamps in the same way.

4 Reassemble the lamp base and the base plate *(right)*, making sure that the screw holes line up. Press tightly together: the two sharp pins in the base of the lamp will pierce the plastic-covered wire in the trough on the base plate. Replace the screw in the screw hole and tighten.

5 To attach the lamp to its supporting spike, insert the two knobs on the top of the spike into "keyholes" on the base of the lamp. Remove the wooden stake you left as a marker and push the spike into the hole. When all the lamps are wired, plug in the transformer and test the system at night. Reposition any lamps that shine into bypassers' eyes or neighbors' windows.

6 Aim the lamps so the light spills horizontally across paths and steps; this will keep people from walking into their own shadows. To hide low-voltage wire, dig a narrow, 6-inch-deep trench and bury it. Where the wire can't be buried, run it along borders; staple it to wood with insulated staples. □

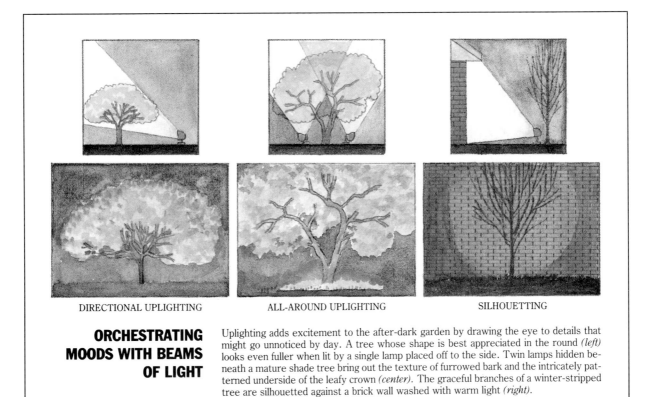

DIRECTIONAL UPLIGHTING   ALL-AROUND UPLIGHTING   SILHOUETTING

ORCHESTRATING MOODS WITH BEAMS OF LIGHT

Uplighting adds excitement to the after-dark garden by drawing the eye to details that might go unnoticed by day. A tree whose shape is best appreciated in the round *(left)* looks even fuller when lit by a single lamp placed off to the side. Twin lamps hidden beneath a mature shade tree bring out the texture of furrowed bark and the intricately patterned underside of the leafy crown *(center)*. The graceful branches of a winter-stripped tree are silhouetted against a brick wall washed with warm light *(right)*.

3

THE GARDEN FLOOR

Few people can resist the sight of a perfect lawn—smooth, healthy and weed-free—but people despair of ever achieving the ideal. Yet there is no mystery to creating a showpiece carpet of green. On the following pages you will find techniques for going about it. The drill begins with a series of steps designed to prepare the soil and improve its contours so that it drains properly and is free of humps and hollows. That accomplished, you can turn to the choice of grass. Some varieties are noted for their beauty, others for their durability under foot traffic, or for their ability to thrive, for example, in shade or in salt air. Finally, you will find criteria for weighing the virtues of sod versus seed, and information about the best procedures for installing both.

But a lawn is not always the best solution to carpeting the garden floor. Sometimes shade is too deep or tree roots are too close to the surface for the shallow roots of the lawn grasses to compete with. Sometimes the ground slopes too steeply for grass roots to anchor themselves and too steeply for a lawn mower to negotiate safely. Sometimes the existing soil is simply too inimical to lawn grasses for them to survive without constant applications of corrective chemicals.

In such cases, ground covers other than grass make more sense. Ivy, pachysandra, lily of the valley, honeysuckle, cotoneaster and liriope—these are but a few of the many plants that can substitute for grass. Indeed, their decorative potential, in terms of color, texture and shape, often makes them preferable to grass. And many of them are relatively maintenance-free.

To round off this section on the design of the garden at ground level, you will learn how various kinds of edgings—of stone, brick or wood—define the boundaries between lawn and flower beds. Finally, you can consider raised beds and terraces, both of which are effective means of dealing with difficult terrains and soils that are better replaced than corrected.

SMOOTHING OUT
THE BUMPS AND HOLLOWS

*A lawn sweeps steeply, but at a regular pitch, past a house,
carrying away rainwater and providing an interesting combination
of planes and angles as background for the plantings.*

Grading—the process of smoothing off land—is the
basic earth-moving technique used to develop landscape. It is
done to ensure adequate drainage and to provide the smooth
foundation necessary for lawns, walks and patios. It eliminates
steep slopes that cause erosion of topsoil and that make walking hazardous and planting impractical. But grading does not imply the cre-
ation of a surface that is perfectly horizontal or one that is unvaryingly
flat; some slope is desirable so that rainwater will run off, and some
contouring gives character to the landscape.

Good grading takes advantage of the leaning of the ground. The job
may be as simple as evening out the odd high spot that looks unsightly
and the random depression that tends to puddle (or to cause pratfalls).
Or it may be as elaborate as constructing stepped terraces (which simul-
taneously aid drainage and discourage soil erosion by allowing land to
drop considerably but in graduated stages).

Changing a slope on a large scale is work for a professional landscape
contractor. But minor irregularities can be easily fixed in a weekend's work.
With a flat-edged spade, a steel rake and a tarp you can transfer soil from a
spot that has too much to another that hasn't enough, as shown here.

1 With a spade, cut the turf away from the area to be graded. Roll it up and place it on a tarp for later use. Dig out the topsoil and save it. Scrape the subsoil from the high spots and shovel it into the dips. Dig down about 6 inches. Remove stones and break up the subsoil to improve aeration and drainage.

2 Tamp down the fill by treading on it. Add more fill and tamp again if necessary to achieve a solid base that is even with the adjoining subsoil. Shovel on the saved topsoil, work in such soil amendments as humus and fertilizer, and rake smooth. Finally, replace the turf and step on it to press it firmly into the topsoil. □

RAISED BEDS: FUNCTIONAL GARDEN ACCENTS

Rustic timbers form a raised bed that sets off a weeping crabapple, gives a finished look to the garden and minimizes any drainage problems.

A handsome solution to many a garden problem is a raised bed. It lets you accent a featured plant or flower cluster with a border of materials that blend with the landscape. When connected to a house, it softens architectural lines and provides a gentle transition from house to garden. A raised bed can also be used as a design element in its own right and to separate garden spaces.

Raised beds have practical value, too, and can turn problem areas into usable space. They improve drainage by elevating the garden, thus saving the expense of drainage system installation. Ease of maintenance is another asset, since a raised bed brings plants to a convenient height and confines leaves and other debris to the garden area.

Raised beds can be made from various materials. Redwood planks and railroad ties make long-lasting beds that blend well with most landscape features. Brick, stone and landscape timbers also make sturdy and attractive beds. Brick and stone beds are secured with mortar; wooden beds *(opposite)* with steel rods. Because some communities have regulations about the size and placement of permanent structures, check with your local authorities before building a raised bed.

To begin, mark the area with stakes and string. Level the bed so the timbers will lie flat, remove loose stones and tamp the soil.

1 Measure the perimeter of the bed and cut timbers to size; for support, use a sawhorse or place one timber across two others. Two to 3 inches from one end of each timber, drill a hole *(right)* for steel rods that will secure the corners vertically. Make the hole about the same diameter as the rod.

2 Place the first course of timbers on the prepared site, alternately butting the end of one timber against the side of another to create a square, as shown. Continue adding timbers to the desired height, alternating the butting sequence and aligning the holes for placement of the steel rods.

3 Anchor the timbers at each of the four corners with a steel rod that is 1 foot longer than the height of the bed. Using a heavy hammer, drive each rod vertically through the holes into the ground until the top of the rod is level with the top surface of the timbers.

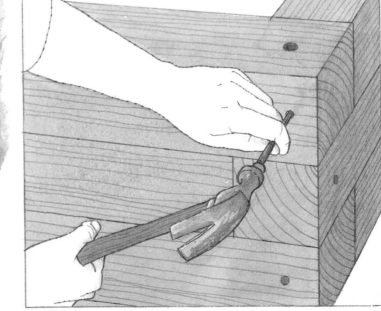

4 Drill a hole horizontally through one end of each corner timber for a spike to secure it to its neighbor. Make the holes slightly smaller than the diameter of the spikes. Drive the spikes through the timbers to secure each end. To prepare for planting, place 4 inches of gravel in the bed. Add soil mixture to no more than 2 inches from the top. □

LAYING OUT LAWN AND BED SPACE

Beds of mixed shrubs and flowers seem to disappear in several places behind foliage, giving a sense of spaciousness to this garden.

Garden beds, those cultivated plots dense with flowers, ferns and shrubs, contribute flavor and vitality to landscape design. Rather than merely decorating an existing space, imaginative bed design can change a yard's look to create an entirely new feeling.

Professional gardeners have a number of tricks for creating illusions of space. One of them is the use of bold curves. The flower bed that spills into the lawn and retreats to the far shrubs takes on a sense of movement. An island bed that stands alone surrounded by a sea of grass can add interest to a patch of green. A bed's placement can make the difference between framing and blocking a good view.

Landscape architects suggest mapping out the yard to make a base plan before designing the beds. Base plans show all the dimensions of the area and indicate the existing elements the design will need to include—the house, garage, trees, areas of sunlight and shade, for example. You can easily make such a plan yourself *(page 20)*.

By drawing several plans on sheets of tracing paper laid over the base plan, you can explore different effects. After picking the design you like best, mark out the beds. This requires nothing more than a tape measure, a garden hose, and a straight-edged spade or an edging tool.

Getting to know the yard is probably the most important part of bed design. Spend time there, study it from the windows, view the yard from different angles. Consider how the area will be used. Then start to work.

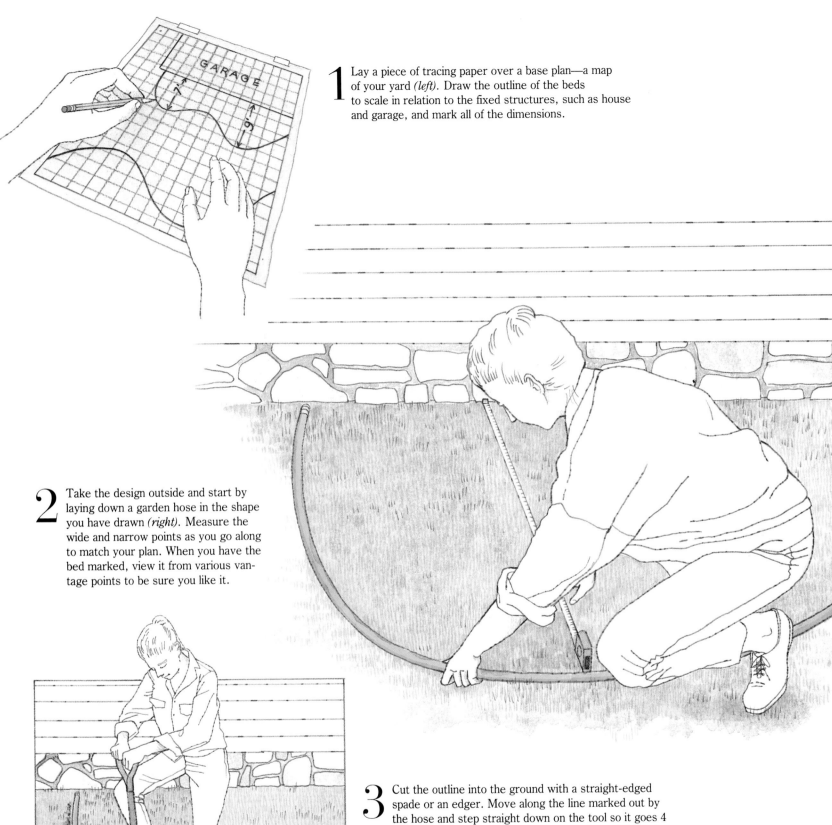

1 Lay a piece of tracing paper over a base plan—a map of your yard *(left)*. Draw the outline of the beds to scale in relation to the fixed structures, such as house and garage, and mark all of the dimensions.

2 Take the design outside and start by laying down a garden hose in the shape you have drawn *(right)*. Measure the wide and narrow points as you go along to match your plan. When you have the bed marked, view it from various vantage points to be sure you like it.

3 Cut the outline into the ground with a straight-edged spade or an edger. Move along the line marked out by the hose and step straight down on the tool so it goes 4 to 6 inches deep. Pull the handle toward you, lifting the dirt outward and forming a narrow trough. □

A HEALTHY LAWN FROM THE ROOTS UP

The best way to get a trouble-free lawn is to plan ahead. After the site has been laid out, graded and provided with adequate drainage, you can decide whether to start your lawn from seed or lay precut strips of sod. Sod yields quick results, but it costs more than seed, and grass grown from seed develops deeper, denser—and thus healthier—roots than grass started from sod.

Whether you decide on seed or sod, pick the type or blend best adapted to local growing conditions and to the ways you intend to use the lawn. Some grasses stand up better to heavy foot traffic than others; if you expect your lawn to be walked on a lot, choose bluegrass, ryegrass or some other durable species. The state agricultural extension service or a garden supply store can help you determine the type and amount of seed to sow. Many garden centers will also rent the equipment you will need, such as a rotary tiller, a roller and a push spreader.

If you seed, wait until the end of the local growing season. In most areas, the growing season generally ends in late summer or early fall; in warm areas, such as Florida and California, it may end in late spring or early summer. Sod can be installed almost any time, but should be laid almost immediately on delivery or it will dry out.

Prepare the soil carefully as much as a month ahead of time. The key to a healthy lawn is a top layer of soil—6 to 8 inches deep—that has a balanced pH and the right mix of inorganic nutrients (such as nitrogen and phosphorous) and organic matter (peat moss, sawdust or ground bark).

Give a freshly seeded lawn a light sprinkling two or three times a day. Once the seeds have sprouted, keep the lawn moist but not flooded. A weekly watering may suffice in a humid climate, but if you live in a dry region, you will probably have to water more often. Try not to walk on the grass for a month or so. Don't begin mowing or weeding until the shoots are at least 2 inches tall and are starting to curve at the top.

A broad lawn of thick, soft grass gives a note of tranquillity to this yard. It also serves to unify the various elements of the landscape— the trees, the shrubs and the house.

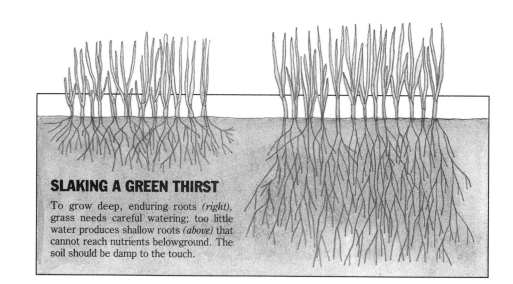

SLAKING A GREEN THIRST

To grow deep, enduring roots *(right),* grass needs careful watering; too little water produces shallow roots *(above)* that cannot reach nutrients belowground. The soil should be damp to the touch.

1 Scatter 2 or 3 inches of organic matter over bare soil with a flathead rake. Use a push spreader *(above)* to add fertilizer. Push the spreader up and down alternate rows, then go around the perimeter to cover the entire area. If your soil is acidic, spread lime the same way. Then use a rotary tiller to work all the supplements 6 inches into the soil.

2 Pick up loose rocks and other debris. Level the soil with a flathead rake. Push a water-filled roller over the area to smooth down rough and uneven spots.

3 Sow seed with a push spreader or by hand. Walk the entire area twice, sowing in opposite directions. Work the seeds into the topsoil with a lawn rake *(left),* then press them ⅛ inch into the ground with an empty roller. Cover lightly with clean straw or burlap. ☐

RIBBONS OF SOD

To keep the rows straight while laying strips of sod, make guidelines of stakes and string. Stagger the ends of the sod strips so they do not line up across rows. Press seams together by hand. Cover exposed edges with mulch or topsoil. Roll with an empty roller.

DOUBLE DIGGING
FOR DEEP, RICH SOIL

A mix of colorful perennials thrives in a carefully prepared bed. Improving the soil before planting is the first step toward spectacular garden color.

Successful gardening begins with an understanding of the soil. Once you know what you have to work with, you can choose plants that will thrive in your zone *(see Zone Map, pages 86-87).* If your soil leaves something to be desired, don't despair. You can improve it by working in amendments, either with the help of a rotary tiller or—as explained below and at right—by hand, using a method known as double digging.

First, determine the pH level—the alkaline or acid nature—of your soil. You can buy a do-it-yourself test kit from a nursery or a state agricultural extension service, or take a sample of soil and have the service analyze it for you. If your soil is too acidic, add lime; if it is too alkaline, add sulfur.

To find out if you have sufficient depth for planting, dig straight down in slightly moist soil with a sharp spade or a spading fork. If you encounter unyielding hardpan or bedrock before 18 inches, consider planting in a bed raised above ground level *(page 50).*

Soil lies in layers. The top two layers, called topsoil and subsoil, are the most important for growing plants. Test a fistful of topsoil: if it fails to hold a shape in your hand, the soil has too much sand. Soil that is excessively sandy lets water and nutrients drain away before plants can use them. If your soil compacts into a tight ball when squeezed, it has too much clay. Such heavy soil is hard to work and does not allow enough air space for roots to breathe.

You can correct most soil-texture problems by adding organic matter, such as peat moss or compost. Amendments like these help aerate heavy clay soil; alternatively, they lend needed substance to sandy soil.

If you decide on double digging, do so in late fall or early winter so the improved soil will be ready for spring planting. Begin by marking off the planting bed with stakes and a string to establish a straight border.

DIGGING BY THE NUMBERS

Double digging is a process for improving the soil by hand. It involves amending and transferring soil within a row of connected trenches. Follow this sequence: remove, amend and set aside the top layer of soil from the first trench *(arrow, far right).* Loosen the subsoil in the lower layer of the first trench and mix with amendments; then move the topsoil from the next trench into the top half of the first trench. Mix this transferred topsoil with amendments. Continue this procedure with each trench. Top the last trench with the soil you first set aside.

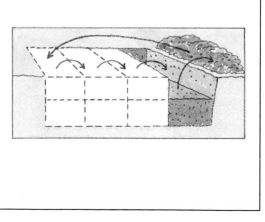

1 When double-digging a new bed, first remove weeds and grass from the planting area and discard. Dig a straight-sided trench 2 feet wide, as long as you like, and as deep as your spade's blade *(left)*. Place the soil alongside the trench and mix with an organic amendment. Add lime or sulfur if necessary to correct pH.

2 With a spading fork, loosen and turn the newly exposed subsoil in the trench. Work your organic amendment into this subsoil, and add any lime or sulfur necessary; mix together in the bottom of the trench to the depth of the spading fork.

3 Dig a second trench next to the first. As you remove the top layer of soil, transfer it to the first trench. Add amendments to the soil. Return to the second trench; loosen and amend the subsoil layer as you did with the first, and fill it with the topsoil from the third trench. Repeat this procedure until the entire planting area has been prepared. □

FRAMES FOR THE GARDEN: EDGING TO SET OFF PLANTINGS

Edging—a border between plantings—functions as a design element by framing the garden's different colors and textures. It also serves the practical purpose of checking the spread of lawn or ground cover into flower beds and shrubbery.

There are many ways to edge your garden. You can use low, dense border plants; you can install bricks, stones, timbers, or strips of concrete, plastic, metal or wood.

To make your own edging of wood, use rot- and termite-resistant wood such as heartwood of cedar or redwood, or cypress, fir, spruce or pine that has been pressure-treated with a nontoxic preservative. The straight edges—called headers or header boards—may be 1-by-4s or 2-by-4s. Stakes that hold the headers in place should be 12 inches long by 1 by 2 inches, 2 by 2 inches or 1 by 3 inches, pointed at one end. For curved edgings, use ⅜-inch bender board —so called because it is flexible enough to be bent into almost any shape of your choosing —and laminate several strips to the thickness of the headers. For laminating the bender board, use thin-shafted nails known as box nails (the kind that carpenters use for making drawers and boxes); they will not split thin slats of wood, as thicker-shafted nails have a tendency to do. Where you join header boards together and where you secure them to stakes, use common nails, but drill pilot holes before driving the nails into them.

Redwood boards make a neat, long-lasting divider. Here, the edging sets off a bed of impatiens and keeps both flowers and grass within clearly defined borders.

1 With stakes and string—and garden hose for the curves—indicate the line to be edged and mark it with lime. Then dig a trench as deep as the header boards and as wide as the combined width of the boards plus the backings used to splice them.

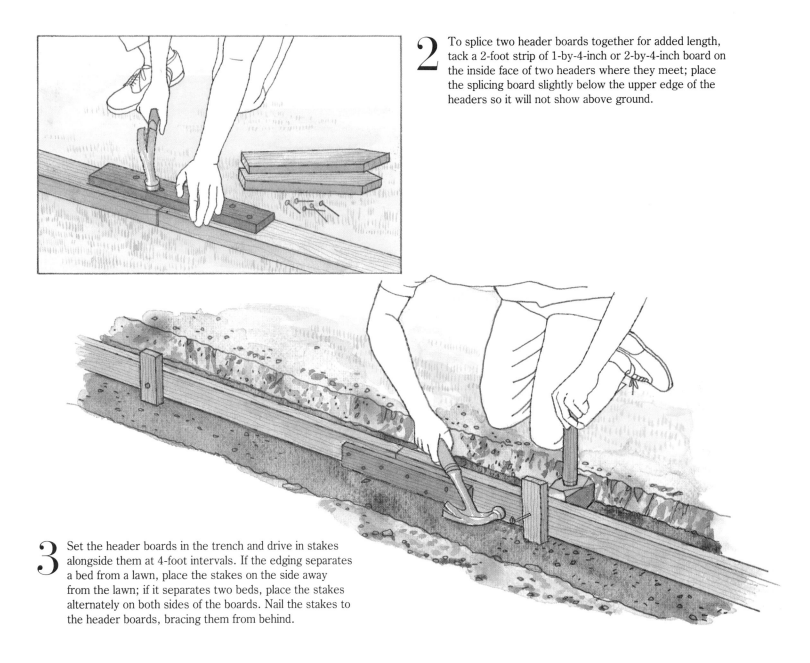

2 To splice two header boards together for added length, tack a 2-foot strip of 1-by-4-inch or 2-by-4-inch board on the inside face of two headers where they meet; place the splicing board slightly below the upper edge of the headers so it will not show above ground.

3 Set the header boards in the trench and drive in stakes alongside them at 4-foot intervals. If the edging separates a bed from a lawn, place the stakes on the side away from the lawn; if it separates two beds, place the stakes alternately on both sides of the boards. Nail the stakes to the header boards, bracing them from behind.

4 With the header boards in place, use a saw to bevel the tops of the bracing stakes at a 45-degree angle; align the higher edge of the bevel with the top edge of the header boards.

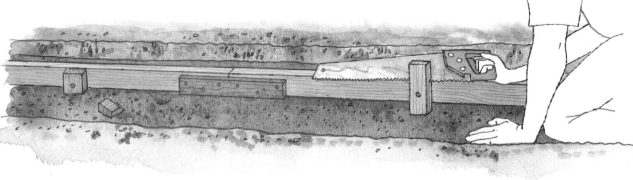

5 For curved edging, drive stakes at both ends of the curved part of the trench and every 6 to 8 inches to mark the inside of the curve. Measure the length of the curve on the inside and outside edges and cut two strips of bender board, one to each measurement.

6 If the bender board is dried out, wet it down with a hose to make the wood more flexible just before bending. Bend the piece that has been measured and cut for the inside edge around your stakes and nail in place.

7 To build up the curved edge to the thickness of the straight header boards, cut additional strips of bender board in varying lengths. Tack them along the outside edge of the curved board, staggering splices and attaching strips securely to prevent the wood from warping. Finish off with a full-length strip on the outside edge. Nail the stakes in position and bevel the tops.

8 Fill in the spaces on both sides of the edging with soil. Make sure the tops of the splicer boards and the stakes are covered with soil so they do not show. With a metal tamper or the end of a 4-by-4-inch board, tamp soil firmly in place until it is level with the top of the edging board. If lawn is on one side, spread grass seed over the soil or top off with strips of sod. □

GROUND COVERS: VERSATILE, CAREFREE CARPETS

The broad, white-edged leaves of hosta overlap in neat but unpredictable patterns on a slope that leads to a stone wall. Ground covers are well suited to this type of terrain because they are easily established and require little maintenance.

Ground covers are living pavements. Like common grass lawn, they spread an appealing protective mantle over an expanse of bare soil that would otherwise fall victim to the forces of erosion or an invasion of unsightly weeds.

Low-growing ground covers like English ivy and pachysandra are often planted in problem areas where mowing and watering a lawn would be an onerous chore. Such areas include steep slopes, deeply shaded spots under large trees and sites that are exposed to intense sunlight.

But with their extraordinary variety of colors and textures, ground covers can do much more than stand in for grass. Cotoneaster's red fruit, the fragrant blossoms of Hall's honeysuckle and lily of the valley, the bronze fall foliage of the evergreen bearberry—these are just some of the sensory delights that ground covers can add to your landscape design. You can use ground covers to give a finished look to a new garden, unify disparate elements in a composition, set off a prized specimen shrub, or soften the lines of walls, paths and steps. Ground covers can even provide microclimate control—shading the soil around plants like azaleas, rhododendrons and clematis that do best when their roots are kept cool.

In selecting ground covers, take care to match your design requirements with the ultimate height and spread of individual plants, their growth rates and the conditions of the site: sunny or shady, soil type, drainage.

Once established, most ground covers require little maintenance; but the ground must be prepared for them by careful tilling, amending, raking and mulching. For woody ground covers such as juniper, use a coarse-textured mulch like woodchips; for small creeping plants like Corsican mint, use a fine-textured mulch such as ground bark. After mulching, lay out holes for seedlings in a staggered pattern to prevent straight-line runoff; this will keep erosion to a minimum.

THE ODD GEOMETRY OF A WELL-MADE BED

To determine how many plants will cover a plot, calculate the square footage. For an irregularly shaped plot, divide the space into squares and rectangles, figure the area of each and add the areas together. Before planting, use a stick to mark the location of each hole. Arrange the holes in a staggered pattern. Leave 6 inches between small plants, 12 inches between larger plants.

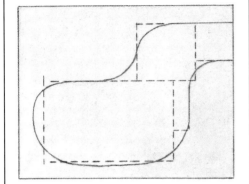

1 To replace a lawn with a ground cover, shave off existing sod with a flat-bladed spade *(above)*. Remove as little soil as possible. Clear rocks. Till to a depth of 6 inches. Mix in soil amendments as you go. Break up clods; rake smooth. Spread 2 to 4 inches of mulch over the entire bed.

2 To avoid disturbing newly planted seedlings, work backward from one corner, following the staggered pattern shown in the diagram below. Thrust the point of the trowel into the ground through the mulch layer. Pull the trowel up and back to hold the scoop of soil and mulch in place while setting a plant in the hole. Cover up the roots, leaving the plant slightly below ground level. □

4
ADDING DIMENSIONS

Often bypassed by owners of small gardens are the gazebos, follies, arbors, fishponds, *faux* stone ruins, waterfalls, artfully weathered statues of chaste Dianas and ribald Cupids, and other fanciful structures widely used in European gardens. It is a mistake to imagine that these frivolities have no place in a city backyard or a standard suburban lot. Indeed, in a limited space, they can often be the most important design element, magically pulling together the disparate plant groupings by their unexpected presence in the scene. Just as magically, these additions can extend the garden's actual size by making references to the larger natural world outside the garden's tight confines. An arbor, for example, lifts climbing and twining plants up into the light and air, freeing them from the ground; at the same time it creates a kind of secret room —mysterious, cool, private. Similarly, a small pool with a splashing fountain or an array of lily pads at its center delights the eyes and ears with its soothing sounds and the sight of multiple reflections of plants, clouds and nighttime stars in its rippling surface.

The following pages are filled with information on some of the more popular of these artifacts. You will find instructions for building a simple post-and-beam arbor strong enough to support a full-grown 50-foot grapevine and a hammock. To go with the arbor, there is a discussion on the various kinds of vines and how they grow—tendril, twining, clinging—with instructions for their care. You will also find how to build a rough-hewn stone wall suitable for shaping a terrace or simply for creating a division between two types of plants; and, on another page, directions for installing and landscaping an in-ground fiberglass pond. Finally, you will discover the fascinating art of espalier, a technique for training and pruning plants to grow against a flat surface. Often used to create elaborately ornamental designs on house walls, espalier is also a classic method of shaping apple and pear trees so that their fruit is easy to harvest.

THE ARBOR: BUILDING A LEAFY SHELTER

Few structures so enhance a garden as an arbor—an open framework that supports vines or shrubs. Passing through an arbor can surround you with greenery, shade you from the sun, and delight you with flowers and fragrance.

An arbor may extend from a house wall or stand free in the yard. It may serve to frame a view, define a space or provide a transition from one part of the garden to another. It can hold a seat or a hammock. And all you need for decoration are plants—climbing roses, grapes and wisteria, to name just a few of the dozens of choices.

The post-and-beam arbor built in the steps shown here is a simple one. It can be as long and as wide as you like. End posts should be at least 4 feet apart to accommodate two persons walking side by side.

Materials are simple. The arbor is made of pressure-treated wood and can be painted or not. For a solid foundation, ready-mix concrete is poured into holes and allowed to dry before the posts are placed upon them; the concrete secures the posts against heaving or sinking in winter freezes and spring thaws. The posts are connected by two beams and the beams by evenly spaced rafters. Galvanized nails and lag-bolts hold the arbor together. As an option, ready-made trellis sheets can close the sides.

An arbor should be sited on ground that slopes no more than approximately 2 inches in 8 feet; if the slope needs correction, use the grading techniques explained on page 49, or call in a professional.

Canopied with vines, a freestanding arbor makes a verdant and cooling transition between house and sunny terrace.

1 Mark the location of the first post with a stake. From it measure the width of the arbor and drive a second stake. If the arbor is to extend from the house, make sure that the stakes square with the house. To ensure right angles *(box, opposite),* use the 3-4-5 triangulation method: tie a string between the stakes; measure along it 4 feet from the first stake; at the 4-foot point, drive a short stake into the ground and mark the string at the same point.

2 To the short stake, tie a string that is slightly longer than 5 feet and mark it exactly 5 feet from the stake. Tie a string to the first stake and mark it exactly 3 feet from its stake. To determine a line that makes a right angle to the width of the arbor, grasp the string marked at 5 feet and the one marked at 3 feet, hold them out from their stakes, cross them at the 3- and 5-foot marks *(inset)*. At the point where they intersect, drive a stake *(left)*.

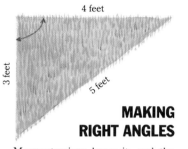

4 feet

3 feet

5 feet

MAKING RIGHT ANGLES

Mesopotamians knew it, and the Greek mathematician Pythagoras proved it: the square of the hypotenuse (the long side of a right triangle) is equal to the sum of the squares of the other two sides. Carpenters reverse the theorem, knowing that a triangle with three sides in the proper ratios will have a right angle opposite the long side. Thus, since 9 and 16 (the squares of 3 and 4) add up to 25 (the square of 5), a 3-4-5 triangle of any units—inches, feet, yards—always forms a right angle opposite the 5-unit side.

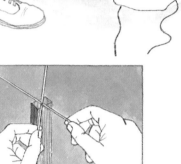

3 Measure between the first and last stakes to locate the third post. For the fourth post, repeat the triangulation. Tie the 5-foot string to a new stake driven 4 feet from the second; tie the 3-foot string to the second stake. Triangulate again for the proper line; measure along it and drive a stake for the fourth post. Measure diagonally from the first post to the fourth, and from the second to the third. The measurements should be equal.

4 With a shovel or a post-hole digger, dig four post-holes 24 inches deep, removing the stakes as you go. In a wheelbarrow, combine ready-mix concrete with water, following the directions on the bag. As a guide for pouring, insert a nail on the inside wall of each hole 6 inches up from the bottom *(inset, right)*. Pour the concrete up to each marker. Eliminate air pockets in the concrete by piercing it with a shovel.

5 Allow the four concrete footings to harden for 24 hours. Set a post into one of the holes—temporarily at this point. Drive stakes into the ground on two sides of the post and, with a single nail, tack a piece of scrap lumber to each stake. Then use a level to plumb the post; that is, align it straight up and down. When it is plumb, secure the scrap lumber to the post and to each stake. Repeat with the other three posts.

6 To make the post tops exactly level with one another, find which is lowest. Span two post tops with a straight 2-by-4. Place a level on top of the 2-by-4 to determine which post is the lower *(below, left)*. Then run the 2-by-4 and level from the lower of the two to a third post. Run it from the lower of this pair to the fourth post. This determines the lowest of the four posts. Run the 2-by-4 from this one to each of the others, and mark a line level with the top of the lowest post *(below, right)*.

7 Number each post. Remove all four posts from the holes, remove the braces from the posts and lay the posts on sawhorses. With a square, extend the leveling marks on each of the three long posts around their four sides. With a circular saw, cut off the tops of the three long posts. You will have to flip each post because the saw blade will only go about halfway through on one pass.

8 Lay posts 1 and 2 on the ground and lay a 2-by-6 beam across them. The beam should project the same distance from the posts at both ends. Hold the beam flush with the top of a post and drill through it two pilot holes—one above the other—for 3½-inch-long lag-bolts. Drill the top pilot hole halfway into the post but make the bottom hole penetrate only the beam *(inset, right);* you will finish drilling later. Repeat with the other two posts and a beam. Screw the beams to the posts using washers and lag-bolts at the top pilot holes only.

9 Set the posts into their holes. Measure the diagonals and adjust the posts until the diagonals are equal; then plumb the posts. Check a beam for level; drill through the bottom pilot hole into the post *(inset)* and screw in a lag-bolt with a washer. Repeat at every post. Tamp dirt into the holes, rechecking for plumb as you add dirt *(left)*. At ground level, slope the dirt away from the posts.

10 Cut 2-by-2 rafters to length, allowing for an overhang of the beams. Use decorative end cuts, if you prefer—an angle cut is shown here. Lay rafters on the beams and determine a spacing—usually about 6 inches—that will be pleasing to the eye. Work from the middle of the beams to the ends and make adjustments after all the rafters are lying on the beams. Nail or screw the rafters to the beams; if you use screws, drill pilot holes first. □

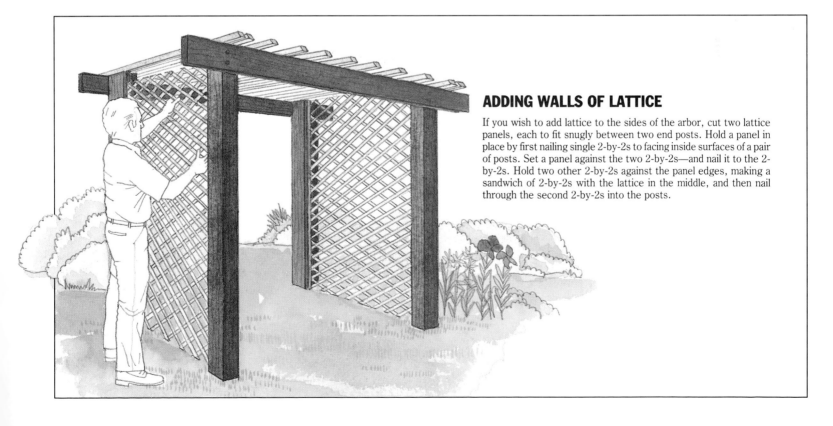

ADDING WALLS OF LATTICE

If you wish to add lattice to the sides of the arbor, cut two lattice panels, each to fit snugly between two end posts. Hold a panel in place by first nailing single 2-by-2s to facing inside surfaces of a pair of posts. Set a panel against the two 2-by-2s—and nail it to the 2-by-2s. Hold two other 2-by-2s against the panel edges, making a sandwich of 2-by-2s with the lattice in the middle, and then nail through the second 2-by-2s into the posts.

UPWARDLY MOBILE GARDENING: USEFUL, EXUBERANT VINES

Vines are opportunists. Give them a chance and they will climb up, over and around any obstacle to get closer to the sun. Chosen with care and vigilantly controlled, they can add beauty and texture to a garden. With only a small patch of ground to grow in, they will put forth a profusion of flowers, fruit or foliage to dress up a wall or a fence, soften hard edges, add interest to a corner.

Some vines are evergreen, others deciduous. Both kinds are classified according to the means they use to climb. There are three vine types: tendril, twining and clinging.

Tendrils are thin, flexible, leafless organs that extend from the body of the plant (its leaves, its flowers or its main stem) and wrap themselves around any slender support. Vines that climb by means of tendrils include clematis and all varieties of grape.

Twining vines, such as wisteria, are ones in which the main stems climb by spiraling up vertical supports—wooden stakes, for example. Keep them away from trees, since they can strangle young branches. Some twining branches spiral clockwise, others counterclockwise; to help a twining vine get established quickly, start it off in the correct direction. Ask your dealer which way your vine twines.

Clinging vines, such as Boston ivy, attach to surfaces by means of disc-shaped adhesive tips or small aerial rootlets called holdfasts. They can be safely grown on brick walls and along stone fences. But don't let them cling directly to clapboard or shingles, since they may damage wood surfaces. If you want a wood wall veiled with a clinging vine, attach the vine to a trellis that stands out several inches from the wall surface. The trellis should be removable so you can repaint the wall easily without harming the vine.

Once established, your vines are likely to need annual pruning. But go easy—too vigorous pruning can reduce total leaf surface and give an elongated, "ropy" look. Prune in early spring, except for spring-flowering vines such as wisteria, which bloom in the spring from buds formed the previous summer. Prune these vines after they finish flowering.

Stems of the twining vine dioscorea, a member of the yam family, spiral up a wooden trellis. The ornamental leaves of this vine flaunt ruby red undersides and dark green tops.

1 To help roots establish themselves quickly, dig a hole twice the diameter of, and about as deep as, the root ball. At the bottom of the hole, make a mound of topsoil. Remove the vine from its container, split the root ball one-half to two-thirds of the way up from the bottom and spread the divided root ball over the mound of topsoil *(right)*. Cover with more soil, and water the plant.

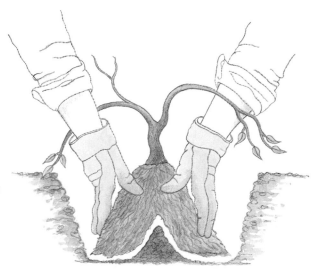

2 To get a twining vine off to a fast start, wind one stem around a vertical support in the direction it naturally grows, clockwise or counterclockwise. Start with a twist across the front of the support *(left)*. Then wind a second stem in the same direction, starting with a twist around the back of the support *(inset, below)*. At intervals of a foot or so, use a plastic-covered wire looped around a protruding nail to support the vine.

HELPING HANDS FOR HIGH CLIMBERS

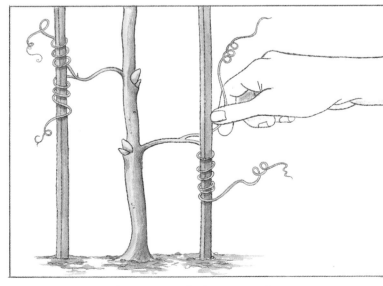

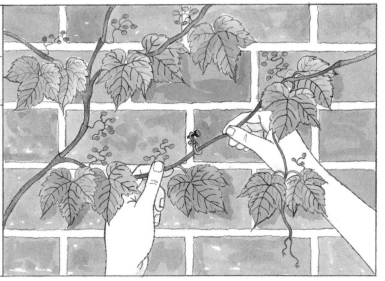

To start a vine that climbs by tendrils, loop two or three tendrils several times around a support—a slim stake, a delicate trellis or a chain link fence. Choose the support carefully: if it is too thick, the tendril will not reach around it.

To channel the growth of a clinging vine up a brick or stone surface, hammer in a line of masonry nails (the kind with grooved shafts). Place the vine along the nails and secure it with wire loops; the plant's rootlets will adhere to the surface of the wall. □

THE FINE ART OF ESPALIER: SILHOUETTING WITH PLANTS

A versatile, hardy fire thorn takes a white brick chimney in its evergreen embrace. The outlines of both plant and backdrop are enhanced by this informal espalier design.

Espalier gardening is a dynamic art. It lets you shape nature's raw material into a design of your own choice. Starting with a young tree, a shrub or a vine, you create a living sculpture that adds year-round interest to a wall or a fence. As the plant grows, you can refine your original design or alter it to suit your changing tastes.

Espaliered plants are meant to be admired in silhouette. They grow flat against a bare surface and occupy very little ground space. Before embarking on espalier, consider the surface you wish to cover. If you want an espalier to climb up a chimney, choose a vertically growing plant such as a fire thorn or a loquat. If what you want to cover is a long, low wall, think of a low-growing plant such as forsythia or honeysuckle.

Espaliers used to be stiff and symmetrical. Plants were trained in the forms of checkerboards, fans, candelabras and other formal patterns over centuries. Although these traditional shapes remain in use, espaliers today are just as likely to be informal, naturalistic and asymmetrical: a loose-limbed spray of foliage suspended in air like a green fountain or a gnarly sprawl of branches resembling a line of strange calligraphy. Imagination is the rule for informal espaliers; the only limits are those imposed by the size and shape of the site and the growth habits of the plant.

The first step in creating an espalier is vigorous pruning to remove the shoots and buds you don't want. To train the remaining branches to follow a desired outline, tie them with plastic-coated wire to nails, a thin trellis or some other inconspicuous framework.

Done properly, espalier will not injure a plant. Apple and pear trees that have been espaliered start bearing good-sized fruit faster than trees allowed to mature without restraint. Other plants that lend themselves well to espalier are yews and cotoneaster.

Virtually any young, healthy shrub, tree or vine with long, supple branches is a candidate for informal espalier. You can use an untrained plant already growing in your garden, or you can buy a preshaped espalier from a nursery and adapt it to your site.

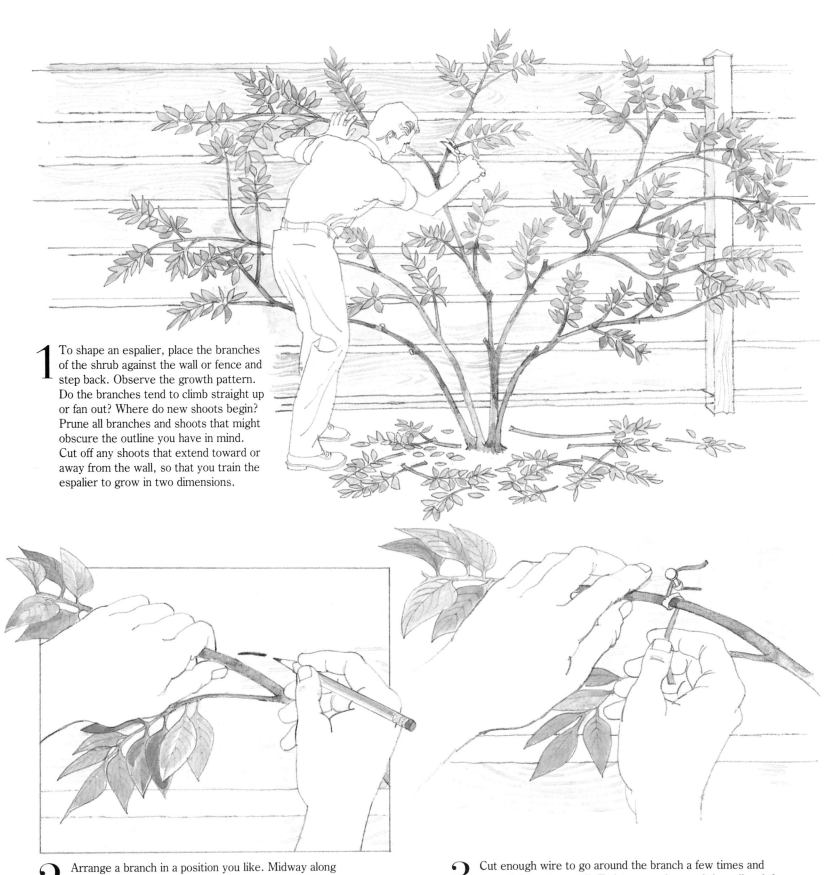

1 To shape an espalier, place the branches of the shrub against the wall or fence and step back. Observe the growth pattern. Do the branches tend to climb straight up or fan out? Where do new shoots begin? Prune all branches and shoots that might obscure the outline you have in mind. Cut off any shoots that extend toward or away from the wall, so that you train the espalier to grow in two dimensions.

2 Arrange a branch in a position you like. Midway along the branch, make a pencil mark on the wall, and hammer in a masonry nail. On brick and stone walls, hammer into mortar joints; on wood walls, aim for the middle of boards. Leave ½ inch of nail protruding.

3 Cut enough wire to go around the branch a few times and around the nail as well. Twist one end around the nail and the other around the branch. Repeat with the remaining branches. Twice a year, refasten ties that have become too tight; prune unwanted shoots; tie desirable new growth to new nails. □

CONSTRUCTING A WALL OF NATIVE STONE

A wall of fieldstone makes an attractive divider for a terraced garden and creates a natural planting area. Openings between the stones allow rainwater to drain off into the soil.

A stone wall is a pleasing sight; it has an aura of permanence and gives a natural backdrop to plants. In addition, it can terrace a slope so you can plant a garden on different levels. No mortar is needed; the joints can be filled with earth, but there are a number of structural requirements. A 3-foot height —about 1 foot higher than the wall shown above—is all an amateur should attempt without professional help. The width of the base should be at least one-third of the height, and the top should be about 18 inches wide.

A gravel footing ensures good drainage and protects against frost heaves. In the first course of rock, small gaps called weep holes serve as outlets for water, which otherwise could build up enough pressure inside the slope to push the wall outward. To be stable, the wall must be made to slant into the hill as it goes up. This arrangement is known as battering. Two slight tiltings are needed—of the individual stones and of the wall itself *(right)*.

Choose stones native to your region. They will blend in well with the topography and will be less expensive than any trucked in. Pick stones that are basically rectangular. And remember: when you lift them, crouch so that, as you rise, your legs bear the weight without straining your back.

BATTERING A WALL

For stability, a retaining wall should lean into the hill it abuts about 2 inches for every foot in height of the wall. Each stone should tilt so that the inside edge is slightly lower than the outer edge and rainwater drains back into the hill.

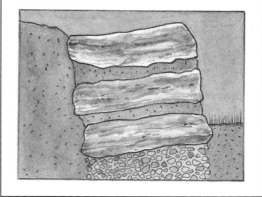

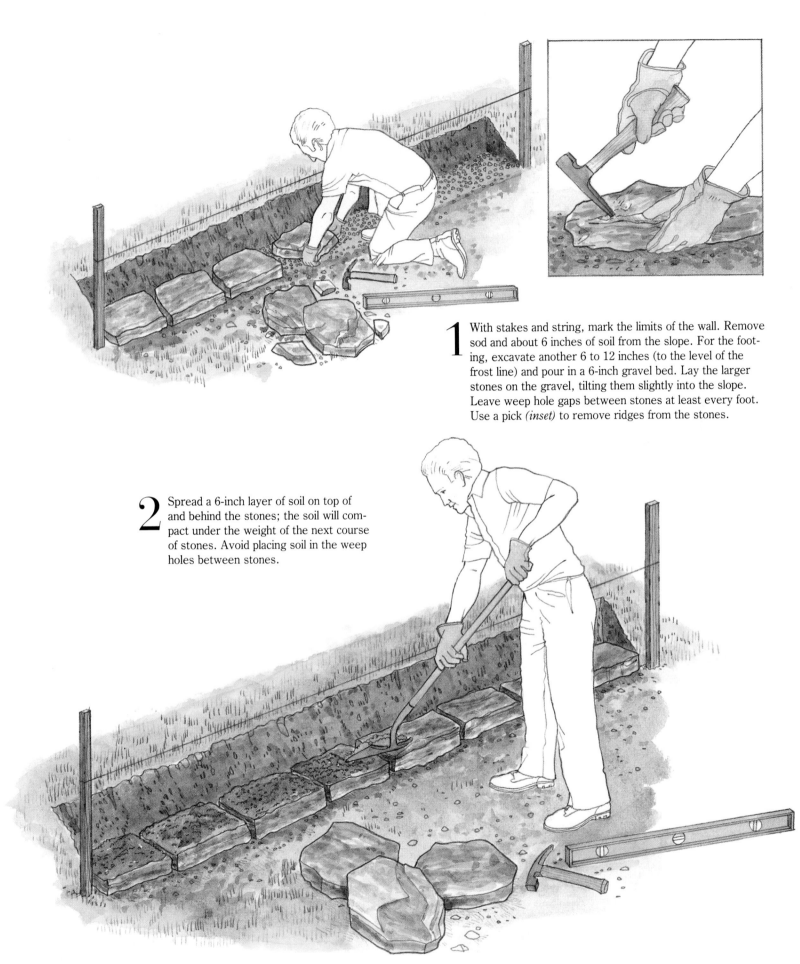

1 With stakes and string, mark the limits of the wall. Remove sod and about 6 inches of soil from the slope. For the footing, excavate another 6 to 12 inches (to the level of the frost line) and pour in a 6-inch gravel bed. Lay the larger stones on the gravel, tilting them slightly into the slope. Leave weep hole gaps between stones at least every foot. Use a pick *(inset)* to remove ridges from the stones.

2 Spread a 6-inch layer of soil on top of and behind the stones; the soil will compact under the weight of the next course of stones. Avoid placing soil in the weep holes between stones.

3 Position the stones of the second course so they lie over the gaps of the first and lean slightly into the hill. Use a level to check that the course is level left to right; add or remove soil underneath stones as needed. Continue laying courses, staggering the placement of the stones and spreading a 6-inch layer of soil over each course up to the next to last.

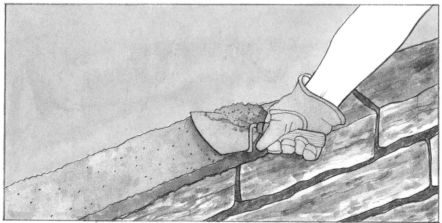

4 To make a more solid topping than one supported by earth alone, spread a 2-inch-thick layer of mortar on top of the next-to-last course. Then lay the top course of stone in the mortar bed. If you want the wall to have a smooth surface, use flagstone for topping stones. Around the sides and bottom of the wall, fill in with earth and then resod.

5 To grow plants in the wall, scoop out one or two trowelfuls of soil from the crevices. Insert the roots of plants; chopsticks are useful for pushing the roots back into the soil. Replace as much of the soil around the roots as you can. Then water behind and on top of the wall thoroughly and frequently until the roots are established. □

FLOWERS TO GROW ON A WALL

The plants you choose to root in your wall will grow better if you pay attention to the amount of sun that the wall receives. The wall itself reflects light and heat, so on southern exposures choose only sun-loving plants. Here are good selections of both sun-loving and shade-loving plants for a wall.

SUN-LOVING PLANTS

Alpine Aster	Columbine
Baby's Breath	Common Houseleek
Basket-of-Gold	Heath
Candytuft	Lavender Cotton

SHADE-LOVING PLANTS

Alpine Poppy	Japanese Painted Fern
Bellflower	Kenilworth Ivy
Crested Iris	Primrose
Ebony Spleenwort	Yellow Corydalis

A GARDEN POOL
FOR A TRANQUIL SCENE

A garden pool—encircled by stones and flowers, freckled with lily pads, stirred by falling water and brightly colored fish—brings a timeless air of peace to this sunny nook between brick wall and patio.

A garden pool is like an oasis in your backyard. Even a small pool reflects objects around it; therefore it lends the illusion of height to a horizontal surface. The easiest pools to install—and the most durable—are made of preformed fiberglass. They have an in-ground life of up to 50 years and require little maintenance.

Once your pool is filled, you will have only to top it off every few days with a garden hose to replace water lost to evaporation. Keep the water level a couple of inches below the rim to allow for heavy rains. The raised lip of the pool, which may be camouflaged beneath decorative stones or bricks, helps prevent soil and mulch from drifting from the surrounding garden into the pool.

If you intend to stock your pool with fish and aquatic plants, add a dechlorinating compound once the water has warmed up to air temperature. Ask your garden center for help in creating a balanced ecosystem in which fish and plants supply each other's nutrients.

Both fish and plants will come through winters in good health in a filled pool—as long as the water does not freeze to the bottom. Keep the pool almost full at all times and make sure ice does not form around the bases of the plants. If it does, use a broom handle to knock off the ice.

With a proper ecosystem, the water is not likely to turn cloudy or scummy. But once a year—probably in the spring—you may want to drain, clean and refill the pool. First remove all plants. Catch the fish with a net and put them in a pail of water. To drain the pool, use a suction pump (the kind that attaches to an electric drill) or make a syphon by submerging a coiled hose in the pool until it fills with water. Leaving one end of the hose submerged, tightly cover the other end with your palm and carry it to any place in your garden that is lower than the pool. When you take away your hand, the water will empty out through the hose.

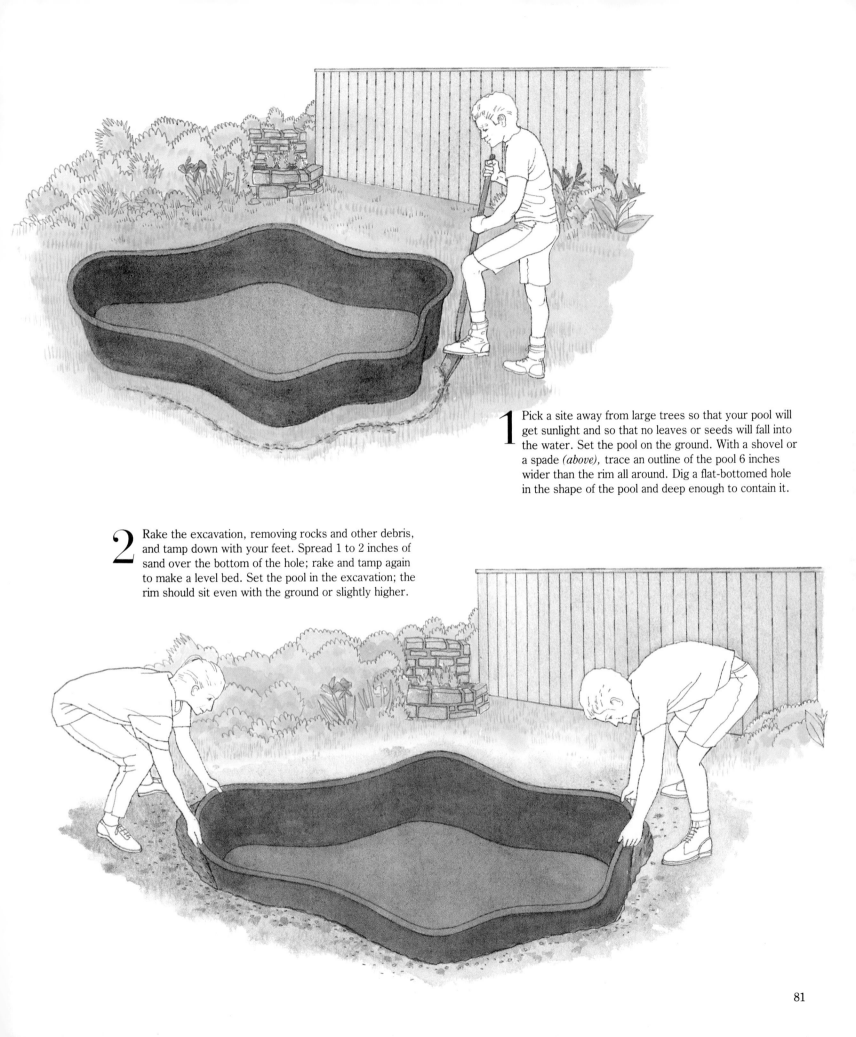

1 Pick a site away from large trees so that your pool will get sunlight and so that no leaves or seeds will fall into the water. Set the pool on the ground. With a shovel or a spade *(above),* trace an outline of the pool 6 inches wider than the rim all around. Dig a flat-bottomed hole in the shape of the pool and deep enough to contain it.

2 Rake the excavation, removing rocks and other debris, and tamp down with your feet. Spread 1 to 2 inches of sand over the bottom of the hole; rake and tamp again to make a level bed. Set the pool in the excavation; the rim should sit even with the ground or slightly higher.

3 To determine if the pool is level, lay a 2-by-4-inch board across it and place a level on top of the board. Check in all directions. If necessary, shovel more sand under the pool to raise one side, or use a rubber mallet to tap the opposite side down into the bed of sand.

4 Backfill around the rim while running water into the pool from a garden hose; this will equalize pressure from outside and inside, and prevent the fiberglass mold from bending or cracking. Fill to 2 inches below the rim.

5 Place stones or bricks as a decorative edge around the rim of the pool *(above)*. Add mulch around stones and prepare the soil for planting. Plants that will thrive at pool's edge include common cattail, hosta, globeflower, pickerel rush, Siberian iris and primula japonica. □

ENLISTING NATURE'S BALANCING ACT

A healthy balance between animal and plant life will keep a pool clean. Japanese black snails control scum. Plants such as cabomba and sagittaria, which grow entirely underwater, compete with algae for nutrients. The shade provided by water-lily pads also discourages algae growth. All plants should be set in containers of heavy soil. The containers of those to be submerged should stand on the bottom of the pool. The lily pads and any other plants meant to show above the surface may need to be elevated. If so, place freestanding bricks on the floor of the pool to raise them. Fish such as koi, comets, Japanese fan-tails and Chinese moors eat insects and plant debris.

5
MAKING THE MOST OF NATURE

Garden design, if it is to be successful and enduring, must make use of plants that adapt themselves to the specific environment and can be kept healthy without herculean caretaking efforts. This means giving thought to such matters as soil composition, length of growing season, depth of winter cold, annual rainfall and prevailing winds. It may mean dealing with such localized problems as salt air and heavy snowfalls that wreak havoc with brittle limbs. In some areas, air pollution can be a major concern; or rabbits and field mice may pose special problems; in humid climates, mold and mildew may harm delicate foliage. All through the year there will also be routine gardening chores of greater or lesser importance, depending on the kind of plant and where it is placed.

The charts and maps and design tips on the following pages are intended to help you work with nature instead of battling it. As a bonus, there are also design tips for creating a garden that lures birds, perfumes the air with sweet smells or is beautiful to look upon even in winter, when branches are bare and shrubs are blanketed in snow.

THE ZONE MAP AND PLANTING

The most important question to ask when considering a plant for your garden is how it will grow in the climate of your area. Besides determining whether a plant can survive, climate can affect its appearance and its performance. For instance, in the cool climate of southern Minnesota, enkianthus *(page 119)* grows as a shrub; in the warmer region of Tennessee the same plant becomes a small tree. Differences in climate can also determine whether a plant is evergreen or deciduous and whether it flowers. To find out how a plant will fare in your zone, consult the Dictionary of Plants *(pages 98-152)*.

The zones have been established by the United States Department of Agriculture, which divides North America into 10 climatic areas *(right)*. Zone 1 is the coldest, with winter lows of −50° F; Zone 10 is the warmest, usually frost-free and having winter minimum temperatures of 30° to 40° F.

Those extremes of temperature should be taken only as guidelines. Within any zone, average annual minimum temperatures may vary by five or more degrees. And in any given zone there may be many so-called microclimates—climates that differ from the one that prevails in the zone. Cool microclimates occur at high altitudes, where the air is thinner and absorbs less of the solar energy reradiated from the earth. They also occur in valleys, because cold air sinks. Warm microclimates exist in large cities, where more heat is generated. Stone walls and large paved surfaces in a yard also create a warm microclimate by reflecting sunlight.

If your plants bloom early, you have a warm microclimate. If morning frost appears in your garden and not in others, you have a cooler one. Check an outdoor thermometer in your garden against local weather bureau reports daily to be sure.

You may be able to have a plant you fancy even if it doesn't fit the guidelines. Some plants adapt to slightly warmer zones. And, paradoxically, low-growing plants that are marginally hardy in cold weather can be used in zones with heavy snowfall; the snow acts as an insulating carpet.

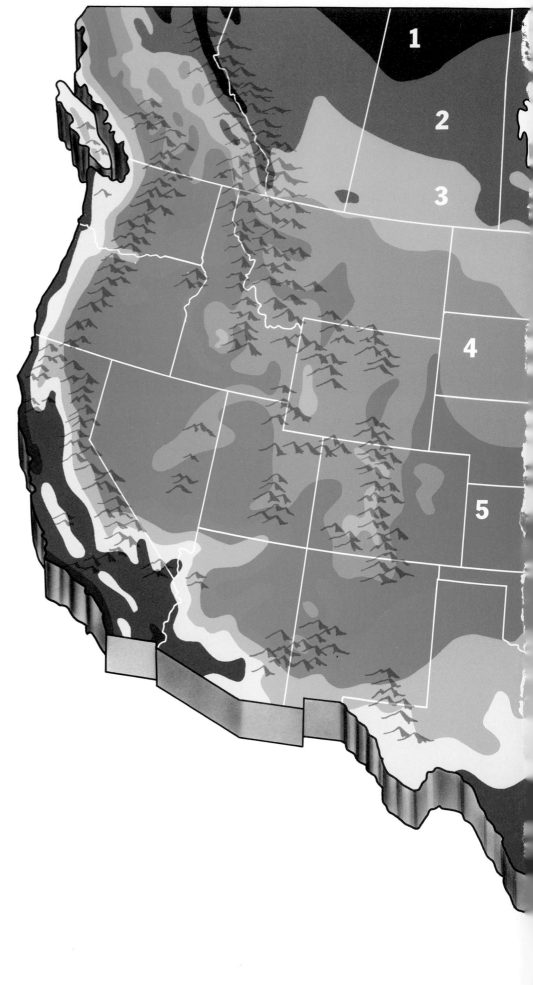

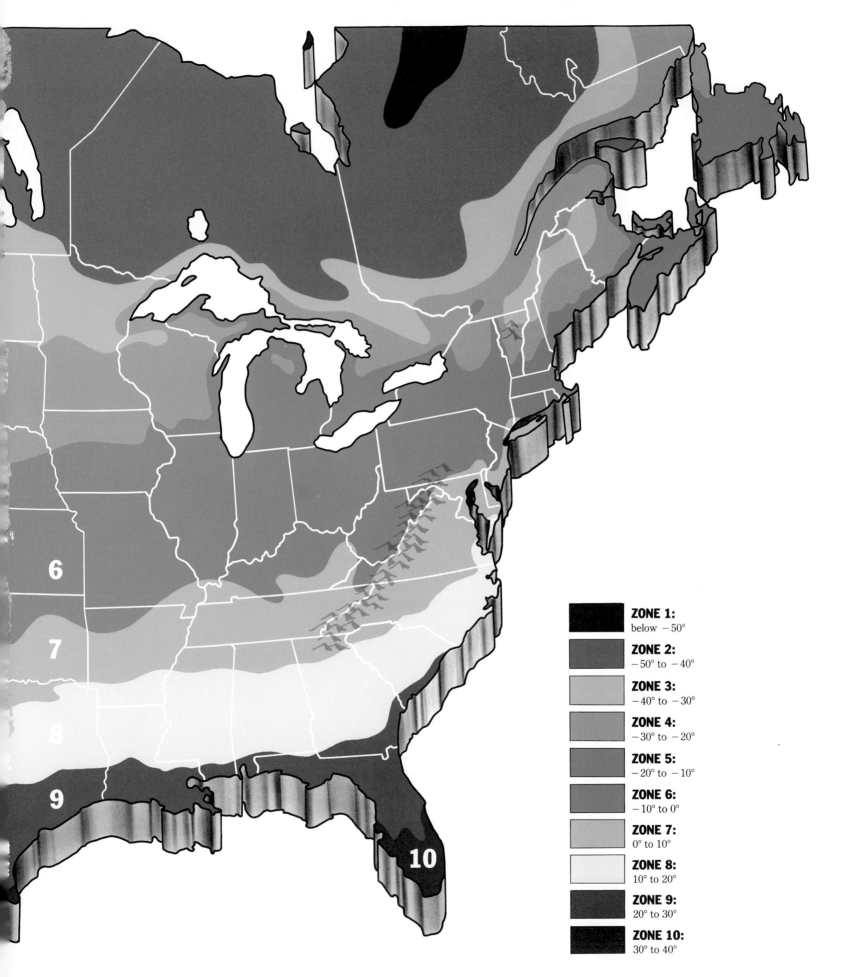

ZONE 1:
below −50°

ZONE 2:
−50° to −40°

ZONE 3:
−40° to −30°

ZONE 4:
−30° to −20°

ZONE 5:
−20° to −10°

ZONE 6:
−10° to 0°

ZONE 7:
0° to 10°

ZONE 8:
10° to 20°

ZONE 9:
20° to 30°

ZONE 10:
30° to 40°

A CHECKLIST FOR MAINTENANCE MONTH BY MONTH

	ZONE 1	ZONE 2	ZONE 3	ZONE 4	ZONE 5
JANUARY/FEBRUARY	• Prune dormant trees and shrubs • Spray broad-leaved evergreens with antidesiccant • Remove snow and ice from evergreens • Replace mulches as needed • Spread sand on ice-covered walkways	• Prune dormant trees and shrubs • Spray broad-leaved evergreens with antidesiccant • Remove snow and ice from evergreens • Replace mulches as needed • Spread sand on ice-covered walkways	• Prune dormant trees and shrubs • Spray broad-leaved evergreens with antidesiccant • Remove snow and ice from evergreens • Replace mulches as needed • Spread sand on ice-covered walkways	• Prune dormant trees and shrubs • Spray broad-leaved evergreens with antidesiccant • Remove snow and ice from evergreens • Replace mulches as needed • Spread sand on ice-covered walkways	• Prune dormant trees and shrubs • Spray broad-leaved evergreens with antidesiccant • Remove snow and ice from evergreens • Replace mulches as needed • Spread sand on ice-covered walkways
MARCH/APRIL	• Clean, oil, sharpen tools • Remove mulch from early bulbs	• Clean, oil, sharpen tools • Remove mulch from early bulbs	• Clean, oil, sharpen tools • Remove mulch from early bulbs	• Plant container and balled-and-burlapped plants • Plant bare-root trees and shrubs • Clean, oil, sharpen tools • Remove mulch from early bulbs	• Plant container and balled-and-burlapped plants • Plant bare-root trees and shrubs • Prune out winter damage • Clean, oil, sharpen tools • Remove mulch from early bulbs • Remove winter mulch, burlap wrappings • Adjust lawn pH if needed
MAY/JUNE	• Plant bare-root trees and shrubs • Plant container and balled-and-burlapped plants • Prune out winter damage • Remove winter mulch, burlap wrappings • Adjust lawn pH if needed • Apply first lawn fertilizer • Seed or sod lawn • Trim lawn and border edging and mow lawn • Fertilize trees and shrubs as growth starts • Prune shrubs after blooming and shear hedges • Transplant trees, shrubs • Trim, plant ground covers • Divide, plant, fertilize perennials • Fertilize bulbs after blooming • Apply summer mulch • Weed and apply pre-emergent herbicide • Plant annuals • Plant tender bulbs • Check for insects, disease	• Plant bare-root trees and shrubs • Plant container and balled-and-burlapped plants • Prune out winter damage • Remove winter mulch, burlap wrappings • Adjust lawn pH if needed • Apply first lawn fertilizer • Seed or sod lawn • Trim lawn and border edging and mow lawn • Fertilize trees and shrubs as growth starts • Prune shrubs after blooming and shear hedges • Transplant trees, shrubs • Trim, plant ground covers • Divide, plant, fertilize perennials • Fertilize bulbs after blooming • Apply summer mulch • Weed and apply pre-emergent herbicide • Plant annuals • Plant tender bulbs • Check for insects, disease	• Plant bare-root trees and shrubs • Plant container and balled-and-burlapped plants • Prune out winter damage • Remove winter mulch, burlap wrappings • Adjust lawn pH if needed • Apply first lawn fertilizer • Seed or sod lawn • Trim lawn and border edging and mow lawn • Fertilize trees and shrubs as growth starts • Prune shrubs after blooming and shear hedges • Transplant trees, shrubs • Trim, plant ground covers • Divide, plant, fertilize perennials • Fertilize bulbs after blooming • Apply summer mulch • Weed and apply pre-emergent herbicide • Plant annuals • Plant tender bulbs • Check for insects, disease	• Plant bare-root trees and shrubs • Plant container and balled-and-burlapped plants • Prune out winter damage • Remove winter mulch, burlap wrappings • Adjust lawn pH if needed • Apply first lawn fertilizer • Seed or sod lawn • Trim lawn and border edging and mow lawn • Fertilize trees and shrubs as growth starts • Prune shrubs after blooming and shear hedges • Transplant trees, shrubs • Trim, plant ground covers • Divide, plant, fertilize perennials • Fertilize bulbs after blooming • Apply summer mulch • Weed and apply pre-emergent herbicide • Plant annuals • Plant tender bulbs • Check for insects, disease	• Plant container and balled-and-burlapped plants • Seed or sod lawn • Mow lawn regularly • Apply first lawn fertilizer • Trim lawn and border edging • Fertilize trees and shrubs as growth starts • Prune shrubs after blooming • Transplant trees and shrubs • Trim, plant ground covers • Divide, plant, fertilize perennials • Fertilize bulbs after blooming • Shear hedges • Apply summer mulch • Weed and apply pre-emergent herbicide • Plant annuals • Plant tender bulbs • Water as needed • Check for insects, disease

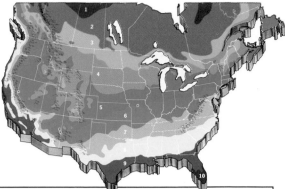

ZONE 6	ZONE 7	ZONE 8	ZONE 9	ZONE 10	
• Prune dormant trees and shrubs • Spray broad-leaved evergreens with antidesiccant • Remove snow and ice from evergreens • Replace mulches as needed • Spread sand on ice-covered walkways	• Prune dormant trees and shrubs • Spray broad-leaved evergreens with antidesiccant • Remove snow and ice from evergreens • Replace mulches as needed • Spread sand on ice-covered walkways	• Prune trees and shrubs • Fertilize trees and shrubs as growth starts • Plant bare-root trees and shrubs • Plant container and balled-and-burlapped plants • Remove winter mulch, burlap • Clean, oil, sharpen tools • Adjust lawn pH if needed	• Prune trees and shrubs • Fertilize trees and shrubs as growth starts • Plant bare-root trees and shrubs • Plant container and balled-and-burlapped plants • Adjust lawn pH if needed • Seed or sod lawn • Mow lawn as needed • Apply pre-emergent herbicide • Transplant trees and shrubs • Divide, plant perennials • Plant, trim ground covers • Plant cool-season annuals • Apply mulch if frost threatens • Water if ground is dry • Check for insects, disease	• Prune trees and shrubs • Fertilize trees and shrubs as growth starts • Plant bare-root trees and shrubs • Plant container and balled-and-burlapped plants • Adjust lawn pH if needed • Seed or sod lawn • Mow lawn as needed • Apply pre-emergent herbicide • Transplant trees and shrubs • Divide, plant perennials • Plant, trim ground covers • Plant cool-season annuals • Apply mulch if frost threatens • Water if ground is dry • Check for insects, disease	**JANUARY/FEBRUARY**
• Plant container and balled-and-burlapped plants • Plant bare-root trees and shrubs • Prune out winter damage • Clean, oil, sharpen tools • Remove mulch from early bulbs • Remove winter mulch, burlap wrappings • Adjust lawn pH if needed • Seed or sod lawn • Mow lawn as needed • Fertilize trees and shrubs as growth starts • Transplant trees and shrubs • Trim ground covers	• Plant container and balled-and-burlapped plants • Plant bare-root trees and shrubs • Prune out winter damage • Clean, oil, sharpen tools • Remove mulch from early bulbs • Remove winter mulch, burlap wrappings • Adjust lawn pH if needed • Seed or sod lawn • Mow lawn as needed • Fertilize trees and shrubs as growth starts • Transplant trees and shrubs • Trim, plant ground covers • Plant perennials • Fertilize early bulbs after blooming	• Plant container and balled-and-burlapped plants • Prune out winter damage • Apply first lawn fertilizer • Mow lawn as needed • Trim lawn and border edging • Trim, plant ground covers • Divide, plant perennials • Fertilize early bulbs after blooming • Prune shrubs after blooming • Shear hedges • Apply summer mulch • Apply pre-emergent herbicide • Plant annuals • Plant tender bulbs • Water if ground is dry • Check for insects, disease	• Plant container and balled-and-burlapped plants • Prune out winter damage • Apply first lawn fertilizer • Mow lawn as needed • Trim lawn and border edging • Trim, plant ground covers • Divide, plant perennials • Fertilize early bulbs after blooming • Prune shrubs after blooming • Shear hedges • Apply summer mulch • Apply pre-emergent herbicide • Plant annuals • Plant tender bulbs • Water if ground is dry • Check for insects, disease	• Plant container and balled-and-burlapped plants • Prune out winter damage • Apply first lawn fertilizer • Mow lawn as needed • Trim lawn and border edging • Trim, plant ground covers • Divide, plant perennials • Fertilize early bulbs after blooming • Prune shrubs after blooming • Shear hedges • Apply summer mulch • Apply pre-emergent herbicide • Plant annuals • Plant tender bulbs • Water if ground is dry • Check for insects, disease	**MARCH/APRIL**
• Plant container and balled-and-burlapped plants • Prune shrubs after blooming • Transplant trees and shrubs • Apply first lawn fertilizer • Mow lawn regularly • Trim lawn and border edging • Divide, plant, fertilize perennials • Fertilize bulbs after blooming • Shear hedges • Apply summer mulch • Weed and apply pre-emergent herbicide • Plant annuals • Plant tender bulbs • Water as needed • Check for insects, disease	• Plant container and balled-and-burlapped plants • Prune shrubs after blooming • Transplant trees and shrubs • Apply first lawn fertilizer • Mow lawn regularly • Trim lawn and border edging • Divide, plant, fertilize perennials • Fertilize bulbs after blooming • Shear hedges • Apply summer mulch • Weed and apply pre-emergent herbicide • Plant annuals • Plant tender bulbs • Water as needed • Check for insects, disease	• Plant container and balled-and-burlapped plants • Prune shrubs after blooming • Mow lawn regularly • Trim lawn and border edging • Trim, plant ground covers • Divide, plant, fertilize perennials • Shear hedges • Weed and apply pre-emergent herbicides • Plant summer annuals • Plant tender bulbs • Water as needed • Check for insects, disease	• Plant container and balled-and-burlapped plants • Prune shrubs after blooming • Mow lawn regularly • Trim lawn and border edging • Trim, plant ground covers • Divide, plant, fertilize perennials • Shear hedges • Weed and apply pre-emergent herbicides • Plant summer annuals • Plant summer bulbs • Water as needed • Check for insects, disease	• Plant container and balled-and-burlapped plants • Prune shrubs after blooming • Mow lawn regularly • Trim lawn and border edging • Trim, plant ground covers • Divide, plant, fertilize perennials • Shear hedges • Weed and apply pre-emergent herbicides • Plant summer annuals • Plant summer bulbs • Water as needed • Check for insects, disease	**MAY/JUNE**

	ZONE 1	ZONE 2	ZONE 3	ZONE 4	ZONE 5
JULY/AUGUST	• Plant container and balled-and-burlapped plants • Transplant evergreens • Fertilize container plants • Weed, apply pre-emergent herbicide • Apply second lawn fertilizer • Seed or sod lawn • Mow lawn regularly • Divide, plant perennials • Plant chrysanthemums for fall color • Water as needed • Check for insects, disease	• Plant container and balled-and-burlapped plants • Transplant evergreens • Fertilize container plants • Weed, apply pre-emergent herbicide • Apply second lawn fertilizer • Seed or sod lawn • Mow lawn regularly • Divide, plant perennials • Plant chrysanthemums for fall color • Water as needed • Check for insects, disease	• Plant container and balled-and-burlapped plants • Transplant evergreens • Fertilize container plants • Weed, apply pre-emergent herbicide • Apply second lawn fertilizer • Seed or sod lawn • Mow lawn regularly • Divide, plant perennials • Plant chrysanthemums for fall color • Water as needed • Check for insects, disease	• Plant container and balled-and-burlapped plants • Transplant evergreens • Fertilize container plants • Weed, apply pre-emergent herbicide • Apply second lawn fertilizer • Seed or sod lawn • Mow lawn regularly • Divide, plant perennials • Plant chrysanthemums for fall color • Water as needed • Check for insects, disease	• Fertilize container plants • Weed and apply pre-emergent herbicide • Mow lawn regularly • Water as needed • Check for insects, disease
SEPTEMBER/OCTOBER	• Spread winter mulch and wrap plants in burlap • Apply third lawn fertilizer • Trim lawn and border edging • Transplant deciduous trees and shrubs • Rake leaves • Lift tender bulbs; store • Plant spring-flowering bulbs • Secure vines to supports • Water if ground is dry • Turn off water, drain hose • Prepare soil for spring planting	• Spread winter mulch and wrap plants in burlap • Apply third lawn fertilizer • Trim lawn and border edging • Transplant deciduous trees and shrubs • Rake leaves • Lift tender bulbs; store • Plant spring-flowering bulbs • Secure vines to supports • Water if ground is dry • Turn off water, drain hose • Prepare soil for spring planting	• Spread winter mulch and wrap plants in burlap • Apply third lawn fertilizer • Trim lawn and border edging • Transplant deciduous trees and shrubs • Rake leaves • Lift tender bulbs; store • Plant spring-flowering bulbs • Secure vines to supports • Water if ground is dry • Turn off water, drain hose • Prepare soil for spring planting	• Spread winter mulch and wrap plants in burlap • Apply third lawn fertilizer • Transplant deciduous trees and shrubs • Rake leaves • Lift tender bulbs; store • Plant spring-flowering bulbs • Secure vines to supports • Water if ground is dry • Turn off water, drain hose • Prepare soil for spring planting	• Plant container and balled-and-burlapped plants • Transplant deciduous trees and shrubs • Rake leaves • Seed or sod lawn • Apply second lawn fertilizer • Divide perennials and ground covers • Lift tender bulbs; store • Plant chrysanthemums for fall color • Plant spring-flowering bulbs • Secure vines to supports • Prepare soil for spring planting
NOVEMBER/DECEMBER	• Prune dormant woody plants • Feed dormant trees, shrubs • Spray evergreens with antidesiccant • Install protection against animals	• Prune dormant woody plants • Feed dormant trees, shrubs • Spray evergreens with antidesiccant • Install protection against animals	• Prune dormant woody plants • Feed dormant trees, shrubs • Spray evergreens with antidesiccant • Install protection against animals	• Prune dormant woody plants • Feed dormant trees, shrubs • Spray evergreens with antidesiccant • Install protection against animals	• Prune dormant woody plants • Feed dormant trees, shrubs • Spray evergreens with antidesiccant • Spread winter mulch and wrap plants in burlap • Install protection against animals • Apply third lawn fertilizer • Rake leaves • Water if ground is dry • Turn off water, drain hose

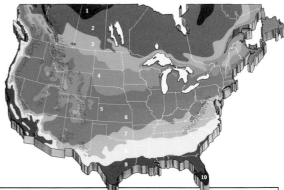

	ZONE 6	ZONE 7	ZONE 8	ZONE 9	ZONE 10	
	• Fertilize container plants • Weed and apply pre-emergent herbicide • Mow lawn regularly • Water as needed • Check for insects, disease	• Fertilize container plants • Weed and apply pre-emergent herbicide • Mow lawn regularly • Water as needed • Check for insects, disease	• Fertilize container plants • Weed and apply pre-emergent herbicide • Mow lawn regularly • Water as needed • Check for insects, disease	• Fertilize container plants • Weed and apply pre-emergent herbicide • Mow lawn regularly • Water as needed • Check for insects, disease	• Fertilize container plants • Weed and apply pre-emergent herbicide • Mow lawn regularly • Water as needed • Check for insects, disease	**JULY/AUGUST**
	• Plant container and balled-and-burlapped plants • Rake leaves • Seed or sod lawn • Apply second lawn fertilizer • Divide perennials and ground covers • Plant chrysanthemums for fall color • Plant spring-flowering bulbs • Secure vines to supports • Prepare soil for spring planting • Transplant evergreens	• Plant container and balled-and-burlapped plants • Rake leaves • Seed or sod lawn • Apply second lawn fertilizer • Divide perennials and ground covers • Plant chrysanthemums for fall color • Plant spring-flowering bulbs • Secure vines to supports • Transplant evergreens	• Plant container and balled-and-burlapped plants • Rake leaves • Seed or sod lawn • Apply second lawn fertilizer • Divide perennials and ground covers • Plant chrysanthemums for fall color • Plant spring-flowering bulbs • Secure vines to supports • Transplant evergreens	• Plant container and balled-and-burlapped plants • Apply second lawn fertilizer • Reseed lawn if needed • Rake leaves • Plant chrysanthemums for fall color • Divide perennials and ground covers • Secure vines to supports • Transplant evergreens • Plant cool-season annuals • Refrigerate spring bulbs	• Plant container and balled-and-burlapped plants • Apply second lawn fertilizer • Reseed lawn if needed • Rake leaves • Plant chrysanthemums for fall color • Divide perennials and ground covers • Secure vines to supports • Transplant evergreens • Plant cool-season annuals • Refrigerate spring bulbs	**SEPTEMBER/OCTOBER**
	• Prune dormant woody plants • Feed dormant trees, shrubs • Spray evergreens with antidesiccant • Spread winter mulch and wrap plants in burlap • Install protection against animals • Apply third lawn fertilizer • Rake leaves • Transplant deciduous trees and shrubs • Remove faded annuals and perennials • Plant spring-flowering bulbs • Lift tender bulbs; store • Water if ground is dry • Turn off water, drain hose	• Prune dormant woody plants • Feed dormant trees, shrubs • Spray evergreens with antidesiccant • Spread winter mulch and wrap plants in burlap • Install protection against animals • Apply third lawn fertilizer • Rake leaves • Transplant deciduous trees and shrubs • Remove faded annuals and perennials • Plant spring-flowering bulbs • Lift tender bulbs; store • Plant container and balled-and-burlapped plants • Prepare soil for spring planting • Water if ground is dry • Turn off water, drain hose	• Prune dormant woody plants • Feed dormant trees, shrubs • Spray evergreens with antidesiccant • Spread winter mulch and wrap plants in burlap • Install protection against animals • Apply third lawn fertilizer • Rake leaves • Transplant deciduous trees and shrubs • Remove faded annuals and perennials • Plant spring-flowering bulbs • Lift tender bulbs; store • Plant container and balled-and-burlapped plants • Prepare soil for spring planting • Water if ground is dry • Turn off water, drain hose	• Feed dormant trees, shrubs • Apply third lawn fertilizer • Rake leaves • Transplant deciduous trees and shrubs • Plant container and balled-and-burlapped plants • Plant bare-root trees and shrubs • Plant prechilled spring bulbs • Water if ground is dry	• Feed dormant trees, shrubs • Apply third lawn fertilizer • Rake leaves • Transplant deciduous trees and shrubs • Plant container and balled-and-burlapped plants • Plant bare-root trees and shrubs • Plant prechilled spring bulbs • Water if ground is dry	**NOVEMBER/DECEMBER**

WHAT TO DO
WHEN THINGS GO WRONG

PROBLEM	CAUSE	SOLUTION
Azaleas, rhododendrons, mountain laurel, andromeda and camellia fail to grow and bloom.	Soil is too alkaline or too poor. Climate is too hot.	Lower the acidity of the soil with powdered sulfur. Add organic matter. Mulch to keep roots cool. Do not use andromeda in areas of extreme summer heat.
Edges of broad-leaved evergreen leaves, especially younger leaves, turn brown and dry out.	Too much sun and wind, especially in winter.	Locate plants on the north or east side of the garden or of the house, out of winter sun and wind. Spray with an antidesiccant in fall. Protect with loose burlap covers in winter if the problem persists.
Tips and edges of leaves, especially older leaves, turn black.	Salt burn.	Do not overfertilize; pay careful attention to label instructions. If you accidentally overfeed, leach out the soil by watering heavily. Wait several months before feeding again. In sandy soil, water daily; in clay soil, water only when previous water is absorbed. Along roadways where salt is spread in winter, protect plants with a low barrier of stone or brick or with a loose cover of plastic. In fall, spray·with an antidesiccant.
Junipers, yews and cypress fail to grow; lower branches die; outside needles turn brown.	Overwatering, poor soil drainage, insufficient light.	Plant only where soil is well drained. To improve drainage, install drainage tiles or raised beds. Do not plant near constantly running automatic sprinklers or next to plants that need frequent watering. Plant in full sun.
Ends of branches or entire branches blacken and die.	Winter kill, a branch disease caused by cold.	Protect affected plants with loose burlap covers or mulch with an organic material such as salt marsh hay, which allows air and water to reach the soil. Prune out diseased branches in early spring. When adding to the landscape, choose plants that are hardy for the area.
Leaves develop ⅛- to ¼-inch, water-filled blisters that burst, leaving dry or colorless areas on the surface. Foliage becomes speckled or glazed in appearance.	Air pollution, exhaust fumes.	If the garden is located in a polluted area, choose plants with care. Use barberry, quince, forsythia, hydrangea, oleander, privet, yew, catalpa, gingko, London plane, magnolia, Norway maple, pin oak, willow oak, willow, Austrian or Japanese black pine.

PROBLEM	CAUSE	SOLUTION
High incidence of leaf diseases such as mildew and leaf spot.	Poor air circulation.	To promote air movement, thin out lower tree branches and allow sufficient room between plants; see the Dictionary of Plants for spacing appropriate to particular plants.
Shrubs fail to berry.	Lack of cross-pollination, improper pruning.	To promote pollination, plant two of each: viburnum, nandina, juniper, holly, yew and skimmia. With nandina and juniper, any two plants will cross-pollinate; male and female plants do not exist. With holly, yew and skimmia, plant one female and one male. Do not prune faded flower heads.
Plants gnawed or eaten to the ground; leaves eaten.	Animal damage.	Build a fence around your garden to keep animals away. Spray plants with lime or red-pepper solution. A wire-mesh or tar-paper cylinder can be wrapped around young trees to prevent animals from getting to the bark. Protection should reach 20 inches higher than the annual average snowfall line. Provide apples, ears of corn, nuts and seed for hungry animals. Some plants deter deer; among them are oleander, juniper, Oregon grape holly, iris, daffodils, tulips, eucalyptus, fir, cedar, zinnia, poppies and foxglove.
Lawn grows thinly; wears out in high-traffic areas.	Insufficient light, too much foot traffic.	In much-used areas, plant traffic-tolerant grass such as tall fescue. In shade, use a durable grass such as roughstalk bluegrass. On steep slopes and in areas where tree roots are shallow and competitive, use ground cover instead of lawn grass.
Evergreen leaves turn yellow.	Iron chlorosis, a condition caused by alkaline soil.	Chelated iron and iron sulfate are sold as powders at garden centers. Mix the powder with water and sprinkle on the foliage and on the soil that covers the root area to correct the pH.
Evergreens grow poorly near cement foundations or retaining walls.	Alkaline content in cement foundations infiltrates soil, raising soil pH.	To lower the pH of the soil, sprinkle sulfur powder on the ground covering the root area. Leave a buffer zone of 18 to 24 inches between foundations and trees.
Unwanted fruit and flowers litter garden.	Excess fruit and flower production.	Some trees can be sprayed with a growth regulator to prevent fruit and flower production; among them are horse chestnut, crab-apple and Norway maple. With apples, sweet cherries, Japanese plums and pears, plant only one tree and cross-pollination will not occur.

TIPS AND TECHNIQUES

SALVAGING A SLOPE

An area with a severe slope can be rescued for planting with shrubs or ground covers that have strong root systems. Roots help hold the soil in place and prevent erosion. Plants needing little care are also ideal on a slope; they require fewer trips on the hilly terrain for pruning and other maintenance chores. Good choices among shrubs are juniper, cotoneaster and Japanese barberry. Among ground covers, choose crown vetch, daylilies, hosta, ice plant or English ivy.

DESIGNING FOR FRAGRANCE

Of the many aspects of garden design, one that is often overlooked is fragrance. Nothing is more relaxing on a cool summer evening—or more inspiriting on a warm spring morning—than the aroma of a garden.

If you plant a border along a walk that leads to and from the front door, you can smell the flowers each time you come or go. Fill a shrub border with lilac, viburnum, osmanthus or gardenia. Trim it with hyacinth and lily of the valley in the spring and with sweet alyssum, heliotrope or garden pinks in the summer. Drape wisteria or star jasmine over a trellis near a window, where the scent can drift into the house. Use aromatic plants in containers on a terrace or a patio to enhance outdoor living areas.

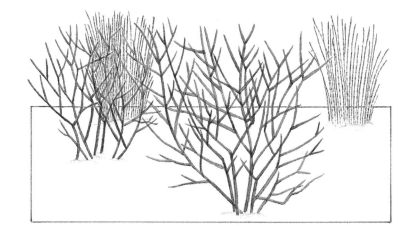

SCENIC WINTERSCAPES

Winter months need not mean dreary winter scenes if you choose trees and shrubs with care. The bare limbs, stems and branches of certain shrubs can provide year-round appeal even after foliage drops. The brightly colored stems of red-twig dogwood, for example, supply a dramatic contrast with snow *(above)*, as does feather reed grass, which retains a sculptural look even after it turns brown. The gnarled limbs of some contorted filberts have twisted contours that show up best when the shrubs are leafless.

Among trees, willow, weeping cherry, dogwood and zelkova provide handsome outlines against the winter sky. To add texture as well as color, choose a tree with a mottled, shedding or colored bark. Examples are crape myrtle, dawn redwood, lacebark pine, paperbark maple and sycamore.

GARDENING BY THE SEA

You can shelter a seaside garden from the hazards of high winds and saltwater spray by encouraging sand dunes to build up. Place two snow fences in the face of the prevailing winds—that is, parallel to the shoreline and to each other. The first fence diminishes the force of the wind so that much of the sand borne on it cannot pass through the second fence and instead comes to rest. Once established, sand dunes may be kept intact with strong-rooted ground covers such as beach grass, bearberry and sand blackberry.

HOLDING BACK THE WIND

In the American Midwest, where winds are fierce (up to 60 miles an hour), protective plantings that reduce wind damage are called shelterbelts. In most of the rest of the country they are known as windbreaks. By any name, a screen of trees or tall shrubs can do much to block the force of the wind. Such a screen may be planted in a single row, but a double row is more effective. Choose evergreens for best protection.

How tall the plants should be depends on how much land you wish to shield from the wind. A screen will reduce wind velocity by 80 percent for a distance about five times its own height. In other words, a screen of 20-foot cedars will cut a brisk 15-mph wind to a tame 3-mph breeze for a distance of 100 feet.

ATTRACTING BIRDS

Birds add color and action to a garden, and there are many ways to attract them. Dense trees and shrubs offer them shelter and sites for their nests. Berries give them food. Evergreen cones provide food for warblers during the spring and winter months; honeysuckle draws hummingbirds in summer. Spring and summer flowers invite birds of all kinds to feed on seeds and nectar.

To make birds feel at home, houses and feeders are essential. So is a year-round supply of drinking and bath water, which can be kept from freezing in winter with special heaters available at hardware stores. Place feeders and birdbaths outside the windows of the kitchen or a living area so that you can watch the activity. Make sure that you select a spot in the sun, away from the wind and beyond the reach of cats and squirrels.

6
DICTIONARY OF PLANTS

A beautiful garden depends on knowledgeable plant selection. The dictionary on the following pages presents more than 150 plants having a combination of appealing features—outstanding form, flowers, fruit, bark, foliage—that make them especially attractive candidates for landscape design. Most of them look interesting in more than one season, but a few, such as the spring-flowering forsythias, are so spectacular in their few weeks of glory that they deserve room in the garden despite their modest appearance during the rest of the year. Many of the plants are so widely popular that they are generally stocked at garden centers. Others are less well known and must be bought on special order through a local nursery or from a mail-order nursery.

The dictionary is divided into 10 major categories *(opposite)*. In each category plants are grouped with their close relatives into genera. The genera and the individual plants belonging to them are identified first by their botanical names and then by their common names. Unrelated plants sometimes share common names, and many plants have three or four common names, which may vary from region to region. Common names do appear in the listing, however, with cross-references to the botanical names, so you will be able to locate a plant easily without knowing its botanical name.

ACER RUBRUM

AESCULUS × CARNEA 'BRIOTII'

DECIDUOUS TREES

Acer (AY-ser)
Maple

A diverse group of small to very large trees with dense, round crowns. Distinctively shaped foliage with brilliant fall color. Clusters of paired, winged seeds follow inconspicuous spring flowers. Zones 3-9.

Selected species and varieties. *A. buergeranum,* trident maple: fast-growing small tree up to 20 or 30 feet tall and spreading as wide. Trilobed leaves turn shades of yellow, orange or red in fall. Zones 6-8. *A. campestre,* hedge maple: slow-growing small tree with dense foliage. Grows to 20 or 30 feet. Leaves golden in fall. Zones 5-8. *A. griseum,* paperbark maple: small tree up to 25 feet tall with open branching pattern. Cinnamon red bark peels from trunks of mature trees. Red fall foliage. Zones 5-7. *A. palmatum,* Japanese maple: tree under 20 feet tall valued for its extremely decorative foliage. Bronze spring leaves become green in summer, turn red in fall. Very slow-growing. Zones 5-9. Among the many varieties available, *A. palmatum* 'Bloodgood' is an upright tree, 10 to 20 feet tall, prized for the deep red color it retains all summer; *A. palmatum dissectum* threadleaf Japanese maple, has leaves finely cut like paper lace on gnarled, drooping branches; *A. palmatum dissectum* 'Crimson Queen' has bright crimson, extremely lacy foliage on low, drooping branches that give the tree a weeping effect; and *A. palmatum dissectum* 'Ever Red' has a cascading form with attractive new growth, downy with silver hairs, that develops into mature deep red foliage. *A. platanoides,* Norway maple, grows rapidly into a towering dome of dense foliage up to 60 feet tall and as wide. Copious tiny yellow flowers in spring. Coarse leaves turn yellow in fall. Zones 4-7. Varieties include *A. platanoides* 'Columnare,' which grows in a narrow column; *A. platanoides* 'Crimson King,' with leaves that unfold red and remain deep red through autumn; and *A. platanoides* 'Drummondii,' with variegated white and green leaves. *A. pseudoplatanus,* sycamore maple or planetree maple: fast-growing tree that eventually reaches 70 feet. Five-lobed leaves do not change color in fall. Zone 5. *A. rubrum,* red maple or swamp maple, grows quickly into a tree up to 60 feet or more tall. Red spring flowers on female trees followed by red seeds. Leaves turn red to orange in fall. Zones 3-9. The variety *A. rubrum* 'Autumn Flame' has a compact, round head and colors earlier in fall than other varieties; *A. rubrum* 'October Glory' and *A. rubrum* 'Red Sunset' are outstanding for their late-fall red coloring. *A. saccharum,* sugar maple: slow-growing tree with an oval head, up to 75 feet tall. Brilliant fall foliage in mingled shades of yellow, orange and red. Zones 3-7. The variety *A. saccharum* 'Bonfire' is a rapid-growing sugar maple with brilliant red fall color; *A. saccharum* 'Green Mountain' has leathery leaves that turn golden orange in autumn.

Growing conditions. Plant maples in full sun in any well-drained soil. Open shade helps preserve the unusual leaf colors of Japanese maples. Red maple will grow in wet soils and in those that are alternately wet and dry. Prune the lower branches of smaller maples to maintain headroom beneath them. Prune in late summer or early fall; maples will bleed profusely if pruned in spring. Norway maple tolerates city pollution. Sugar maple is sensitive to road salts and air pollution. The waxy leaves of Green Mountain sugar maple make it more heat- and drought-resistant than other sugar maples.

Landscape uses. Plant large maples as specimen trees and as shade trees. Little can grow in their dense shade, however. Use delicate Japanese maples as specimen trees and as border accents.

Aesculus (ES-kew-lus)
Horse chestnut

Large tree with pyramidal crown of coarse foliage. Erect clusters of late-spring flowers followed by rough husked nuts. Zones 5-8.

Selected species and varieties. *A. × carnea* 'Briotii,' ruby horse chestnut: fast-growing tree that can reach 40 feet in height. Deeply veined 10-inch leaves with leaflets arranged like the fingers on a hand. Leaves drop early in fall without changing color. Ten-inch clusters of red flowers with yellow throats begin blooming when the tree is 6 to 10 feet tall. Nuts 2 inches across.

Growing conditions. Plant ruby horse chestnut in full sun in any moist but well-drained soil. It tolerates both urban and seaside conditions.

Landscape uses. Ruby horse chestnut may be used for shade or as a specimen tree. Caution: some gardeners find its litter of leaves, twigs and nuts objectionable.

—

Amelanchier (am-el-ANK-ee-er)
Serviceberry

Small to medium-sized tree with oval or round crown and single or multiple trunks. Branches billowy with nodding clusters of 1-inch white flowers in early spring before leaves appear. Edible crabapple-like red or purple fruit. Yellow to orange and red fall foliage. Zones 3-8.

Selected species and varieties. *A. canadensis,* downy serviceberry: silvery gray bark with dark stripes on mature trees up to 40 feet tall. Erect branches form an oval crown. Leaves when young gray-green with downy undersides, half-grown when flowers appear. Yellow to red fall color. *A. × grandiflora,* apple serviceberry: spreading crowns on trees up to 25 feet tall. Buds of the larger, later-blooming flowers are touched with pink. Yellow to orange fall color. *A. laevis,* Allegheny serviceberry: oval-shaped tree 20 to 30 feet tall at maturity. Young leaves tinged with red before turning fully green. Yellow to red autumn color.

Growing conditions. Plant serviceberry in any moist but well-drained soil in full sun or light shade. Prune suckers to train young trees to a single trunk.

Landscape uses. Use serviceberry at the back of a natural border, as a specimen tree set against a background of evergreens or as an understory tree beneath larger specimens.

—

Basswood see *Tilia*
Beech see *Fagus*

—

Betula (BET-yew-la)
Birch

Graceful, pliant tree with a lacy, irregular head. Single trunk or multiple stems with white, gray or reddish peeling bark on mature trees. Clear yellow autumn foliage. Birch grows quickly but is short-lived. Zones 2-9.

Selected species and varieties. *B. papyrifera,* canoe birch: from 30 to 60 feet tall at maturity, with ivory-colored bark becoming streaked with black bands as outer layers break into ragged sheets. Grows in Zones 2-7, but not always satisfactorily in warmer zones. *B. pendula,* European birch: pyramidal tree up to 60 feet tall with flaking white bark. Slightly pendulous branches. Grows in Zones 3-5. *B. pendula* 'Youngii,' Young's birch: remains small with conspicuously marked trunk. Graceful, slender branches sweep the ground. *B. platyphylla japonica,* Japanese white birch: unique ruffled white bark. Hardy in Zones 5-7. *B. nigra,* river birch: 30 to 60 feet tall with red to brown bark that peels into papery strips. Found at the edges of streams. Grows in Zones 4-9. More satisfactory in California than other birches.

Growing conditions. Most birches should be planted in full sun in well-drained soil; the river birch tolerates wet soil, while the paper birch grows in rocky and poor soils. Select a site protected from strong winds, which might break fragile branches. European birch tolerates heat and city growing conditions better than other species. All birches transplant poorly; move balled-and-burlapped young trees in the spring. Prune anytime except in late winter or early spring, when birch will bleed excessively. Spray regularly for control of borers and miners, which can severely weaken the tree.

Landscape uses. Use birch as a single specimen or in clumps where dappled shade is desired. Birches enhance the appearance of a naturalized garden. Their bark provides winter color, especially when the trees are planted against a backdrop of dark evergreens. Furry, caterpillar-like catkins appear in the spring. Foliage turns yellow in fall.

—

Birch see *Betula*
Black gum see *Nyssa*

—

Carpinus (kar-PY-nus)
Hornbeam

Medium-sized tree with rippled bark, slowly growing to 20 or 30 feet with a spread almost as wide. Dense, shiny green foliage. Drooping caterpillar-like catkins followed by clusters of hanging nutlets. Zones 5-7.

Selected species and varieties. *C. betulus,* European hornbeam: catkins up to 5 inches long. Large, toothed leaves, which sometimes turn yellow in fall.

Growing conditions. European hornbeam can thrive in any moist but

AMELANCHIER CANADENSIS

BETULA PAPYRIFERA

CARPINUS BETULUS

CERCIDIPHYLLUM JAPONICUM

CERCIS CANADENSIS

CHIONANTHUS RETUSUS SERRULATUS

CLADRASTIS LUTEA

well-drained soil in full sun. Hornbeam tolerates heavy shearing. Transplant young trees under 8 feet tall for best results.

Landscape uses. Plant European hornbeam as a small shade tree or as a specimen. Group hornbeams for a dense screen or tall hedge.

—

Cercidiphyllum
(ser-sid-i-FILL-um)

Single-trunked oval or multiple-trunked wide-spreading tree growing rapidly to 25 feet and eventually up to 50 feet. Round, scalloped leaves on red-tipped branches. Unusual autumn color. Zones 5-9.

Selected species and varieties. *C. japonicum,* Katsura tree: reddish tinge to young leaves. Pale yellow to pink or red fall color. Shaggy, gray-brown bark on mature trees.

Growing conditions. Katsura may be planted in full sun in Zones 5-7, in light shade in Zones 8 and 9. Plant in any good, moist but not wet soil. Multiple-trunked trees spread as wide as they are tall. To develop an oval crown, prune Katsura to a single trunk when young.

Landscape uses. Katsuras are outstanding shade and specimen trees. Allow room for the spread of multiple-trunked trees.

—

Cercis (SER-sis)
Eastern redbud, American redbud, Judas tree

Small to medium tree with clusters of bright pink or white flowers on leafless branches in spring. Zones 5-9.

Selected species and varieties. *C. canadensis,* eastern redbud: up to 30 feet tall, with a broad crown sometimes exceeding 30 feet in width. Often has multiple trunks. Blooms when only four or five years old, bearing showy clusters of bright pink flowers in April or May before leaves appear. The heart-shaped leaves turn yellow in fall. The variety *C. canadensis alba* bears white flowers.

Growing conditions. Plant in full sun or light shade in moist, well-drained soil. It does not require fertile soil and needs little pruning. Transplant when young and under 6 feet tall, any time from fall through spring.

Landscape uses. As it matures, eastern redbud develops a broad, rounded crown that makes it an attractive specimen tree, although with

age it may develop an irregular, flat-topped crown. It is often interplanted with flowering dogwood, which blooms at the same time. It is relatively short-lived.

—

Cherry see *Prunus*

—

Chionanthus (ky-o-NAN-thus)
Fringe tree

Small tree between 12 and 25 feet tall with a trunk that begins branching close to the ground. Foliage unfolds very late in spring or early in summer. Clusters of white flowers with narrow petals like dangling fringe are followed by dark blue, olive-sized fruits on female plants. Yellow autumn color. Zones 5-9.

Selected species and varieties. *C. retusus serrulatus,* Oriental fringe tree: erect branches form tree with vase-shaped crown. Red-brown peeling bark on older trees. Oval 4-inch leaves. Flower clusters up to 4 inches long on tips of twigs. Zones 6-9. *C. virginicus,* white fringe tree, old man's beard: slow-growing, with arching branches spreading as wide as the tree is tall. Oblong 8-inch leaves. Very narrow-petaled flowers in clusters up to 8 inches long.

Growing conditions. Plant in full sun in any moist but not wet soil.

Landscape uses. Use fringe trees as specimen trees where their interesting branching pattern will show to advantage. Grow them at the back of a naturalized border. Male trees have slightly larger, showier flowers. Only females bear fruit.

—

Cladrastis (klad-RAS-tis)
Yellowwood

Medium-sized tree 20 to 40 feet tall with branches arching into a rounded head. Dense foliage with leaves composed of many rounded 4-inch leaflets. Drooping white flower clusters in early summer followed by thin pods. Zones 4-8.

Selected species and varieties. *C. lutea,* American yellowwood: fragrant, inch-long, butterfly-like flowers in drooping clusters up to 16 inches long. Sometimes blooms only every second or third year. Smooth silver-gray bark.

Growing conditions. Yellowwood can thrive in full sun and moist but well-drained soil. Established trees are able to tolerate drought. Prune in summer. Trees pruned in winter or spring may bleed excessively. Removing most of the flower clusters on very young trees for several years may increase the frequency of blooming as trees mature.

Landscape uses. Yellowwood is superb as a shade tree and as a lawn specimen. Because its roots are deep, turf and ground cover will grow in its dense shade.

Cornus (KOR-nus)
Dogwood

Small to medium-sized tree with open crown of horizontal branches spreading wider than the tree's height and becoming flat-topped with age. Clusters of flat white or pink flowers in spring or early summer followed by blue-black or red berries in summer. Foliage dull red or wine-colored in fall. Interesting square buds on winter twigs. Zones 4-9.

Selected species and varieties. *C. alternifolia,* pagoda dogwood: distinctly layered horizontal branches on trees up to 20 feet tall. Flat flower clusters 2½ inches across in spring followed by blue-black berries on red stalks. Zones 4-7. *C. florida,* flowering dogwood: 15 to 30 feet tall. White or pink flowers with distinctively notched, petal-like bracts in spring. Glossy red fruit. *C. florida* 'Cherokee Chief' has deep pink bracts. Large white flower bracts appear before the leaves of both *C. florida* 'Cherokee Princess' and *C. florida* 'Cloud Nine.' Zones 5-9. *C. kousa,* Japanese dogwood: pointed white petal-like bracts on 3- to 4-inch flowers in early summer; slow-growing. Red fruits that look like dangling raspberries. *C. kousa* 'Milky Way' produces unusually large quantities of flowers. The small flowers of *C. kousa* 'Summer Stars' remain on trees until late summer. *C. kousa chinensis,* Chinese dogwood, produces flowers slightly larger than others of the species. Zones 5-8.

Growing conditions. Dogwood may be planted in moist but well-drained soil in full sun or light shade. Light shade is best for flowering dogwood at the southern end of its range. Choose a site that is protected from winds and allows for the spread of mature trees. Japanese dogwood tolerates heat and drought better than other species.

Landscape uses. Use dogwoods as specimen trees or as border accents, especially in naturalized borders. They provide an airy understory beneath larger deciduous trees.

Cotinus (ko-TY-nus)
Smoke tree

Small tree, usually 15 feet tall, with loose, open head of round leaves. Tall clusters of inconspicuous fruiting flowers intermingled with striking sterile flowers composed of plumy hairs give the tree a smoky effect for weeks in late summer. Orange, red or purple autumn foliage. Zones 5-7.

Selected species and varieties. *C. coggygria,* smoke tree: blue-green 3-inch leaves. Yellow to orange fall color. Greenish purple to buff-colored feathery flowers. The cultivar *C. coggygria* 'Flame' has pink flower clusters and red-orange fall foliage; *C. coggygria* 'Royal Purple' has deep burgundy leaves that turn red in autumn.

Growing conditions. Plant smoke trees in full sun in any moist, well-drained soil. The royal purple smoke tree is less tolerant of cold weather than other varieties. Spring pruning will enhance its leaf color, but at the expense of flowers.

Landscape uses. Plant smoke trees as specimen plants or as background in a border where late-summer flowering interest is desired.

Crabapple see *Malus*
Crape myrtle see *Lagerstroemia*

Crataegus (krat-EE-gus)
Hawthorn

Medium-sized tree up to 30 feet tall with thorny horizontal branches that form a dense, round head. Toothed, triangular, lustrous leaves. Small white late-spring or early-summer flowers followed by colorful berry clusters. Zones 4-9.

Selected species and varieties. *C. phaenopyrum,* Washington hawthorn: shiny red edible fruits stay on tree into winter. Leaves red-orange in fall. Zones 4-8. *C. viridis* 'Winter King': very large, dull orange fruits remain through winter. Little fall color. Smooth silvery bark flakes off to show orange bark underneath on trunks of older trees.

Growing conditions. Hawthorn can flourish in full sun in any alkaline or acid soil that is moist but well

CORNUS FLORIDA

COTINUS COGGYGRIA 'ROYAL PURPLE'

CRATAEGUS PHAENOPYRUM

FAGUS SYLVATICA 'PENDULA'

FRANKLINIA ALATAMAHA

GINKGO BILOBA

GLEDITSIA TRIACANTHOS INERMIS 'SHADEMASTER'

drained. Once established, the tree tolerates dry soil conditions. It can be difficult to transplant. Move small plants in early spring.

Landscape uses. Plant hawthorns as specimen trees or mass them for a dense screen.

Dogwood see *Cornus*
Elm see *Ulmus*

Fagus (FAY-gus)
Beech

Massive tree that grows very slowly, reaching 80 feet tall and wide in as many years. Branches sweep the ground from a trunk with smooth gray bark. Very dense round head of toothed foliage. Nuts in small, prickly husks. Zones 5-9.

Selected species and varieties. *F. sylvatica,* European beech: dark green 4-inch leaves with wavy margins turning dark brown in winter. *F. sylvatica* 'Atropunicea,' copper beech, has red to purple leaves; *F. sylvatica* 'Pendula,' weeping beech, has horizontal branches that droop at their tips; and *F. sylvatica* 'Rotundifolia' has unusually dainty 1-inch round leaves on erect branches.

Growing conditions. Plant beech in full sun in a moist but not wet, slightly acid soil. Adequate soil moisture is essential at the southern end of its range.

Landscape uses. Use beeches as specimen trees where there is sufficient room for their spread. Dense foliage, shallow roots and low branches prevent other plants from growing beneath beeches.

Franklinia (frank-LIN-ee-a)

Low-branching oval tree up to 30 feet tall. Lustrous 8-inch oblong leaves. Late-summer to fall flowers tip branches. Zones 6 and 7.

Selected species and varieties. *F. alatamaha,* franklinia: creamy cupped flowers 3 to 4 inches across with prominent yellow centers. Rich orange-red fall foliage.

Growing conditions. Franklinia may be planted in full sun in well-drained acid soil. Remove lower branches on young plants for more treelike form.

Landscape uses. Use franklinia as a specimen tree or in a border where

its flowers will provide color that lasts into the fall.

Ginkgo (GINK-o)
Ginkgo, maidenhair tree

When young, a sculpturesque tree up to 30 feet tall with irregularly branched ascending limbs. Older trees up to 80 feet tall with rounder heads. Distinctive fan-shaped leaves. Zones 4-8.

Selected species and varieties. *G. biloba,* ginkgo or maidenhair tree: light green 3-inch leaves turning yellow in fall. *G. biloba* 'Autumn Gold' is a spreading tree with particularly good fall color. *G. biloba* 'Fastigiata,' sentry ginkgo, grows as a narrow, conical tree.

Growing conditions. Plant ginkgo in full sun in a moist but well-drained slightly acid soil. Ginkgoes are sensitive to air pollution. Select only male trees. Female trees, after many years, bear fleshy fruits that smell like rancid butter.

Landscape uses. Use ginkgoes as specimens, as street trees or wherever light, open shade is desired.

Gleditsia (gled-IT-see-a)
Honey locust

Rapid-growing large tree that can reach 25 feet in height and almost as wide in six or seven years. Mature trees 70 feet or more tall and almost half as wide. Trunks sometimes crooked. Open canopies of lacy leaves composed of many small leaflets. Some varieties with stiff 3-inch thorns and twisted, flat pods up to 18 inches long; others thornless and podless. Yellow fall color. Zones 4-9.

Selected species and varieties. *G. triacanthos inermis* 'Shademaster,' thornless honey locust: thornless, podless tree with very straight trunk and narrow crown. *G. triacanthos inermis* 'Sunburst': thornless, podless, slower-growing tree with golden young foliage that becomes green during summer.

Growing conditions. Plant honey locust in full sun in any ordinary soil. It tolerates alkaline soils and city conditions. At the northern end of its range, avoid practices that promote too vigorous growth, such as regular watering or over-fertilization.

Landscape uses. Use honey locust as a street tree or where light, open shade is desired; its ferny leaves admit enough sunlight for grass to grow under the tree.

Golden-rain tree
see *Koelreuteria*

Gum see *Nyssa*

Halesia (hal-EE-zha)
Silverbell

Tree with loose, open head. Pointed oval leaves that turn yellow in fall. Clusters of white flower bells line previous year's growth in spring, often before leaves appear. Winged green summer fruits ripen to brown in fall. Zones 5-9.

Selected species and varieties. *H. carolina,* Carolina silverbell: small tree 15 to 20 feet tall and spreading as wide. Half-inch flowers and 1½-inch four-winged fruits. Zones 5-9. *H. diptera,* two-winged silverbell: small tree to 15 feet with sparse 1-inch flowers and 2-inch two-winged fruits. Zones 8 and 9. *H. monticola,* mountain silverbell: large tree 40 feet or more. Larger flowers and 2-inch four-winged fruits. Zones 5-8.

Growing conditions. Plant silverbells in full sun or light shade in a moist but well-drained soil that is slightly acid. Young Carolina silverbell can be trained to a single stem or left to grow as a multistemmed tree.

Landscape uses. Silverbell may be planted as a specimen or in a site where light shade is desired, or use several in a naturalized garden. Carolina silverbell and the two-winged silverbell will grow in the open shade of other trees. Use mountain silverbell as a canopy for broad-leaved evergreen shrubs.

Hawthorn see *Crataegus*

Honey locust see *Gleditsia*

Hornbeam see *Carpinus*

Horse chestnut see *Aesculus*

Japanese pagoda tree
see *Sophora*

Katsura tree see *Cercidiphyllum*

Koelreuteria (kol-roo-TEE-ree-a)
Golden-rain tree

Medium-sized tree up to 30 feet tall with round head of ferny leaves composed of many small leaflets. Tiny yellow flowers with red centers clustered in foot-long spikes growing at the tips of branches. Summer or fall flowers followed by inflated green pods that turn brown and remain on trees into late fall. Leaves occasionally yellow before dropping. Zones 5-9.

Selected species and varieties. *K. paniculata,* golden-rain tree: midsummer flower spikes followed by 2-inch yellow-green pods. *K. paniculata* 'September': late-summer or early-fall flowers. Less hardy in Zones 6-9.

Growing conditions. Plant golden-rain tree in full sun in any moist, well-drained soil. Golden-rain tree tolerates both acid and alkaline soils and thrives in city conditions. Protect from strong winds, which can break limbs or overturn shallow-rooted trees.

Landscape uses. Use golden-rain as a medium shade tree or as a street or lawn specimen.

Lagerstroemia
(lay-ger-STREEM-ee-a)
Crape myrtle

Small, multiple-stemmed fast-growing tree with broad, spreading crown. Crape myrtle is valued for the loose clusters of crinkled flowers that cap the current year's growth in middle to late summer. Glossy oval leaves are bronze when young, and turn red or yellow in fall. The tree's silver-gray bark flakes to reveal pink, tan or gray bark underneath. Zones 7-10.

Selected species and varieties. *L. indica,* crape myrtle: profuse 5- to 10-inch clusters of 1½-inch white, pink, red, lavender or bluish flowers on trees 10 to 20 feet tall. *L. indica* 'Cherokee' is a smaller tree and has bright red flowers. *L. indica* 'Natchez' grows to 25 feet in height, with white flowers and cinnamon-colored bark.

Growing conditions. Crape myrtle does best in full sun in a moist but well-drained soil that has been enriched with organic matter. It will tolerate alkaline soil. Cold winters at the northern end of its range may kill the plant top; select a site with a southern exposure, preferably against a wall or an embankment. Prune in spring; flowers will bloom that year on new growth.

Landscape uses. Crape myrtle may be planted as a specimen tree or at the back of a border.

HALESIA MONTICOLA

KOELREUTERIA PANICULATA

LAGERSTROEMIA INDICA

LIQUIDAMBAR STYRACIFLUA

LIRIODENDRON TULIPIFERA

MAGNOLIA SOULANGIANA

MALUS FLORIBUNDA

Linden see *Tilia*

—

Liquidambar (lik-wid-AM-bar)
Sweet gum

A large conical tree growing up to 30 feet in 10 years, ultimately reaching a height of 80 feet or more. Maple-like leaves with striking fall color. Inconspicuous flowers are followed by prickly, woody 1-inch fruits that remain on the tree into winter. Ridged, corky bark on mature trees. Zones 5-9.

Selected species and varieties. *L. styraciflua,* sweet gum: star-shaped leaves unfold pale green, becoming deep green and leathery. Yellow and red fall color is sometimes mixed with green on the same tree. The foliage of *L. styraciflua* 'Burgundy' turns deep wine red in autumn. *L. styraciflua* 'Moraine' is an especially hardy, fast-growing variety with glossy green leaves that turn red in fall.

Growing conditions. Sweet gum may be planted in full sun in moist but not wet soil well enriched with organic matter. Lack of moisture will diminish the growth rate of sweet gum. Some gardeners object to the tree's seed pods.

Landscape uses. Use sweet gum as a shade tree or as a specimen.

—

Liriodendron (li-ri-o-DEN-dron)
Tulip tree

A very tall tree reaching 25 to 30 feet in eight years and ultimately growing to over 100 feet tall with a spread half as wide. The tree branches high on its trunk—at maturity 50 feet or more from the ground. Erect tulip-like flowers in early summer followed by conelike seed pods that remain into winter. Zones 5-9.

Selected species and varieties. *L. tulipifera,* tulip tree: greenish petals tinged with orange form 2-inch flowers after 10 or more years. Broad, glossy 5-inch leaves with blunt lobes.

Growing conditions. Tulip tree should be planted in a moist but not wet soil that is enriched with organic matter and deep enough to accommodate its long roots. Be sure to provide ample space for the tree's mature spread.

Landscape uses. Use tulip trees for shade or, on very large properties, as specimens.

Magnolia (mag-NO-lee-a)

Small to medium-sized tree with branches low on the trunk, or sometimes multiple trunks, in a wide-spreading pyramid. Fragrant, showy spring flowers appear before leaves. Knobby, conelike fruits split to release conspicuous red or orange seeds in fall. Zones 5-9.

Selected species and varieties. *M. × loebneri* 'Merrill,' Merrill magnolia: vigorous hybrid, fast-growing, 20 to 30 feet tall. Begins blooming when very young. Creamy white flowers up to 4 inches across. *M. × soulangiana,* saucer magnolia: 20 to 30 feet tall; upright, spreading oval head of coarse leaves. Large, cupped 5- to 10-inch flowers, white inside, tinged purple outside. Starts to bloom when very young. *M. stellata,* star magnolia: slow-growing, 15 to 20 feet tall, with branches that sweep the ground. Numerous ribbon-like white or pink petals on very fragrant flowers 4 inches across. Among the varieties available are *M. stellata* 'Pink Star,' with pink flower buds that open light pink to white; *M. stellata* 'Royal Star,' with very large flowers; and *M. stellata* 'Waterlily,' fast-growing, with pink buds that open to white flowers.

Growing conditions. Magnolias do well in full sun in any moist, well-drained soil. Star magnolia blooms very early but is susceptible to frost damage at its northern limits; place it where it has a northern exposure. This will retard blooming until the last frost is past.

Landscape uses. Plant magnolia as a specimen tree or as an accent at the back of a border where there is room for its spread.

—

Malus (MAY-lus)
Crabapple

Small tree 15 to 25 feet tall with a rounded head of pointed oval leaves. Abundant pink or white spring flowers, sometimes double-petaled, followed by edible, decorative pea-sized fruit that remains through fall. Zones 4-8.

Selected species and varieties. *M. × Donald Wyman:* pink flower buds unfold to white. Bright red fruit and dense foliage. *M. floribunda,* Japanese flowering crabapple: pink to red flower buds and pink to white flowers up to 1½ inches across and very fragrant. Yellow fruit touched with red. *M. halliana parkmanii,* Parkman crabapple: pink flowers 1 inch or more across with double petals. Small, dull red fruit. Vase-shaped tree with leathery leaves. Less hardy, Zones 5-8.

Growing conditions. Crabapple may be planted in full sun in a moist but well-drained soil that is slightly acid. Shape young trees by pruning in winter or early spring. Unless eaten by birds, fruit may create litter.

Landscape uses. Use crabapple as a specimen tree on a lawn or at the back of a border. The tree may be espaliered on a fence, wall or trellis. Several may be massed for screens.

Maple see *Acer*

Nyssa (NIS-sa)
Tupelo

Horizontal branches layered into a conical dome 25 to 75 feet tall and spreading half as wide. Spectacular autumn color. Inconspicuous small green flowers followed by tiny blue-black fruit clusters. Zones 5-9.

Selected species and varieties. *N. sylvatica,* tupelo, pepperidge, sour gum, black gum: leathery 5-inch leaves turn a mixture of brilliant yellows and scarlets in fall.

Growing conditions. Plant tupelo in full sun in a moist but not wet acid soil that is enriched with organic matter. A long taproot makes this tree difficult to transplant but tolerant of drought. Provide adequate water until tree is well established.

Landscape uses. Use tupelo as a specimen or as a shade tree.

Oak see *Quercus*

Oxydendrum (ox-si-DEN-drum)
Sourwood, sorrel tree

Very slow-growing tree, sometimes with multiple trunks, up to 30 feet tall. Neat pyramidal crown of glossy foliage. Young trees have branches to the ground. Drooping clusters of white flower bells like lily of the valley in summer, followed by strings of gray-brown seed pods that remain decorative into fall. Zones 5-9.

Selected species and varieties. *O. arboreum,* sourwood, sorrel tree: flower clusters 10 inches long or more. Glossy, pointed oval leaves up to 8 inches long turn deep red in fall.

Growing conditions. Sourwood does best in full sun in a moist but well-drained acid soil. Sourwood will grow in light shade but will have fewer flowers and less striking color. Sourwood will tolerate dry conditions once it is established.

Landscape uses. Use sourwood as a specimen tree or at the back of a border. Plant it as an understory tree beneath tall evergreens or combine with broad-leaved evergreens as part of a naturalistic border.

Pear see *Pyrus*
Pepperidge see *Nyssa*

Prunus (PROO-nus)
Cherry

Small to medium-sized trees bearing masses of delicate, long-lasting, single- or double-petaled, white or pink flowers that blossom in spring before leaves appear. Finely toothed oval leaves, sometimes with autumn color. Scanty, inconspicuous fruits. Zones 5-9.

Selected species and varieties. *P. sargentii,* Sargent cherry: up to 40 feet, pink or rose flowers 1½ inches across with a single row of petals. Leaves red or orange in fall. Lustrous reddish brown bark banded horizontally. Zones 5-9. *P. serrulata,* Japanese flowering cherry: to 50 feet, white clusters of 2½-inch white or pink flowers with single or double rows of petals. No autumn color. Zones 6-8. The variety *P. serrulata* 'Kwanzan' grows up to 40 feet and has ascending branches in a vase shape and extremely profuse double-petaled deep pink flowers 2½ inches across. *P. serrulata* 'Shirotae,' also called 'Mount Fuji': 15-foot tree that bears fragrant double-petaled white flowers 2½ inches across with ruffled edges. *P. subhirtella autumnalis,* autumn Higan cherry: 20-40 feet, nearly double-petaled light pink flowers 1½ inches across appearing in both fall and spring. Zones 6-8. *P. subhirtella pendula,* weeping Higan cherry, has graceful, drooping branches. Zones 6-8. *P. yedoensis,* Yoshino cherry: up to 40 feet; very early fragrant spring flowers 1 inch across, opening pale pink, then fading to white. Zones 6-8.

Growing conditions. Plant in full sun in any moist but well-drained soil. Choose a site sheltered from winds to protect brittle branches. Young trees can be difficult to establish. Avoid

NYSSA SYLVATICA

OXYDENDRUM ARBOREUM

PRUNUS SUBHIRTELLA PENDULA

PYRUS CALLERYANA 'BRADFORD'

QUERCUS ALBA

SALIX BABYLONICA

summer fertilizing or fall watering that would encourage late-season growth. Prune, if necessary, after flowering. Cherry trees tend to be short-lived, about 20 years. The Sargent cherry tolerates pollution and tends to be hardier and more trouble-free than other Oriental cherry trees. The Kwanzan cherry is considered the hardiest of the double-petaled varieties.

Landscape uses. Use cherry trees as specimens or as patio trees. Plant several in front of an evergreen border to accent their flowers. Mass them for special effects. Espalier it against a wall or a trellis.

Pyrus (PY-rus)
Pear

Small to medium-sized tree 15 to 50 feet tall with an upright oval head. Clusters of erect white 1-inch flowers in spring before leaves appear. Glossy, dark green oval 3-inch leaves turning deep red, then orange, in fall. Insignificant ½-inch russet fruits. Zones 5-9.

Selected species and varieties. *P. calleryana* 'Aristocrat': fast-growing tree with open head. Leaves with rippled edges. *P. calleryana* 'Bradford,' Bradford pear: compact pyramidal tree with dense foliage that retains its color into late fall. *P. calleryana* 'Chanticleer': very narrow cone of dense foliage.

Growing conditions. Plant Callery pear in full sun in any moist but well-drained soil. It should be pruned to prevent the development of a narrow crotch, which could split in a high wind. In winter or early spring, prune lower branches for headroom.

Landscape uses. Use as specimen trees, small shade trees or street trees. Espalier a pear tree against a wall or trellis.

Quercus (KWER-kus)
Oak

Very large, long-lived tree up to 60 feet or more at maturity with loose, round head spreading nearly as wide. Attractive lobed, sometimes toothed, leaves in some species noteworthy for rich autumn color. Short, inconspicuous female flower spikes. Zones 3-9.

Selected species and varieties. *Q. alba,* white oak: rigid horizontal branches with a broad spread. Round-lobed 9-inch leaves turn

brownish red in fall. Slow-growing. Zones 4-9. *Q. palustris,* pin oak: fast-growing, pyramidal form with erect upper branches and drooping lower ones. Shiny green leaves with narrow lobes turn yellow or bronze in fall, and then brown, sometimes remaining on trees through winter. Intolerant of alkaline soil. Zones 5-8. *Q. phellos,* willow oak: fast-growing, spreading pyramidal form. Very narrow leaves, only ½ inch wide, turn yellow or brown in fall. Zones 6-9. *Q. robur,* English oak: spreading, open head. Lobed leaves remain green in fall. Zones 5-9. The variety *Q. robur* 'Fastigiata' grows as a narrow column. *Q. rubra,* red oak: fast-growing, pyramidal when young, becoming wide-spreading with age. Large, 8-inch lobed leaves turn bright red in fall. Zones 3-9. *Q. velutina,* black oak: very tall tree that can reach 125 feet at maturity. Shiny, dark green 9-inch leaves with hairy undersides. Red fall color. Zones 4-9.

Growing conditions. Oak does best in full sun and in well-drained soil deeply enriched with organic matter. Most oaks prefer a slightly acid soil; pin oak requires it. For shallow-rooted willow oak, choose a site protected from high winds. Red oak and willow oak tolerate urban growing conditions. Long taproots make white oak and black oak difficult to transplant.

Landscape uses. Plant most oaks as specimens or as shade trees where they will have adequate room for mature spread. English oak 'Fastigiata' is suitable for use in a constricted area. Oaks provide filtered sunlight for shade-loving shrubs and small trees growing underneath. Prune dead lower branches to improve appearance. Some gardeners object to oak litter.

Regent scholar tree
see *Sophora*

Salix (SAY-lix)
Willow

Fast-growing tree, 15 to 75 feet in height, with pendulous arched branches that sweep the ground. Very narrow 3- to 6-inch fine-textured leaves. Zones 5-9.

Selected species and varieties. *S. babylonica,* Babylon weeping willow: light green caterpillar-like catkins among very pale green emerging leaves in spring. Foliage dull green in summer, yellow in autumn. Height to 40 feet. Zones 7-9. *S. matsudana* 'Torulosa,' corkscrew willow: small tree to 15 feet. Unlike most willows, 'Torulosa' has branches that ascend rather than droop, and twigs in twisted spirals. Zones 5-9.

Growing conditions. Plant willow in full sun in any soil that is moist or even wet. Water during dry periods. Protect brittle limbs from strong winds. Prune Babylon weeping willow for headroom, if desired, during summer or fall; willows will bleed excessively if they are pruned in winter or spring.

Landscape uses. Use willows as specimens. Grow them at the edge of a pond or a stream, where their moisture requirements will be met.

Serviceberry see *Amelanchier*
Silverbell see *Halesia*
Smoke tree see *Cotinus*
Snowbell see *Styrax*

Sophora (sof-FO-ra)
Japanese pagoda tree, Regent scholar tree

Round-headed tree prized for the showy clusters of cream to pale yellow blooms that tip its branches in late summer. Zones 5-9.

Selected species and varieties. *S. japonica* 'Regent,' Regent scholar tree: between 20 and 60 feet tall at maturity, with a spread that is equally wide. White to yellow ½-inch flowers, in clusters up to 15 inches long, appear in July and August. Clusters profuse on mature trees. Drab green bark on growing twigs. Beautiful, evenly furrowed charcoal gray bark on older trees.

Growing conditions. May be planted in full sun in any well-drained soil in a site protected from high wind. The Regent scholar tree is susceptible to frost damage in Zone 5. Requires little pruning. Tolerates city growing conditions.

Landscape uses. Plant as a shade tree or as an ornamental specimen. The late-summer flowers extend the season of bloom.

Sorrel tree see *Oxydendrum*
Sour gum see *Nyssa*

Sourwood see *Oxydendrum*

Stewartia (stew-ART-ee-a)

A low-branching pyramidal tree that grows slowly up to 25 feet with a spread as wide or wider. It has waxy white summer flowers that resemble camellias and flaking bark in mottled tones of brown. Good fall color. Zones 6-8.

Selected species and varieties. *S. pseudocamellia,* Japanese stewartia: tight, round green buds an inch across unfold to reveal 2½-inch cupped white flowers with orange centers. Oval 4-inch leaves turn reddish purple in autumn.

Growing conditions. Japanese stewartia may be planted in partial shade in a moist but well-drained, slightly acid soil. Choose a site that is sheltered from wind. Japanese stewartia is difficult to transplant. Buy a container-grown small plant with an ample soil ball.

Landscape uses. Plant Japanese stewartia as a specimen tree or group several of them for summer screening.

Styrax (STY-rax)
Snowbell

A small to medium-sized tree with dangling clusters of small, bell-shaped white flowers that blossom in summer. Snowbell has dense, lustrous green foliage with little autumn color. Zones 6-9.

Selected species and varieties. *S. japonicus,* Japanese snowbell, has a spread wider than its 20- to 30-foot height, a flat top and mildly fragrant ¾-inch flower bells with upturned petals dangling in clusters beneath stiff 3-inch leaves. Occasional yellow or red fall color. Zones 6-8. *S. obassia,* fragrant snowbell: upright tree to 25 feet, with strongly scented flower bells in drooping 8-inch clusters somewhat obscured by large leaves up to 4 inches wide and 8 inches long. Zones 6-8.

Growing conditions. Snowbell should be planted in full sun in a moist but well-drained soil. Protect from winter winds. To transplant, ball-and-burlap the tree when it is small and young, in early spring.

Landscape uses. Use any snowbell as a specimen or as a patio tree where there is sufficient room for the tree's spread.

SOPHORA JAPONICA 'REGENT'

STEWARTIA PSEUDOCAMELLIA

STYRAX OBASSIA

TILIA CORDATA

ULMUS PARVIFOLIA

ZELKOVA SERRATA

ACACIA BAILEYANA

Sweet gum see *Liquidambar*

Tilia (TIL-ee-a)
Basswood, linden

Large pyramidal tree 45 to 75 feet tall or more and spreading half as wide. Dense heart-shaped foliage. Yellowish white early-summer flowers with fine fragrance dangle from narrow, leaflike bracts. Little autumn color. Zones 3-8.

Selected species and varieties. *T. americana,* American linden, basswood: fast-growing tree with loose clusters of ½-inch yellow flowers that hang from pale yellow-green bracts among coarse, medium green leaves up to 8 inches long. Leaves sometimes turn yellow or brown in fall before dropping. *T. cordata,* littleleaf linden: very tiny, yellowish white flowers in clusters beneath yellowish bracts. Deep green leaves 2½ inches long. Slow-growing. The variety *T. cordata* 'Greenspire' is a narrow tree with symmetrical branches.

Growing conditions. Although lindens tolerate some shade, they prefer full sun in a moist and well-drained soil that is neutral to alkaline. Littleleaf linden withstands pollution.

Landscape uses. Lindens make excellent street trees. They may be planted as shade or specimen trees. Use American linden in a naturalistic garden.

Tulip tree see *Liriodendron*
Tupelo see *Nyssa*

Ulmus (UL-mus)
Elm

Very fast-growing large tree with loose, rounded head. Foliage yellow and purple in fall. Inconspicuous greenish flowers in late summer or early fall, followed by clusters of seeds surrounded by papery wafers. Zones 5-9.

Selected species and varieties. *U. parvifolia,* Chinese elm: glossy oval 2-inch leaves on branches that droop slightly. Up to 50 feet tall at maturity. Forked trunks with mottled, flaking bark on older trees. Resistant to Dutch elm disease, which has decimated the American elm population.

Growing conditions. Chinese elm can flourish in any moist but well-

drained soil in full sun. Protect from high winds, which can uproot the tree or break any brittle branches. Prune dead or damaged branches in any season. Little grows beneath Chinese elm in competition with its extensive feeder roots. At the southern end of its range, Chinese elm may remain green almost year-round.

Landscape uses. Chinese elm may be used as a fast-growing shade tree or as a specimen.

Willow see *Salix*
Yellowwood see *Cladrastis*

Zelkova (zel-KO-va)

Medium to large tree growing rapidly up to 80 feet. Trunk with multiple forks developing into vase-shaped crown. Toothed oval leaves up to 5 inches long that unfold pale green, then deepen. Zones 4-9.

Selected species and varieties. *Z. serrata* 'Green Vase': 60 to 70 feet tall with narrow vase shape. Bronzy red autumn foliage. Zones 5-9. *Z. serrata* 'Village Green': slightly arching branches develop wineglass-shaped crown on trees 50 to 60 feet tall. Rusty red fall color. Zones 4-9.

Growing conditions. Plant zelkova in full sun in any moist but well-drained soil. Tolerates city growing conditions.

Landscape uses. Use zelkova for shade or as a street tree and as a disease-resistant substitute for American elm.

BROAD-LEAVED EVERGREEN TREES

Acacia (a-KAY-sha)
Acacia, wattle

Small to medium-sized tree with a round head of soft, feathery foliage. Fragrant yellow flowers in striking clusters appear in late winter or in spring and are followed by pods. Zones 8-10.

Selected species and varieties. *A. baileyana,* Cootamundra wattle: gray-blue fernlike leaves. Foliage nearly hidden by feathery flower balls in 3-inch clusters from January through March. To 30 feet tall. Zone 10. *A. farnesiana,* sweet acacia: leaves composed of tiny leaflets less than ½ inch long. Branches bristly with thorns. Tiny flower balls in extremely fragrant clusters in February and March. Up to 10 feet tall. Zones 8-10. *A. melanoxylon,* blackwood acacia: fernlike foliage with broad 4-inch leaflets. Very pale yellow flowers in short spikes. Twisted 5-inch pods. Zones 8-10.

Growing conditions. Plant acacia in full sun in a moist but well-drained soil. The amount of water a young tree receives can regulate its growth rate. Once established, acacia tolerates dry conditions. Prune after blooms fade, training to a single trunk if necessary.

Landscape uses. Use acacias as specimen trees on a patio or at the back of a flower border. They grow extremely fast, reaching 20 feet in five years, but this advantage is offset by a relatively short life span compared with those of other flowering trees.

—

Arbutus (ar-BEW-tus)

Medium to large tree with glossy evergreen foliage and showy pink or white flowers. Zones 7 and 8 in coastal climates.

Selected species and varieties. *A. menziesii,* Pacific Madrone: an open-headed tree up to 75 feet tall. Two- to 6-inch leathery elliptical leaves with hairy undersides. Erect white flower clusters up to 9 inches long in late spring, followed by red-orange berries in fall. Older bark peels back to reveal lighter, cinnamon-colored bark underneath. Grows in Zone 7. *A. unedo,* strawberry tree: a small tree up to 30 feet tall with lustrous toothed leaves. Drooping 2-inch clusters of white or pink flowers bloom in very late fall, followed by scarlet, berry-like fruits that remain on trees for a month or more. Grows in Zone 8.

Growing conditions. Arbutus species grow better along the West Coast than in the East. They are difficult to transplant. Move young balled-and-burlapped trees when they are 18 to 24 inches tall. Plant in full sun. They do best in a sandy, slightly dry soil. Avoid alkaline soils.

Landscape uses. Plant arbutus as a specimen tree.

—

Bauhinia (Baw-HIN-ee-a)

A small to medium-sized tree with an irregularly shaped head. Flowers that resemble orchids among kidney-shaped leaves on thorny branches. Zone 10.

Selected species and varieties. *B. forficata:* white flowers like butterflies up to 5 inches across in summer followed by flat 8-inch pods. Grows to 30 feet with drooping branches lined with ¼-inch spines.

Growing conditions. Plant bauhinia in full sun in moist, well-drained soil. It will tolerate light shade.

Landscape uses. Bauhinia is one of the showiest flowering trees. Plant as a specimen tree or group with other tropical flowering evergreen trees for a succession of blooms.

—

Eriobotrya (er-i-o-BOT-ree-a)

Small to medium-sized tree with a round ball of leathery, corrugated foliage. White flowers in fall and winter followed by edible yellow-orange fruits in spring. Zones 8 and 9.

Selected species and varieties. *E. japonica,* loquat, Japanese plum: fragrant, drooping clusters of ½-inch white flowers begin blooming in late fall among 10-inch oval leaves with woolly brown undersides. Grows to 25 feet.

Growing conditions. Loquat will thrive in full sun in a moist but well-drained soil that is not too alkaline.

Landscape uses. Grow loquat as a specimen or as a patio tree. Use as an evergreen background or as a canopy for a flower border.

—

Eucalyptus (yew-ka-LIP-tus)

Very fast-growing, medium-sized tree up to 50 feet tall. Loose, open head of fragrant leaves. Zone 9.

Selected species and varieties. *E. cinerea,* mealy stringybark, silverdollar eucalyptus: round, silver-gray leaves. Has fibrous, shredding red bark. *E. ficifolia,* red-flowering gum: showy clusters of flowers and deep green, yellow-veined leaves. Up to 30 feet tall.

Growing conditions. Plant eucalyptus trees in full sun in a well-drained to dry, slightly alkaline soil. Protect from strong winds. Mealy stringybark may require staking when young.

Landscape uses. Use eucalyptus trees as quick-growing shade trees or mass them for screens. Plant them as specimens where their foliage will

ARBUTUS UNEDO

BAUHINIA FORFICATA

ERIOBOTRYA JAPONICA

EUCALYPTUS FICIFOLIA

ILEX × ATTENUATA 'FOSTERI'

LAURUS NOBILIS

MAGNOLIA GRANDIFLORA

show to advantage. Some gardeners dislike their litter.

Gum see *Eucalyptus*
Holly see *Ilex*

Ilex (EYE-lex)
Holly

Small pyramidal tree notable for its shiny, crisp, sometimes spiny green foliage and the red or yellow berries that develop in fall and remain on trees through the winter. Zones 5-9.

Selected species and varieties. *I. × attenuata* 'Fosteri,' Foster No. 2: 20 to 30 feet tall, with a narrow cone of fast-growing spiny foliage. Heavy crop of pea-sized red berries. *I. opaca,* American holly: dense cone of spiny, arched or twisted leaves, from 10 to 40 feet tall. Inconspicuous white flowers followed by scarlet berries. Over 100 varieties exist, including *I. opaca* 'Amy,' with copious fruits and greater hardiness; *I. opaca* 'Goldie,' with thick curved leaves and abundant yellow berries; and *I. opaca* 'Jersey Princess,' with very dark green color. Zones 6-9. *I. pedunculosa,* long-stalked holly: 20 to 30 feet tall, with dark green spineless oval leaves. Clusters of red berries held above leaves on 1-inch stalks. Very hardy species. Zones 5-9. *I. vomitoria,* yaupon: 15 to 20 feet with stiff branches. Glossy, gray-green 1-inch leaves with spiny edges. Most prolific producer of ¼-inch red or yellow berries. Zones 8-10.

Growing conditions. Holly should be planted in full sun in a moist, well-drained, neutral to acid soil. Light shade slows growth but protects foliage from winter burn. Shelter hollies from winter winds. Yaupon adapts to extremes of sun and wind. Both male and female plants are necessary to produce berries. Choose nursery stock carefully to get fruiting female plants. These should be located within 100 feet of a male holly to ensure good berry production. Most hollies grow slowly, but Foster No. 2 can grow as much as a foot annually.

Landscape uses. Most hollies are naturally graceful and require little pruning to maintain a pleasing symmetrical shape. The red-berried hollies are prized for their winter color, and the branches of some red-berried varieties are harvested in December to serve as holiday decorations.

Japanese plum see *Eriobotrya*

Laurus (LAW-rus)
Laurel

Small tree that is prized for its dense head of leathery, aromatic foliage. Zones 8-10.

Selected species and varieties. *L. nobilis,* bay laurel, sweet bay: grows slowly to 20 or 30 feet tall. Dull, dark green, oval, pointed leaves. Aromatic and used for seasoning. Inconspicuous greenish white flowers blooming in spring followed by small black berries.

Growing conditions. Plant bay laurel in full sun or light shade in a moist but well-drained soil. To grow laurel as a tree, prune away all suckers and train the young plant to a single stem.

Landscape uses. Grow as a patio specimen or as an accent at the back of a formal border. Easily sheared and often clipped into topiary.

Loquat see *Eriobotrya*

Magnolia (mag-NO-lee-a)

Medium to large tree with an open, spreading crown of shiny, dark green oval leaves. Noteworthy for conspicuous, creamy white, late-spring to early-summer flowers. Colorful red or orange seeds dangle by a thread when conelike fruits split open. Zones 5-10.

Selected species and varieties. *M. grandiflora,* bull bay, southern magnolia: 30 to 80 feet tall, with oval crown. Waxy, thick-petaled, strongly scented flowers 8 to 10 inches across in early summer. Red-brown fuzz on the undersides of 8-inch leaves. Zones 7-10. The variety *M. grandiflora* 'Samuel Somer' has especially large flowers 14 inches across. *M. virginiana,* sweet bay: a deciduous or evergreen tree 25 to 40 feet tall with an irregular crown. Waxy gray bloom on the undersides of glossy 5-inch leaves. Very fragrant 3-inch white flowers in late spring. *M. virginiana* sometimes grows as a shrub in northern areas. The variety *M. virginiana australis* is often more vase-shaped and more reliably evergreen than other members of the species. Zones 5-10.

Growing conditions. Choose a site in full sun with well-drained soil for bull bay. Sweet bay tolerates wet, even swampy, soil but does not need it. Fleshy roots of young magnolias are easily damaged so trees are difficult to transplant. Place where mature tree will not become crowded. Sweet bay becomes deciduous at the northern end of its range.

Landscape uses. Evergreen magnolias are elegant specimen and shade trees.

Mealy stringybark
see *Eucalyptus*

Oak see *Quercus*

Pacific Madrone see *Arbutus*

Quercus (KWER-kus)
Oak

Massive tree with spreading horizontal branches. Up to 40 feet tall and almost twice as wide. Dense foliage. Zones 8-10.

Selected species and varieties. *Q. virginiana,* live oak: leathery, oblong 5-inch leaves with white fuzz on their undersides. Flowers are dangling caterpillar-like catkins and are followed by 1-inch acorns.

Growing conditions. Live oak prefers full sun and moist but well-drained soil enriched with organic matter. Sometimes deciduous at the northern end of its range.

Landscape uses. Use live oak for shade or as a specimen tree where there is room for its spread. Spanish moss often trails from aged limbs.

Strawberry tree see *Arbutus*

Swamp mahogany
see *Eucalyptus*

Sweet bay see *Laurus*

Wattle see *Acacia*

Yaupon see *Ilex*

NEEDLE-LEAVED EVERGREEN TREES

Abies (AY-beez)
Fir

Stately conical tree 50 or more feet tall with dense whorls of horizontal branches. Flat sprays of aromatic needles and erect cones. Zones 2-8.

Selected species and varieties. *A. balsamea,* balsam fir: a slow-growing, sparsely branched tree that will survive as far north as Zone 2 and grows south through Zone 5. *A. concolor,* white fir: grows up to 1½ feet annually with blue-green foliage in Zones 4-8. *A. nordmanniana,* Nordmann fir. Dark green needles. Grows in Zones 5-7.

Growing conditions. Plant in a sunny site protected from wind, in well-drained sandy soil that is slightly acid. Firs need little or no pruning. Balsam fir does best in a cool climate. White fir tolerates heat, drought and city growing conditions.

Landscape uses. Use firs as specimen trees or in masses for screens or hedges. Few plants can grow in the dense shade of these trees.

Arborvitae see *Thuja*

Calocedrus (kal-o-SEE-drus)

Formal columnar evergreen with fans of aromatic upright leaves. Zones 6-9.

Selected species and varieties. *C. decurrens,* California incense cedar: grows to 100 feet tall with flat, erect branches. Retains lower branches, even with age. Shredding red-brown bark on older trees.

Growing conditions. Select a sunny site with moist, well-drained soil. Choose a location protected from winter winds, especially at the northern end of the tree's range.

Landscape uses. Plant the California incense cedar as a striking specimen tree or group several together for a screen.

Cedar see *Calocedrus;*
see *Cedrus;* see *Juniperus*

Cedrus (SEE-drus)
Cedar

A stately tree with widely spreading branches that sweep the ground. Conical when young, becoming broader and flat-topped with age. Tufts of 1- to 2-inch green needles. Oval brown cones stand erect on topmost branches. Aromatic wood. Zones 7-9.

QUERCUS VIRGINIANA

ABIES CONCOLOR

CALOCEDRUS DECURRENS

CEDRUS ATLANTICA 'GLAUCA'

CHAMAECYPARIS PISIFERA 'FILIFERA AUREA'

× CUPRESSOCYPARIS LEYLANDII

CUPRESSUS

Selected species and varieties. *C. atlantica* 'Glauca,' blue Atlas cedar: grows to 60 feet tall with pyramid of branches that spread slightly upward. Attractive bluish needles. *C. deodara,* deodar cedar: graceful horizontal branches that droop at their tips. Has soft green needles and grows to 50 feet.

Growing conditions. Plant cedars in full sun in any moist, well-drained soil. Choose a site that is protected from the drying effects of winter winds.

Landscape uses. Use cedars as landscape accents where their spreading branches will show to advantage or mass several to make thick screens.

—

Chamaecyparis
(kam-ee-SIP-a-ris)
False cypress

A pyramidal tree up to 50 feet in height with flat sprays of scalelike leaves marked with white on undersides. Foliage primarily glossy dark green but many varieties have golden yellow, sage green or bluish green leaves. Shredding red-brown bark. Zones 5-8.

Selected species and varieties. *C. nootkatensis,* Nootka false cypress, Alaska false cypress: extremely fast-growing, with slightly drooping branches and dense, dark blue-green needles. The variety *C. nootkatensis* 'Pendula' is a weeping form. *C. obtusa,* Hinoki false cypress: slower-growing than other cypress species. Broad pyramids of glossy foliage. *C. pisifera,* Sawara false cypress: loose, open branches. Foliage can be either fluffy and feathery—resembling threads—or soft and mossy. *C. pisifera* 'Filifera Aurea,' golden thread: a variety up to 10 feet tall with weeping, golden, threadlike foliage; *C. pisifera* 'Squarrosa,' moss Sawara cypress, has feathery, soft, gray-green foliage and can grow up to 10 feet tall.

Growing conditions. Plant in full sun in moist, well-drained soil. False cypress does best in cool, humid conditions but will grow under average conditions. Choose a site protected from winter winds.

Landscape uses. Use false cypress as a specimen tree or as background for a flower border. Smaller trees are suitable for use as part of a foundation planting. Older trees lose their lower branches.

× Cupressocyparis
(kew-press-o-SIP-a-ris)
Leyland cypress

Grows rapidly into a medium-sized tree, reaching 15 feet in about five years and ultimately 50 feet or more. Hybrid of *Chamaecyparis nootkatensis* and *Cupressus macrocarpa.* Zones 7-9.

Selected species and varieties. × *C. leylandii,* Leyland cypress: column or narrow pyramid of dark green scalelike leaves. × *C. leylandii* 'Haggerston Gray' is a variety with soft green branches that turn up at their ends; × *C. leylandii* 'Leighton Green' has gray-green foliage, lighter on the underside.

Growing conditions. Plant Leyland cypress in any moist, well-drained soil in full sun. Choose a site protected from the drying effect of winter winds.

Landscape uses. Use Leyland cypress as a specimen tree or mass several for a fast-growing screen or hedge. Leyland cypress tolerates heavy pruning.

—

Cupressus (kew-PRESS-us)
Cypress

A tree that grows in a narrow, formal column up to 70 feet tall. Dark green scalelike leaves. Zones 7 and 8.

Selected species and varieties. *C. glabra,* smooth-barked Arizona cypress: gray-green to blue-green foliage. Flaking bark on older trees. Zone 7. *C. macrocarpa,* Monterey cypress: pyramidal species with varieties having weeping or horizontal forms and golden, green or blue-green foliage. Tolerates seaside conditions. Zone 8. *C. sempervirens,* Italian cypress: columnar tree with very dark green foliage. Zone 8.

Growing conditions. Plant cypress in full sun in well-drained soil. It will tolerate slightly dry soil. Monterey cypress will adapt to seaside conditions, often growing into a windswept form. Cypress grows well along the West Coast, less successfully in the East.

Landscape uses. Use cypress as a specimen tree or group several into a screen. Monterey cypress can be sheared into a hedge.

—

Cypress see *Cupressocyparis;* see *Cupressus*

Douglas fir see *Pseudotsuga*

Fir see *Abies*

Hemlock see *Tsuga*

Juniper see *Juniperus*

—

Juniperus (joo-NIP-er-us)
Juniper

A hardy family with great diversity of forms and colors. Foliage either prickly needles or smooth, overlapping scales in colors ranging from bright green through gray-green. Tolerant of hot, dry locations and city pollution. Zones 3-9.

Selected species and varieties. *J. chinensis*, Chinese juniper: pyramidal tree with scalelike leaves. Grows in Zones 4-9. Varieties include *J. chinensis* 'Columnaris Glauca,' blue column Chinese juniper: narrow, conical tree up to 20 feet tall with silvery gray foliage; *J. chinensis* 'Kaizuka' ('Torulosa'), a narrow, erect juniper that grows up to 15 feet with uniquely twisted bright green foliage; and *J. chinensis* 'Robusta Green,' an upright juniper with tight, brilliant green foliage. *J. communis*, common juniper: the most widely distributed tree in the northern hemisphere, grows to over 30 feet tall with an open, irregular head. Foliage is dull green to blue-green, turning purple or brown in winter. Zones 2-6. *J. scopulorum*, western red cedar or Rocky Mountain juniper: slow-growing columnar tree up to 20 feet tall that maintains silvery blue color year-round. Zones 3-6, but generally grows best west of the Mississippi. Varieties include *J. scopulorum* 'Gray Gleam,' a columnar tree with gray-green foliage that becomes grayer in winter; *J. scopulorum* 'Moonglow,' with silvery blue foliage growing in a thick, pyramidal form; and *J. scopulorum* 'Pathfinder,' a very narrow tree with blue-gray foliage that often grows five times taller than it is wide. *J. virginiana*, eastern red cedar: an extremely hardy juniper that grows naturally over three quarters of the United States. Forms range from narrow spires to wide pyramids as trees mature. Usually not over 50 feet. Bark shreds on older specimens. Zones 3-9. Varieties include *J. virginiana* 'Skyrocket,' a very narrow tree almost eight times taller than it is wide.

Growing conditions. Plant juniper in full sun in a location protected from wind. It will grow in any well-drained soil that is not too acid. The eastern red cedar thrives in dry, gravelly soils. All junipers are tolerant of dry,

hot locations and city growing conditions, but none do well in moist or wet soils. Most can adapt to seaside conditions. Transplant while young and prune branches to shape trees. Mature trees may lose lower branches. Tall, narrow junipers may break from the weight of snow in winter; remove snow with a broom before it has time to freeze.

Landscape uses. The diversity of juniper shapes makes at least one species suitable for almost any landscaping use. Unusual varieties of juniper, such as J. chinensis 'Kaizuka,' make outstanding accent or specimen trees. Group any of the juniper species as background plants or mass them for screens. Junipers are most easily sheared into topiary.

—

Picea (PY-see-a)
Spruce

Wide-spreading conical tree up to 100 feet tall and about a third as wide. Drooping branches densely packed with square, green or blue-green needles. Pendant cones on older trees. Zones 3-8.

Selected species and varieties. *P. abies*, Norway spruce: fast-growing but short-lived tree. Foliage droops from slightly ascending branches. Cones up to 7 inches long. Zones 3-8. *P. omorika*, Serbian spruce: slow-growing tall, tapering column up to 100 feet. Markedly pendulous branches turn up at the ends. Glossy green needles are marked with white on the undersides. Zones 4-8. *P. pungens*, Colorado spruce: stiff branches spiky with sharp, green to blue-green needles. Broad, wide-spreading cone. *P. pungens glauca*, Colorado blue spruce, has needles covered with a powdery, waxy coating, or bloom, that gives the tree a blue-green to bright blue appearance. Zones 3-7.

Growing conditions. Plant spruce in full sun in a well-drained sandy soil. Norway spruce tolerates wind; for other spruces, choose sites protected from strong winds.

Landscape uses. Use spruce as a specimen tree where there is sufficient space for its mature height and spread. Group several for a screen but place them with care, since spruce tends to lose lower branches if crowded or shaded. Norway spruce withstands high wind and can be planted as a windbreak.

JUNIPERUS CHINENSIS 'KAIZUKA'

PICEA ABIES

PINUS STROBUS

PSEUDOTSUGA MENZIESII

TAXUS BACCATA

Pine see *Pinus*

—

Pinus (PY-nus)
Pine

Tree that is generally conical when young, developing a round or spreading head with age. Up to 100 feet. Tiers of branches with twigs lined with bundles of soft needles. Popular and widely grown. Zones 3-9.

Selected species and varieties. *P. bungeana,* lacebark pine: light green 4-inch needles on gray-green twigs. Flaking bark with gray-green and cream-colored patches on older trees; slow-growing, 30 to 50 feet tall. Zones 5-9. *P. densiflora,* Japanese red pine: irregular crown; twisting, often leaning trunk with distinctive red-orange bark; slow-growing, up to 60 feet. Blue-green 5-inch needles. The variety *P. densiflora* 'Umbraculifera,' Tanyosho pine, has a flattened, umbrella-like head and seldom exceeds 15 feet in height. Zones 5-7. *P. flexilis,* limber pine: slow-growing tree, 30 to 50 feet tall, with flexible branches and gray-green bark. Stiff 3-inch blue-green needles. Zones 4-7. *P. nigra,* black pine, Austrian pine: 35 to 50 feet tall, with deep green, almost black 6-inch needles. Open tiers of branches on older trees. Zones 4-8. *P. palustris,* longleaf pine: tufts of needles up to 18 inches long. Retains its 10-inch cones up to 20 years and may grow up to 100 feet. Zones 7-9. *P. strobus,* Eastern white pine: fast-growing tree, 50 to 75 feet tall, with blue-green 5-inch needles. Zones 3-9. *P. sylvestris,* Scotch pine: 30 to 60 feet tall, rough red-orange bark on older trees and twisted 3-inch needles. Zones 3-8. *P. thunbergiana,* Japanese black pine: 20 to 40 feet, with a large, irregular crown and deep green 3-inch needles. Zones 6-9.

Growing conditions. Although all pines tolerate heat, drought and poor soil, they grow best in full sun in a well-drained sandy or gritty soil. Eastern white pine will tolerate light shade. Black pine will tolerate alkaline soils. Choose sites protected from strong winter winds. Austrian pine, limber pine, black pine and Japanese black pine tolerate more wind than other pines.

Landscape uses. Use pines as specimens or group them for screens and windbreaks. Branches will sweep the ground when trees are grown in the open, but trees grown in the shade will lose their lower branches.

Eastern white pine withstands shearing as a tall hedge. Austrian pine and Japanese black pine tolerate seaside conditions.

—

Pseudotsuga (soo-do-SOO-ga)

Conical ornamental that grows rapidly when young. Up to 100 feet tall at maturity. Horizontal branches with soft, dark green or blue-green needles. Zones 4-6.

Selected species and varieties. *P. menziesii,* Douglas fir: deep green needles. Fast growth into open pyramid with wide-spreading branches. Hanging 4-inch cones on older trees. Zones 3-7. *P. menziesii glauca* is a slower-growing, hardier variety with bluish needles. Zones 3-7.

Growing conditions. Plant Douglas fir in full sun in a well-drained soil that is not too alkaline. Choose a site protected from high winds, which can break branches and uproot shallow-rooted *P. menziesii glauca.*

Landscape uses. Douglas fir is an excellent specimen tree. Group several for a screen; shear for a tall hedge.

—

Spruce see *Picea*

—

Taxus (TAX-us)
Yew

Grows very slowly, reaching 10 to 12 feet in approximately 20 years, with dark green, glossy needles spiraling thickly on its branches. Zones 6 and 7.

Selected species and varieties. *T. baccata,* English yew: pyramidal tree with dense branches. Inconspicuous flowers in spring are followed by fleshy red berries in autumn. *T. baccata* 'Fastigiata,' Irish yew: a columnar tree with stiff, upright branches that give it a rugged appearance.

Growing conditions. Yews may be planted in full sun to light shade. Select sites protected from both summer heat and winter winds. Grow in any well-drained soil. Wet soils will retard the growth of young yews.

Landscape uses. Yews make good specimen trees and may be grouped for screens and backgrounds. They are easily pruned and can be sheared for topiary. Berries and foliage are poisonous.

Thuja (THOO-ya)
Arborvitae

Dense and symmetrical tree with flat sprays of dark green, pungent, scale-like leaves, which are sometimes twisted and ruffled. Zones 3-9.

Selected species and varieties. *T. occidentalis,* American arborvitae: conical tree up to 60 feet tall. Young branches grow vertically, then droop gracefully. Zones 3-7. Varieties include *T. occidentalis* 'Pyramidalis,' pyramidal American arborvitae, which grows as a narrow cone with especially deep green color; and *T. occidentalis* 'Techny,' which has a tall, pyramidal form and grows quickly. *T. orientalis,* Chinese arborvitae: tree up to 50 feet tall with fine, dense foliage on ascending branches that give it a formal appearance. Zones 7-9. *T. plicata,* giant western arborvitae: mature older specimens grow up to 180 feet tall. Short branches with coarse foliage marked with white on the undersides. Zones 4-7.

Growing conditions. Plant in full sun or light shade in any moist soil. Arborvitae grows best where humidity is high. Susceptible to damage by snow and ice.

Landscape uses. Because arborvitae does not lose branches close to the ground, it is a good choice for use in hedges and screens. Remove topmost branches to limit height; new foliage quickly hides stubs. Use giant western arborvitae to give a formal presence.

Tsuga (TSOO-ga)
Hemlock

Graceful conical tree 30 feet or more tall, with horizontal or slightly drooping branches. Soft, feathery sprays of lustrous green needles marked with white on their undersides. Quantities of ¾-inch brown cones at the tips of branches. Zones 3-8.

Selected species and varieties. *T. canadensis,* Canada hemlock: broad pyramidal tree, often with a forked trunk. Needles in flat sprays. Zones 3-8. *T. caroliniana,* Carolina hemlock: drooping branches spaced well apart along trunk. Needles spiral around twigs. Zones 5-8.

Growing conditions. Plant hemlocks in full sun or light shade in a moist but well-drained soil. Protect them from the drying effects of winter winds. They grow best in humid areas and benefit from light

shade where summers are hot and dry. Carolina hemlock tolerates city pollution.

Landscape uses. Use hemlock as a lawn specimen or mass several for a screen. Hemlocks are among the best evergreens for hedges, because they can be easily sheared. Prune them into formal shapes or loose, informal mounds.

—

Yew see *Taxus*

DECIDUOUS SHRUBS

Aesculus (ES-kew-lus)
Buckeye

Large, boldly textured shrub whose width may be twice its height. Long spikes of many small white flowers in midsummer. Zones 4-9.

Selected species and varieties. *A. parviflora:* bottlebrush buckeye. Height 8 to 12 feet, width 8 to 15 feet or more. Many erect stems. Compound leaves with five radially arranged leaflets up to 8 inches long. Slender pink-tinged stamens extend an inch beyond the white flower petals, giving the 8- to 12-inch spikes a bristly appearance. Smooth light brown fruit 1 inch in diameter. Fast-growing.

Growing conditions. Buckeye does best in a moist, well-drained acid soil that has been enriched with organic matter, but it will also tolerate alkaline soil. Can thrive in full sun or partial shade. Plant balled-and-burlapped and container-grown shrubs in early spring. Pruning is seldom required.

Landscape uses. Plant buckeye singly or in masses in a woodland setting or use as a lawn specimen. Allow ample room to accommodate its spreading form.

—

Aronia (a-RO-nee-a)
Chokeberry

Upright shrub with white flowers followed by clusters of red or black berries. Brilliant red fall foliage. Zones 4-9.

Selected species and varieties. *A. arbutifolia,* red chokeberry: height 6 to 9 feet; forms clumps that slowly increase in diameter. Many upright stems, with most branches above the midpoint of the stems.

THUJA OCCIDENTALIS

TSUGA CANADENSIS

AESCULUS PARVIFLORA

ARONIA ARBUTIFOLIA

BUDDLEIA ALTERNIFOLIA

CALLICARPA JAPONICA

CALYCANTHUS FLORIDUS

Shiny, dark green oval 1- to 3-inch leaves with pale undersides. Small white flowers in 2-inch clusters in late spring. Small, bright red, bitter-tasting berries that last until early spring. Fairly slow-growing. *A. melanocarpa*, black chokeberry: height 1½ to 5 feet; produces many stems and spreads into broad colonies. Foliage and flowers similar to those of red chokeberry. Purplish black fruit in late summer and fall.

Growing conditions. Adapts to conditions that range from poor, dry soils to wet soils. Will grow well in partial shade, but fruit is more abundant and fall color brighter in full sun.

Landscape uses. Plant red chokeberry in a shrub border or in a group of three or more, to minimize its sometimes leggy appearance. Use black chokeberry where it will have room to spread without encroaching on other plants. Both species are well suited to naturalistic plantings.

—

Azalea see *Rhododendron*
Bayberry see *Myrica*
Beautyberry see *Callicarpa*
Black alder see *Ilex*
Blue spirea see *Caryopteris*
Broom see *Cytisus*
Buckeye see *Aesculus*

—

Buddleia (BUD-lee-a)
Butterfly bush

Large, fast-growing shrub with arching branches that are covered in late spring or early summer with spikes of fragrant flowers in a range of colors. Zones 5-9.

Selected species and varieties. *B. alternifolia*, fountain butterfly bush: height 8 to 12 feet, width to 15 feet. Wide-spreading, graceful branches give a fountain effect. Abundant clusters of lilac-purple flowers in late spring. Lance-shaped leaves 1 to 4 inches long with silvery undersides. *B. davidii*, orange-eyed butterfly bush: height 5 to 15 feet with a width equal to its height. Rangy, open, somewhat coarse in texture. Large flower clusters up to 10 inches long in summer. The species has lilac flowers with orange centers; varieties with white, blue, purple, red or pink flowers are available. The tapering 4- to 8-inch-long leaves have a handsome silvery or bluish cast. Both species are slow to leaf out and hold their leaves till

late in the fall. Their flowers lure butterflies and moths.

Growing conditions. Buddleia will grow in almost any well-drained soil but does best when organic matter such as peat moss or compost has been added. Full sun. Plant in spring in Zones 5-7, and at any time of year in Zones 8 and 9. Prune in spring before new growth begins.

Landscape uses. Use *B. alternifolia* as a specimen or as part of a shrub border. *B. davidii* can be used in a shrub border or in masses. A vigorous grower, it can reach a height of 6 feet in a single growing season. To use it in a perennial border in warmer zones, where its stems survive the winter, cut it to the ground in spring before new growth appears.

—

Butterfly bush see *Buddleia*

—

Callicarpa (kal-ee-KAR-pa)
Beautyberry, jewel berry

Rounded shrub prized for its clusters of small, strikingly colored fall fruit. Zones 5-8.

Selected species and varieties. *C. dichotoma*, purple beautyberry: height and width 3 to 4 feet. Slender, gracefully arching branches. Three-inch-long medium green oval leaves tapering to a point. Small pink flowers in midsummer followed by lilac-violet berries on purplish stems. Fast-growing. *C japonica*, Japanese beautyberry: height and width usually 4 to 6 feet, but sometimes larger in mild climates. Arching branches. Medium green oval leaves up to 5 inches long, tapering to a point; foliage golden in fall. Midsummer flowers pink or white, often hidden by foliage. Purple or violet berries. Fast-growing.

Growing conditions. Plant in well-drained soil and full sun or very light shade. Prune in spring to remove any stems killed during winter. Beautyberry may be cut to within 4 to 6 inches of the ground in spring before growth begins. The plant will grow to about 3 feet and will produce a full crop of berries, since flowers and fruit are borne on the current year's growth.

Landscape uses. The showy fruits, which persist for about two weeks after the leaves fall off, have the greatest impact when the shrubs are planted in groups in the front of a shrub border. Grouping also ensures cross-pollination and, consequently, a good crop of berries.

Calycanthus (kal-ee-KAN-thus)

Dense, rounded shrub with very fragrant flowers and aromatic stems and leaves. Zones 4-9.

Selected species and varieties. *C. floridus,* sweet shrub, Carolina allspice: height 6 to 9 feet, width equal to or greater than its height. Shiny dark green elliptical leaves 2 to 5 inches long with fuzzy pale gray or brownish undersides. Foliage clings until late in fall, sometimes turning an attractive yellow. Dark, reddish brown flowers 2 inches across in late spring, with an intense fragrance reminiscent of strawberries or pineapple. Slow-growing.

Growing conditions. Tolerant of different soils but grows best in moist soil enriched with organic matter. Light shade is preferable and height is achieved in a shaded site, but plants also do well in full sun. Greatest height achieved in a shaded site. Protection from wind is desirable. For the most prolific flowering, remove one-third of the stems each spring.

Landscape uses. Plant close to house, terrace or other spot where the fragrance can be enjoyed. The intensity of fragrance varies somewhat from plant to plant, so it is preferable to purchase Carolina allspice when it is in flower. The neat form and lustrous foliage make the shrub a handsome addition to a border.

Carolina allspice
see *Calycanthus*

Caryopteris (kair-ee-OP-ter-is)
Bluebeard, blue spirea

Bright blue flowers in late summer and early fall when few other shrubs are in bloom. Zones 5-8.

Selected species and varieties. *C. × clandonensis:* rounded form, with height and width 2 to 3 feet; clusters of many small flowers in late summer. Lance-shaped leaves 2 to 3 inches long with gray or silvery undersides. Flowers, leaves and stems are fragrant. Fast-growing.

Growing conditions. Plant in loose, rich well-drained soil in full sun. Spring planting is recommended for Zones 5 and 6; in other zones caryopteris may be safely planted in spring or fall. Winter damage is common, especially in a heavy clay soil. It is usually best to treat caryopteris as a herbaceous perennial, cutting it to within 2 to 4 inches of the ground each spring after the risk of a killing frost has passed. By late summer it will grow to 2 or 3 feet and produce abundant flowers.

Landscape uses. Plant singly or in groups of three or more at the front of a perennial border or a shrub border. In addition to its late-season flowers, caryopteris provides attractive foliage throughout the growing season.

Chaenomeles (key-NOM-el-eez)
Quince

Among the earliest of spring-blooming shrubs, with white, pink or red flowers appearing before the leaves unfold. Zones 4 to 9.

Selected species and varieties. *C. japonica,* Japanese quince: height between 2 and 4 feet, width equal to or greater than its height. Dense, intricate pattern of thorny stems and branches. Five-petaled orange-red flowers 1 inch in diameter. Glossy, dark green oval leaves 1 to 2 inches long with toothed edges. *C. speciosa,* flowering quince: rounded form, with a height of 6 to 10 feet and a width equal to or greater than the height. Dense and twiggy, with thorns. Flowers to 1¾ inches across, either alone or in small clusters. The shrub's usual color is red, but pink and white are also common. Many named varieties of various shades. Glossy, 1½- to 3½-inch oval leaves with toothed edges; young foliage bronze-tinged.

Growing conditions. Quince tolerates different conditions, including alkaline soils, but extreme alkalinity causes the leaves to turn yellow. Quince also grows in dry soil but will begin to shed its leaves in the middle of summer and may be bare by early autumn. Full sun is best, although quinces also grow in light shade. Prune after flowering.

Landscape uses. Low-growing Japanese quince is well suited to foundation plantings and the front of a shrub border. Its thorns make quince an excellent hedge plant. It can also be used as a specimen, and trained as an espalier on a wall or a fence.

Chaste tree see *Vitex*

Chimonanthus
(ky-mo-NAN-thus)
Wintersweet

Large shrub valued for its sweetly fragrant winter flowers. Zones 6-9.

CARYOPTERIS × CLANDONENSIS

CHAENOMELES SPECIOSA

CHIMONANTHUS PRAECOX

CLETHRA ALNIFOLIA

CORNUS SERICEA

CORYLOPSIS SPICATA

Selected species and varieties. *C. praecox,* wintersweet: 8 to 15 feet in height and almost as wide as it is tall. Many arching stems. One-inch yellow flowers marked with red-brown, opening over many weeks on mild, sunny winter days. Shiny dark green oval leaves up to 6 inches long. Slow-growing.

Growing conditions. Plant in almost any well-drained soil. To minimize damage to flower buds, choose a site with morning shade, afternoon sun and shelter from winter winds. In Zone 6 plant wintersweet in a warm, sheltered location. Every spring cut a few of the older stems to the ground.

Landscape uses. Plant wintersweet where its flowers can easily be seen and smelled. Use it in a shrub border or group it with low-growing broad-leaved evergreens such as dwarf Chinese holly that will mask its bare lower stems. Wintersweet can be espaliered on a wall.

Chokeberry see *Aronia*

Clethra (KLETH-rah)

Fragrant white summer flowers, handsome form and foliage. Zones 3-9.

Selected species and varieties. *C. alnifolia,* summersweet, sweet pepperbush: oval shape with many upright stems; height 3 to 8 feet, width 4 to 6 feet. Deep green oblong leaves with toothed edges to 4 inches in length; autumn color clear yellow to gold-brown. Small flowers in 3- to 6-inch spikes in mid- to late summer. Tends to spread in clumps by stems that form underground. Growth rate slow to medium.

Growing conditions. Plant in moist or wet acid soil supplemented with organic matter such as peat moss. Full sun to heavy shade. Does well in sandy soils, withstands wind and salty seashore conditions, and cannot tolerate extended periods of dryness. Pruning is seldom required.

Landscape uses. May be used in woodland plantings, wet areas or shrub borders.

Cornus (KOR-nus)
Dogwood

Shrubby dogwood valued mainly for the color its red or yellow bark brings to the winter garden. Zones 2-8.

Selected species and varieties. *C. alba,* Tatarian dogwood: slender, erect stems 8 to 10 feet tall, with few branches; spreads by underground stems to a width of 5 feet or more. Shiny bark green in summer, turning red in fall. White flowers in 2-inch clusters in late spring, followed by small white or bluish fruit. Foliage dark green in summer; sometimes turns attractive reddish purple in fall. Fast-growing. *C. sericea,* red osier dogwood: very similar to *C. alba;* the variety 'Flaviramea' has yellow stems.

Growing conditions. Both species thrive in rich, well-drained or moist soil but will also do well in poor and wet soils. Though light shade is tolerated, winter bark color is most intense in full sun. For best winter appearance, remove the oldest stems from established plants in early spring to encourage young, brightly colored growth. Alternatively, cut the entire plant to the ground each spring.

Landscape uses. Site either of these species where it will be prominent in winter. Both are striking in masses in a naturalistic planting but are also good additions to a shrub border, where they combine well with broad-leaved and needle-leaved evergreens.

Corylopsis (kor-i-LOP-sis)
Winter hazel

Intricately branched spreading shrub with clusters of fragrant yellow bell-shaped flowers in late winter or early spring before the leaves unfold. Zones 6-9.

Selected species and varieties. *C. pauciflora,* buttercup winter hazel: 4 to 6 feet tall; 4 to 6 feet or more in width. Smooth, deeply veined leaves up to 2 inches long with toothed edges. Small clusters of two or three ¾-inch flowers. *C. spicata,* spike winter hazel: 4 to 6 feet tall; width may be twice the height. Smooth, deeply veined 4-inch blue-green leaves with toothed edges. Small flowers in drooping clusters 1 to 3 inches long.

Growing conditions. Plant in moist, well-drained acid soil rich in organic matter such as peat moss. Full sun or light shade. A sheltered site reduces the chance of frost damage to the flower buds.

Landscape uses. Use winter hazel in a shrub border for early spring color and attractive summer foliage. Dark evergreens provide a good backdrop and can also shelter winter hazel from cold winds.

Cotoneaster (ko-TO-nee-as-ter)

Horizontal branches with a distinctive fish-bone pattern; bright red berries in fall. Zones 5-9.

Selected species and varieties. *C. horizontalis,* rockspray cotoneaster: low-growing, flat-topped plant between 2 and 3 feet high; width is at least twice the height. Small, glossy dark green leaves that turn red in autumn. In mild winters the leaves may be evergreen. Small white or pinkish flowers in late spring are followed by ¼-inch berries. Growth rate slow to medium.

Growing conditions. Performs best in a well-drained fertile soil, but rockspray cotoneaster also tolerates poor, dry soil. Full sun or light shade. Adapts to windy locations. Container-grown plants are easiest to establish and may be set out at any time. Balled-and-burlapped plants should be installed in spring only.

Landscape uses. Plant on a slope or bank or in front of taller shrubs. Its interesting branching pattern makes rockspray cotoneaster a good subject for espaliering. Wherever it is used, allow ample room for the branches to spread, since pruning to keep the plant small detracts from its handsome form.

Cranberry bush see *Viburnum*

Cytisus (SY-tis-us)
Broom

Abundant flowers in shades of yellow, red or pink in late spring; bright green stems for winter color. Zones 5-8.

Selected species and varieties. *C. × praecox,* Warminster broom: numerous slender stems, vertical or arching, 5 to 10 feet tall; width about equal to its height. One-inch, sulfur yellow pealike flowers with an unpleasant odor. Small, sparse gray-green leaves. Fast-growing. *C. scoparius,* Scotch broom: mound-shaped, 5 to 6 feet tall, with an equal or greater breadth when grown as a specimen; height up to 10 feet when crowded by other plants. Slender, upright stems. Small, sparse foliage ½ inch long. Abundant rich yellow flowers. The cultivar 'Burkwoodii'

has red flowers. 'Dorothy Walpole' has bicolored flowers of pink and crimson. Fast-growing.

Growing conditions. Brooms grow best in very well drained, comparatively infertile soil that is acid to slightly alkaline. They require full sun. Purchase container-grown plants only and plant in early spring. Prune after flowering, cutting back only the stems that have blossomed in the current year; older stems will not produce new growth. Brooms grow vigorously but begin to decline after six or seven years and should be discarded and replaced.

Landscape uses. Planted singly or in groups, brooms are dazzling in flower and provide a mass of bright green during the rest of the year, even in poor, sandy spots where few plants thrive. The stems' vertical lines contrast effectively with the horizontal line of a creeping ground cover.

Deutzia (DEWT-zee-a)

Low, mounded shrub covered with clusters of pure white flowers in middle to late spring. Zones 4-9.

Selected species and varieties. *D. gracilis,* slender deutzia: height 2 to 4 feet, width 3 to 4 feet; slender arching or ascending branches. Matte green leaves, 2½ inches long, are virtually hidden by profuse 3-inch-long erect clusters of small flowers lasting about two weeks. Growth rate slow to medium.

Growing conditions. Plant in spring in almost any soil; adapts to both acid or alkaline conditions. Full sun or very light shade. Prune in early spring to remove stem tips damaged during winter. Postpone pruning to shape or control size until after flowering.

Landscape uses. Deutzia makes a handsome low hedge and is also well suited to foundation plantings or to the front of a shrub border, singly or in groups.

Dogwood see *Cornus*
Dyer's greenwood see *Genista*

Enkianthus (en-kee-AN-thus)

Bell-shaped flowers in the spring and brilliant orange, yellow and red foliage in the fall. Zones 4-7.

COTONEASTER HORIZONTALIS

CYTISUS SCOPARIUS

DEUTZIA GRACILIS

ENKIANTHUS CAMPANULATUS

EUONYMUS ALATUS

FORSYTHIA × INTERMEDIA 'SPECTABILIS'

GENISTA TINCTORIA

Selected species and varieties. *E. campanulatus,* redvein enkianthus: height 6 to 8 feet in colder zones; can grow as a small tree of 20 feet or more in milder zones. Narrow and upright in form. Drooping 3-inch clusters of small creamy yellow or pale orange flowers with dark red veins bloom as the foliage is developing. Leaves are 1 to 3 inches long and grouped in tufts at the ends of the branches. Slow-growing.

Growing conditions. Enkianthus requires an acid soil rich in organic matter such as peat moss or compost. Full sun or partial shade.

Landscape uses. Its flowers, bright green summer foliage, neat form and fine fall color make enkianthus an excellent specimen plant. It can also be used in a shrub border with other acid-loving plants.

Euonymus (yew-ON-i-mus)

Rounded shrub with exceptionally brilliant fall foliage and attractive winter outline. Zones 3-9.

Selected species and varieties. *E. alatus* 'Compactus,' dwarf winged euonymous, burning bush: 6-10 feet tall, with a width about equal to its height. Densely branched, often with small corky ridges or wings running the length of the branches. Dark green 1- to 3-inch leaves turn brilliant red in fall. Small orange fruits in fall. Slow-growing.

Growing conditions. Adapts to virtually any well-drained soil. Best fall color in full sun but will grow well in partial shade. Pruning is seldom required.

Landscape uses. Use this versatile plant as a specimen, as a hedge plant, in masses or in a shrub border. In spite of its name, it is not a small shrub. Allow it ample room, since pruning to keep it small detracts from its handsome form.

Forsythia (for-SITH-ee-a)

Masses of showy yellow flowers in early spring before the leaves appear. Zones 5-9.

Selected species and varieties. *F. × intermedia,* border forsythia: hybrids in this group have a breadth equal to their height and numerous upright and arching stems. Flowers 1 to 2 inches across; leaves 3 to 5 inches long. Recommended hybrids include 'Lynwood' and 'Spectabilis,'

up to 10 feet tall with bright yellow flowers, and 'Spring Glory,' 6 feet tall with sulfur yellow flowers. All are fast-growing.

Growing conditions. Forsythia grows well in almost any type of garden soil and tolerates city conditions. Bare-root, balled-and-burlapped, and container plants are all easy to establish. For best flowering, plant in full sun. Prune as soon as the flowers have faded, cutting back old stems to within 4 inches of the ground.

Landscape uses. Plant forsythia in masses or in a shrub border. It is a good choice for planting on an embankment or where a fast-growing hedge is needed. Avoid using forsythia as a foundation or specimen plant, since its appearance is outstanding only while it is in bloom.

Genista (je-NIS-ta)
Woadwaxen

Low-growing rounded shrub covered in late spring with bright yellow flowers. Zones 4-9.

Selected species and varieties. *G. tinctoria,* common woadwaxen, dyer's greenwood: 2 to 3 feet tall and wide, with a neat outline. Upright twiggy stems are green all year. Small, bright green leaves. Half-inch yellow flowers in upright clusters 2 to 3 inches long. Blooming may continue through summer.

Growing conditions. Plant in poor, light, dry infertile soil in full sun. Tolerates drought and seaside conditions.

Landscape uses. Use singly or in groups for an intense splash of color. Common woadwaxen is suited to planting in a rock garden or in the front of a shrub border; flowers and stems provide color year-round.

Hamamelis (ham-am-EE-lis)
Witch hazel

Large shrub valued for its fragrant winter or early-spring flowers with many slender, ribbon-like petals, handsome summer foliage and fine fall color. Zones 4-8.

Selected species and varieties. *H. × intermedia,* hybrid witch hazel: large, spreading shrub with yellow or red flowers blooming in mid- to late winter. Zones 5-8. Recommended cultivars include 'Arnold Promise,' a vase-shaped shrub or small tree 15 to 20 feet tall and wide with 1½-inch golden yellow flowers. Leathery gray-green leaves turn shades of red, yellow and orange in fall. 'Jelena' is similar in size, form and foliage to 'Arnold Promise' but has copper-orange flowers. *H. mollis,* Chinese witch hazel: rounded shrub usually 10 to 15 feet tall, though sometimes reaching 20 feet or more. Downy, rounded 3- to 6-inch leaves turning yellow in fall. Very fragrant bright yellow flowers 1½ inches across. Zones 5-8. *H. mollis* 'Pallida' has sulfur yellow flowers and slightly glossy foliage. *H. vernalis,* vernal witch hazel: round, dense shrub 6 to 10 feet tall with a spread equal to or greater than its height. Dark green leaves 2 to 5 inches, with toothed edges; yellow fall color. Fragrant ½-inch yellow or reddish flowers. Zones 4-8. Witch hazels grow at a slow or medium rate.

Growing conditions. These witch hazels grow well in a moist, well-drained acid soil rich in organic matter. *H. vernalis* can tolerate wetter sites than the other two species. None tolerates drought. Full sun to partial shade.

Landscape uses. Any of these witch hazels makes an excellent specimen plant or a focal point in a woodland setting. Witch hazels can also be used for hedges and screens. Allow ample room so pruning will not be required to keep a plant within bounds. Evergreens make a good background for the flowers. Flowering time depends on the weather but can occur as early as January. Flowers last three to four weeks; the petals roll up during severe weather and open again in mild spells.

—

Hardy orange see *Poncirus*

Hazel see *Corylopsis*

Holly see *Ilex*

—

Hydrangea (hy-DRAN-jee-a)

Late-spring and summer flowers in white and shades of blue and pink. Zones 5-9.

Selected species and varieties. *H. macrophylla,* bigleaf hydrangea: broad shrub 3 to 6 feet tall, spreading by suckers; many erect stems with broad leaves 4 to 8 inches long. Fast-growing. Zones 6-9. There are a very large number of cultivars, which are divided into two groups. 'Hortensias' have sterile flowers arranged in globe-shaped clusters 4 to 8 inches or more in diameter.

'Lacecaps' have flat clusters 4 to 8 inches across, with tiny fertile flowers in the center and a lacy edging of large sterile flowers. Some cultivars are white; others are pink or blue, depending on soil acidity. A pH of 6 or more produces pink flowers; more acid soils produce blue flowers. One of the best lacecaps is 'Mariesii.' *H. quercifolia,* oakleaf hydrangea: 4 to 6 feet tall, spreading by suckers to 6 feet or more. Lobed leaves similar to an oak's, up to 8 inches long; dark green in summer, turning to beautiful shades of red, purple and orange-brown in fall. Conical flower clusters 8 to 12 inches long. Clusters remain for months, changing from white in late spring to green to rose and tan in fall. Growth rate slow to medium. Zones 5-9.

Growing conditions. Hydrangeas do best in moist, fertile, well-drained soil rich in organic matter. Bigleaf hydrangea grows best in partial shade except in seashore gardens, where it does well in full sun. Plant oakleaf hydrangea in full sun or partial shade. To alter soil pH to achieve the desired flower color in bigleaf hydrangea cultivars, add lime to raise the pH for pink flowers; add aluminum sulfate to produce the acidity required for blue flowers. Although oakleaf hydrangea is hardy in Zone 5, extreme winter cold may kill the flower buds.

Landscape uses. Plant bigleaf hydrangea in shrub borders or in masses under high-branching trees for mid-summer color. Oakleaf hydrangea can be used in a shrub border, in masses or in shady locations. Even where it is too cold for this species to flower, bold foliage makes hydrangea a valuable plant.

—

Ilex (EYE-lex)
Holly

Lustrous bright red berries that remain on bushes from late summer into winter; attractive glossy foliage in summer. Zones 3-9.

Selected species and varieties. *I. verticillata,* winterberry, black alder: a rounded shrub 8 to 12 feet tall with a similar width; many stems bearing slender, twiggy branches. Small dark green leaves. A winterberry plant bears either male or female flowers; only female plants produce berries, but a male plant is required for pollination. Quarter-inch berries ripen in late summer and provide color until midwinter or later, unless they are eaten by birds or damaged by winter cold and wind.

HAMAMELIS MOLLIS

HYDRANGEA MACROPHYLLA

ILEX × 'SPARKLEBERRY'

KERRIA JAPONICA

MYRICA PENSYLVANICA

PONCIRUS TRIFOLIATA

Slow-growing. Recommended cultivars: 'Red Sprite,' 3 to 4 feet tall; 'Winter Red,' bronze foliage in fall and long-lasting berries. *I.* × 'Sparkleberry': abundant berries through the winter. Grows slowly to 10 feet.

Growing conditions. Plant winterberry in a moist to wet acid soil high in organic matter such as peat moss or compost; it can adapt to sandy and clayey soils. Full sun or partial shade.

Landscape uses. Winterberry is a handsome addition to shrub borders, where it combines especially well with evergreens. Mass plantings make a fine show of color after the leaves fall and expose the berries. Use winterberry in low, wet areas where few plants are able to thrive. In any planting, be sure to include one male plant for every eight or 10 female plants.

Jewel berry see *Callicarpa*

Kerria (KAIR-ee-a)

A vase-shaped shrub that has bright yellow flowers in the spring and shiny green stems throughout the year. Zones 4-9.

Selected species and varieties. *K. japonica,* kerria: 3 to 6 feet tall, spreading slowly to 9 feet in width. Many slender stems grow upright and then arch gracefully, forming a dense, broad mass. Shiny bright green bark. Bright green lance-shaped leaves with toothed edges, and 1½-inch yellow flowers with five petals in midspring, lasting two to three weeks. Fast-growing once it is established. *K. japonica* 'Pleniflora,' globeflower kerria: 6 to 8 feet in height, with an open, upright form. This cultivar has golden yellow ball-shaped double flowers 1 to 2 inches across.

Growing conditions. Plant in well-drained soil supplemented with organic matter such as peat moss or compost. Kerria grows well and flowers last longest in light to full shade, but it will tolerate full sun. Avoid windy, exposed locations. In early spring prune any branch tips killed in winter.

Landscape uses. Use kerria in a shrub border or in masses, siting it where its bright green stems will be effective in winter. Its shade tolerance makes kerria an excellent choice for planting under trees or on the north side of a wall or a house.

Lilac see *Syringa*

Myrica (my-RY-ka)

Leathery dark green foliage in summer; waxy pale gray berries clustered along the branches from fall through winter. Zones 2-6.

Selected species and varieties. *M. pensylvanica,* northern bayberry: mounded shrub 5 to 9 feet tall and wide with many erect branches. Oblong leaves up to 4 inches long, lasting till late fall or, in milder zones and sheltered locations, into winter. Plants are either male or female, with only female plants producing the tiny berries. Male plants are required for pollination. Leaves and berries are very aromatic.

Growing conditions. Northern bayberry, a native of coastal dunes, thrives in poor, dry, sandy soil and salt spray, but also grows well in acid, well-drained soils and clay soils. Full sun or partial shade. Buy balled-and-burlapped or container-grown plants only, preferably after fruit has formed, so that female plants can be identified with certainty. Plant one male for every eight to 10 females. Little or no pruning is required.

Landscape uses. Plant northern bayberry in groups or in a shrub border. Broad-leaved and needle-leaved evergreens make excellent backgrounds for the pale berries. This plant often spreads by suckers to form large masses.

Poncirus (pon-SY-rus)
Hardy orange

Thorny upright shrub with white spring flowers, orange fruit and dark green branches. Zones 6-10.

Selected species and varieties. *P. trifoliata,* hardy orange: 8 to 20 feet tall with an upright oval form. Stems have striated bark. Small branches have smooth bark and numerous stiff, sharp thorns. Compound leaves with three small, dark green, shiny leaflets. Flowers 1½ to 2 inches across are followed by 2-inch fuzzy, bitter-tasting fruit that turns from green to orange in autumn. Hardy orange is a member of the citrus family.

Growing conditions. Plant hardy orange in a moist, well-drained acid soil in full sun or light shade.

Landscape uses. Hardy orange may be used as a specimen or to form an impenetrable barrier hedge. Also, it is handsome espaliered on a wall. Hardy orange withstands heavy pruning.

—

Quince see *Chaenomeles*

—

Rhododendron
(ro-do-DEN-dron)
Azalea, rhododendron

Spring flowers in a wide range of colors and handsome fall foliage in some species. Zones 3-9.

Selected species and varieties. *R. calendulaceum,* flame azalea: usually 4 to 6 feet tall, sometimes reaching 10 feet, with a width equal to its height; upright open form, with 3-inch oblong leaves that turn muted red and yellow in fall and 2-inch flowers in late spring ranging from yellow through orange to red. Zones 5-8. *R. kaempferi,* torch azalea: 4 to 8 feet tall, with a compact upright form. Two-inch shiny oval leaves are dark green in summer, reddish in fall and may last into winter in milder zones. Two-inch flowers in white, pink and shades of salmon or orange in spring. Zones 6-9. *R. mucronulatum* 'Cornell Pink,' Korean rhododendron or azalea: 4 to 8 feet tall and wide; upright stems. Three-inch lance-shaped leaves yellow or bronze in fall. Clusters of clear pink 1½-inch flowers in very early spring before the leaves unfold. Zones 5-7. *R. periclymenoides,* pinxterbloom azalea: 4 to 6 feet in height, spreading to form colonies. Upright stems. Bright green 3-inch leaves. One-and-a-half-inch flowers ranging from pinkish white to violet in midspring. Zones 4-8. *R. schlippenbachii,* royal azalea: upright shrub 4 to 6 feet tall and wide. Three- to 5-inch leaves dark green in summer, turning yellow, orange and red in fall. Clusters of 3-inch pale pink to rose flowers in midspring as the leaves unfold. Zones 5-8. *R. vaseyi,* pinkshell azalea: upright shrub 5 to 8 feet tall. Three- to 5-inch dark green leaves turn red in fall. One-and-a-half-inch rose flowers in midspring before the leaves unfold. Zones 5-8. All of the species listed here are slow-growing.

Growing conditions. Azaleas require moist, well-drained acid soil rich in organic matter such as peat moss. Mulch to conserve moisture. Full sun or light shade; light shade is preferable in the South. Korean azalea flowers best in a site shaded from the late-winter sun; otherwise its buds

may open prematurely and be frozen. Prune only to remove dead or damaged branches.

Landscape uses. Deciduous azaleas are valuable in shrub borders and as specimen plants because of their spring flowers, attractive summer foliage and neat growth patterns, and the smaller species, such as Korean azalea, are good foundation plants. Use any of these species in groups at the edge of woodland plantings. Pinxterbloom azalea is best reserved for naturalistic plantings because of its tendency to form broad colonies.

—

Rosa (RO-za)
Rose

Hardy species valued for their flowers, attractive foliage and fruits; they require far less attention than the floribundas, grandifloras, hybrid teas and climbers prized for their beautiful flowers. Zones 2-10.

Selected species and varieties. *R. carolina,* Carolina rose: 3 to 6 feet tall, spreading by suckers to form colonies. Erect branches with numerous thorns. Compound leaves with 1-inch toothed leaflets turn red in fall. Pink flowers 2 inches across in late spring and early summer. Small red fruit, or hips, in fall and winter. Zones 4-9. *R. rubrifolia,* redleaf rose: 5 to 7 feet tall; erect, almost thornless canes tinged with purple. Smooth 1-inch leaflets with red or purple tones. Fragrant 1½-inch clear pink single flowers in late spring followed by ½-inch round red hips that last well into winter. Zones 2-7. *R. rugosa,* Japanese rose, rugosa rose: 4 to 6 feet tall and wide. Very prickly upright stems. Wrinkled, dark green glossy leaves turn orange in fall. Single fragrant purplish red, pink or white flowers 2½ to 3½ inches across. Flowers heavily in late spring but continues to produce flowers into fall. Brick red 1-inch hips from late summer into fall. Zones 2-7. All three species are fast-growing.

Growing conditions. All three of these species do well in full sun in a moist, well-drained soil supplemented with organic matter such as peat moss or compost. Rugosa rose also thrives in sandy soil and tolerates salt spray. Carolina rose grows well in damp to wet soil. Little pruning is required.

Landscape uses. Carolina rose is valuable in wet spots where few plants are able to do well. The foli-

RHODODENDRON MUCRONULATUM 'CORNELL PINK'

ROSA RUGOSA

SPIRAEA JAPONICA 'ALPINA'

SYRINGA VULGARIS

VIBURNUM PLICATUM TOMENTOSUM

age of the redleaf rose is an interesting accent in an otherwise green shrub border. Japanese rose makes an excellent dense hedge and is well suited to difficult sites, such as seashore gardens.

Rose see *Rosa*

Spiraea (spy-REE-a)
Spirea

Profuse clusters of small flowers in white or shades of pink in spring or summer. Zones 3-8.

Selected species and varieties. *S.* × *bumalda,* bumald spirea: dense, twiggy shrub up to 3 feet tall and 5 feet wide; white or pink flowers late spring to midsummer. *S.* × *bumalda* 'Anthony Waterer': deep rose flowers; can reach 4 feet in height and 6 feet in width. *S. japonica* 'Alpina,' alpine Japanese spirea: 1½ to 2½ feet tall and 3 feet or more across; pink flowers in early summer. *S. nipponica* 'Snowmound,' boxwood spirea: neat, rounded form 3 to 5 feet tall and wide; small blue-green leaves similar to those of boxwood; white flowers in late spring or early summer. *S.* × *vanhouttei,* Vanhoutte spirea: rounded shrub 6 to 8 feet tall; white flowers in mid- to late spring. Spireas are fast-growing.

Growing conditions. These tough shrubs adapt to almost any soil except a wet one. Full sun or light shade.

Landscape uses. Use spireas in the front or middle of shrub borders, depending on their height. Alpine Japanese spirea's spread makes it a good ground-cover plant.

Summersweet see *Clethra*
Sweet pepperbush see *Clethra*
Sweet shrub see *Calycanthus*

Syringa (sy-RING-ga)
Lilac

Clusters of deliciously fragrant spring or summer flowers in colors ranging from white to purple. Zones 3-8.

Selected species and varieties. *S.* × *chinensis,* Chinese lilac: 6 to 10 feet tall and wide; rounded form with graceful arching branches and 6-inch clusters of very fragrant light purple flowers in mid- to late spring. Zones 5-8. *S. microphylla,* littleleaf lilac:

handsome mounded shrub 6 feet tall and up to 12 feet in width; 2-inch leaves with fuzzy undersides; 2-inch clusters of fragrant pinkish lilac flowers in late spring; sometimes blooms again in late summer. Zones 4-8. *S. vulgaris,* common lilac: upright shrub 8 to 15 feet tall. Four- to 8-inch clusters of very fragrant flowers in midspring. There are hundreds of varieties available in white, pink, blue, violet, lilac, magenta and purple. Zones 3-7.

Growing conditions. Plant lilacs in full sun in a soil that is close to neutral and supplemented with organic matter. Prune common lilac after flowering, cutting to the ground old stems that no longer flower well and removing some of the numerous suckers from the base of the plant. Cut off faded flower clusters to ensure profuse flowering the following year. Littleleaf lilac and Chinese lilac need little pruning except to remove flower clusters.

Landscape uses. Common lilac and Chinese lilac are used in shrub borders and, because of their size, as hedge or screen plants. Use littleleaf lilac as a specimen plant.

Viburnum (vy-BUR-num)

Versatile shrub grown for its spring flowers, handsomely wrinkled foliage and fall fruit. Zones 3-9.

Selected species and varieties. *V. carlesii,* Korean spice viburnum: 5 to 8 feet tall and wide, with stiff ascending branches. Pink flower buds, opening to rounded 3-inch clusters of white, extremely fragrant flowers in early spring. Slow-growing. Zones 4-8. *V. dilatatum,* linden viburnum: 6 to 9 feet tall and wide; attractive dark green toothed leaves; 3- to 5-inch clusters of white flowers in late spring, followed by bright red fruit in fall. Slow to medium growth rate. Zones 5-7. *V.* × *juddii,* Judd viburnum: 6 to 8 feet tall and wide with extremely fragrant 3-inch white flower clusters followed by reddish black fruit. Zones 4-8. *V. opulus* 'Compactum,' compact European cranberry bush: 4 to 5 feet tall and wide; glossy, lobed maple-like leaves; 2- to 3-inch white flower clusters in midspring followed by long-lasting bright red fruit from fall into winter. *V. plicatum tomentosum,* doublefile viburnum: 8 to 10 feet tall, with tiers of horizontal branches spreading to a width that is equal to or greater than the height. Double rows of flat white flower clusters held above the leaves in middle to late spring. Zones 5-8. *V. prunifolium,* blackhaw viburnum: 12 to 15 feet tall and wide; sometimes grows as a small tree. Lustrous dark green leaves turning red or purple in fall; 3-inch clusters of white flowers in middle to late spring, followed by ½-inch fruits that change from pink to blue-black in fall. Growth rate slow to medium. Zones 3-9.

Growing conditions. All of these species do well in moist, well-drained soil. Plant in full sun for best flowering; partial shade is tolerated. Prune only to remove dead or diseased branches.

Landscape uses. Viburnum makes a good addition to a shrub border. With the exception of Korean spice viburnum, which is valued mainly for its flowers, viburnums are ornamental in at least three seasons and are suitable for specimen planting, and for hedges, screens and masses.

Vitex (VY-tex)
Chaste tree

Spikes of lilac, lavender or white flowers from midsummer to early fall, when few other shrubs are in bloom. Zones 6-10.

Selected species and varieties. *V. agnus-castus,* chaste tree: 3 to 20 feet tall, depending on the climate. May die to the ground in winter in Zones 6 and 7. Compound leaves composed of 4-inch leaflets dark green above and gray-green beneath. Tiny, fragrant lilac to lavender flowers in 6- to 8-inch spikes. The cultivar 'Silver Spire' has white flowers. Fast-growing. *V. negundo,* chaste tree: size similar to *V. agnus-castus,* varying with the climate. Gray-green compound leaves with toothed edges. Lilac to lavender flowers in 5- to 8-inch spikes. Fast-growing.

Growing conditions. Plant in moist, well-drained soil in full sun. Avoid heavy, wet soils, which increase chances of winter damage. In spring, cut dead branches to within 6 inches of the ground; new growth can reach 3 or more feet in height by the end of the season.

Landscape uses. In a warm climate use chaste tree in a shrub border or as a specimen. In zones where the cold will kill it back in winter, place it in the front of a shrub border or in a perennial border.

Weigela (wy-JEE-la)

Shrubs with profuse white, pink or red trumpet-shaped flowers in late spring and early summer. Zones 5-8.

Selected species and varieties. *W. florida,* old-fashioned weigela: 6 to 9 feet tall and 9 to 12 feet wide; dense and rounded, with many stems and arching branches. One-inch pink flowers. *W. florida* 'Bristol Ruby': more erect stems and branches, ruby red flowers. *W. florida* 'Bristol Snowflake': white flowers tinged with pink. *W. florida* 'Java Red': deep pink flowers; purplish red cast to leaves.

Growing conditions. Plant in almost any well-drained soil. Full sun. Prune after flowering.

Landscape uses. Use weigela in shrub borders and in masses. It is not a good specimen plant.

Winterberry see *Ilex*
Winter hazel see *Corylopsis*
Wintersweet see *Chimonanthus*
Witch hazel see *Hamamelis*
Woadwaxen see *Genista*

BROAD-LEAVED EVERGREEN SHRUBS

Abelia (ah-BEE-lee-a)

Graceful, rounded shrub bearing clusters of fragrant bell-shaped flowers from early summer into fall. Fine glossy foliage. Deciduous or semi-evergreen in more northern areas. Zones 6-10.

Selected species and varieties. *A.* × *grandiflora,* glossy abelia: 3 to 6 feet tall and wide, with many arching stems. Small white flowers tinged with pink have attractive reddish sepals that last for months after flowers. Grows tallest in mild climates; may occasionally be killed to the ground in severe Zone 6 winters but grows back quickly. One-inch pointed leaves are bronze when young, dark green in summer and reddish bronze in winter. Leaves last until late fall or early winter in Zones 6 and 7. Leaves last longer in a spot sheltered from the wind.

Growing conditions. Plant in moist, well-drained fertile acid soil and full sun or partial shade. Leaves last longer in a spot sheltered from

VITEX AGNUS-CASTUS

WEIGELA FLORIDA

ABELIA × GRANDIFLORA

ARDISIA

AUCUBA JAPONICA 'VARIEGATA'

BERBERIS JULIANAE

BUXUS SEMPERVIRENS 'ARBORESCENS'

the wind. Prune only to remove old woody stems or damaged stems.

Landscape uses. Its fine foliage, attractive form and long flowering season make abelia an excellent addition to a shrub border. Where it is reliably evergreen, use it for hedges.

Andromeda see *Pieris*

Ardisia (ar-DIZ-ee-a)

Boldly textured dwarf shrub with glossy dark green foliage, white flowers and red fruit. Zones 8 and 9.

Selected species and varieties. *A. japonica,* Japanese ardisia: 9 to 18 inches tall; spreads to form colonies. Leathery elliptical leaves up to 4 inches long with toothed edges. Small clusters of ½-inch white flowers in mid- to late summer, followed by small round red fruit in fall. The variety 'Hakuokan' has variegated silvery green and white leaves.

Growing conditions. Plant in a moist, well-drained acid soil rich in organic matter such as peat moss. Partial to deep shade.

Landscape uses. Plant Japanese ardisia in the foreground of a shaded shrub border or use it in a foundation planting on the shady side of a house. It also makes a handsome ground cover for a woodland garden. The paler variegated Japanese ardisia is especially effective with dark-leaved shrubs such as *Pieris japonica.*

Aucuba (a-KOO-ba)

Shade-loving shrub with large, glossy leaves and, on female plants, bright red fruit from fall to spring. Zones 7-10.

Selected species and varieties. *A. japonica,* aucuba: 6 to 12 feet tall, forming a neat clump of erect stems with 6-inch, dark green leathery leaves. Clusters of tiny purple flowers in early spring. Plants bear either male or female flowers. Male plants are required for females to produce the ½-inch oval fruit. *A. japonica* 'Variegata,' gold-dust aucuba: leaves speckled with yellow.

Growing conditions. Aucuba does best in a moist, well-drained soil rich in organic matter such as peat moss. Plant in light to deep shade only; too much sun burns and discolors the foliage. Tolerates city conditions and competes well with tree roots. Es-

tablished plants are drought-tolerant. Pruning is seldom required, but overgrown plants may be cut to the ground to control their size. In Zone 7 aucuba is sometimes killed to the ground in winter but grows back quickly.

Landscape uses. Plant this tough, handsome shrub under trees or on the north side of a house, singly or in groups. Set out one male plant for every eight to 10 females.

Azalea see *Rhododendron*
Barberry see *Berberis*

Berberis (BER-ber-is)
Barberry

Dense, mounded shrub bearing slender, glossy leaves with spiny edges and yellow spring flowers. Branches have sharp spines. Zones 5-8.

Selected species and varieties. *B. candidula,* paleleaf barberry: dwarf shrub 2 to 4 feet tall and up to 5 feet wide with arching branches. Half-inch-long leaves green above and white beneath turning reddish in winter. Half-inch flowers followed by purplish gray berries in late summer. *B. julianae,* wintergreen barberry: 5 to 8 feet tall and wide; 2- to 3-inch leaves green above and pale beneath, turning reddish in winter. Clusters of yellow flowers followed by bluish black fruit in late summer.

Growing conditions. Evergreen barberries do best in moist, well-drained soil in full sun or light shade. Pruning is rarely needed, but overgrown plants can be cut back to the ground and will grow back quickly.

Landscape uses. Handsome foliage and form make both of these barberries attractive specimens. They can also be planted in groups and, because of their fierce spines, as highly effective barrier hedges. These species are often semi-evergreen or deciduous in the northern part of their range.

Bottlebrush see *Callistemon*
Box see *Buxus*
Boxwood see *Buxus*

Buxus (BUCK-sus)
Box, boxwood

Dense, slow-growing rounded or conical shrub that ranges in form from treelike to low-growing dwarf plant. Small, shiny fragrant leaves. Often sheared for a formal effect. Zones 4-9.

Selected species and varieties. *B. microphylla*, littleleaf box or boxwood: compact form 3 to 4 feet tall and equally wide. Oval leaves ½ to 1 inch long turn yellow-green in winter. Zones 6-9. *B. microphylla* 'Green Pillow': very slow-growing variety that eventually becomes about 1 foot tall and 4 feet wide; dark green foliage. Zones 6-9. *B. microphylla koreana:* an unusually cold-tolerant littleleaf box hardy to Zone 4. Foliage becomes brownish in winter. *B. sempervirens*, common box or boxwood: 15 to 20 feet tall, branching from the ground up. Elliptical leaves about 1 inch long, dark green all year long. Zones 5-9. *B. sempervirens* 'Arborescens,' American box: cultivar with a conical form. *B. sempervirens* 'Suffruticosa,' edging box: grows very slowly to 4 or 5 feet in height and width. Bright green rounded leaves. Zones 5-9.

Growing conditions. Set plants out in spring in moist, well-drained soil where there is protection from drying winter winds. Mulch after planting. Full sun or light shade. Common box does best in a warm, moist climate that does not have extremes of cold and heat. Plants withstand pruning well.

Landscape uses. Depending on their size, use boxwoods for low edgings, tall hedges or screens. Edging boxwood can easily be kept a foot or less tall. The lower-growing varieties are suitable for foundation plantings. All boxwoods are invaluable in formal gardens.

Callistemon (kal-is-TEE-mon)
Bottlebrush

A spreading shrub that has profuse flower spikes in spring and summer. Zones 9 and 10.

Selected species and varieties. *C. citrinus*, lemon bottlebrush: 8 to 10 feet tall, with arching branches. Grows to 20 feet or more if pruned to a single stem. Named for its lemon-scented, lance-shaped 3-inch leaves. Scarlet flower spikes up to 4 inches long with prominent, bristly stamens. Intermittent blooms in fall and winter.

Growing conditions. Plant in full sun in well-drained soil. Tolerates dry or alkaline soil.

Landscape uses. Use as a screen or for a hedge. Can also be espaliered on a wall or a fence.

Calluna (ka-LOO-na)
Heather

Low-growing, finely textured shrub with slender spikes of tiny flowers in summer and early fall. Zones 4-7.

Selected species and varieties. *C. vulgaris*, Scotch heather: 2 feet tall and equally wide; has many ascending branches with tiny overlapping scalelike leaves. Rosy or purplish pink flowers on spikes 6 to 10 inches tall. There are dozens of cultivars of Scotch heather. They range down to 4 inches in height and have flowers in white and shades of pink, purple and red. Some have golden or bronze foliage.

Growing conditions. Scotch heather requires a poor, moist but very well drained acid soil. Set out container plants in spring in a site protected from drying winter winds. Full sun or light shade. Where there is little snow cover, a shaded location prevents leaf burn in winter. Prune in early spring only.

Landscape uses. Plant Scotch heather in seaside gardens and other poor, sandy spots. Use it in rock gardens, as an edging or as a ground cover.

Camellia (ka-MEEL-ee-a)

Neat, dense shrub with white, pink or red flowers in fall, winter or spring. Lustrous dark green foliage. Zones 8 and 9.

Selected species and varieties. *C. japonica*, common camellia or Japanese camellia: 8 to 15 feet tall and 6 to 10 feet wide; usually pyramidal in form. Broad oval leaves 2 to 4 inches long. Immense number of cultivars; flowers up to 5 inches across; single or double; white and many shades of pink or red; some variegated. Time of flowering ranges from late fall to early spring, depending on the zone and the weather. *C. sasanqua*, sasanqua camellia, autumn camellia: 6 to 10 feet or more in height, forming a broad pyramid. Elliptical leaves 2 to 3 inches long. Many cultivars; flowers 2 to 3 inches across; same form and color range as in common camellia. Blooms in fall.

Growing conditions. Plant in moist, well-drained acid soil rich in organic matter such as peat moss. Mulch to conserve moisture. Full sun

CALLISTEMON CITRINUS

CALLUNA VULGARIS 'H.E. BEAL'

CAMELLIA JAPONICA 'PINK PERFECTION'

CHOISYA TERNATA

CLEYERA JAPONICA

DAPHNE ODORA 'AUREO-MARGINATA'

ERICA CARNEA 'SPRINGWOOD PINK'

or partial shade for sasanqua camellia; common camellia grows best in partial shade but can tolerate full sun in coastal areas with high humidity. Severe cold snaps may damage flower buds. Both species may do well in the southern part of Zone 7 in a protected spot with ideal growing conditions.

Landscape uses. Use camellia singly as a specimen or an accent plant, or use it in groups as screens or informal hedges.

▬

Cape jasmine see *Gardenia*
Cherry laurel see *Prunus*

▬

Choisya (CHOY-zee-a)
Mexican orange

Open, spreading shrub with sweet-scented white flowers in late spring. Zones 8-10.

Selected species and varieties. *C. ternata,* Mexican orange: 6 to 8 feet tall and equally wide. Aromatic, glossy 3-inch leaflets arranged in threes. Intermittent flowers in summer and fall.

Growing conditions. Plant in moist, well-drained acid soil rich in organic matter such as peat moss. Full sun or partial shade. In the colder parts of Zone 8, plant in a warm, sheltered spot.

Landscape uses. Situate Mexican orange in a shrub or as a screen near a house or terrace, where its fragrance can easily be enjoyed.

▬

Cleyera (KLAY-er-a)

A dense, upright shrub that has fragrant white flowers and red berries. Zones 8-10.

Selected species and varieties. *C. japonica,* Japanese cleyera (also called *Ternstroemia gymnanthera):* 8 to 10 feet or more in height; width about two-thirds of the height. Leathery, lustrous dark green leaves turning bronze in winter; ½-inch flowers in late spring; ½-inch oval berries that ripen in early fall.

Growing conditions. Japanese cleyera needs moist, well-drained soil and a shaded site. Can be pruned to keep its height 6 feet or less.

Landscape uses. Use on the north side of a building or under high-branching trees as an accent plant, hedge, screen or foundation plant.

Daphne (DAFF-nee)

Small, mounded shrub with handsome foliage and intensely fragrant flowers in middle to late winter. Zones 7-9.

Selected species and varieties. *D. odora,* winter daphne: 3 to 4 feet tall and wide. Narrow, glossy 3-inch leaves. Small rosy or purplish flowers in 1-inch clusters lasting for weeks. *D. odora* 'Aureo-marginata' has narrow creamy yellow margins.

Growing conditions. Plant in moist, well-drained acid soil in partial shade. Mulch after planting. Pruning seldom needed.

Landscape uses. Use winter daphne as an accent plant beneath high-branching trees or in the front of a shaded shrub border.

▬

Erica (AIR-ik-a)
Heath

Dwarf shrub with dense foliage and spikes of tiny tubular flowers in winter or spring. Zones 5-8.

Selected species and varieties. *E. carnea,* winter heath, spring heath: 6 inches to 1 foot tall, spreading to 2 or more feet in width; tiny needle-like leaves. One- to 2-inch-long spikes of rosy red flowers blooming as early as January in warm zones. *E. carnea* 'Springwood Pink': clear rose pink flowers. *E. carnea* 'Springwood White': white flowers.

Growing conditions. Plant in spring in a poor, light, moist soil with excellent drainage. Winter heath does best in acid soil but will tolerate one that is slightly alkaline. Full sun. Mulch to control weeds. Prune immediately after flowering to keep plants bushy.

Landscape uses. Plant winter heath in a rock garden, as an evergreen accent in a perennial border or as a ground cover. The flower buds add color to the garden for weeks before they open.

▬

Euonymus (yew-ON-i-mus)

Dense shrub with handsome dark green foliage and colorful fruit in fall. Zones 6-9.

Selected species and varieties. *E. kiautschovicus,* spreading euonymus: rounded shrub 8 to 10 feet tall and wide. Leaves to 3 inches in length with toothed edges. Three-inch-wide clusters of greenish white flowers in late summer, followed by pink fruits that open to reveal orange-red seeds in mid- to late fall. In northern areas the foliage is often burned by the winter sun. *E. kiautschovicus* 'Manhattan': a compact variety 4 to 6 feet tall with very glossy foliage.

Growing conditions. Plant in almost any well-drained soil. Can thrive in full sun to partial shade. A tough, highly adaptable plant.

Landscape uses. Spreading euonymus is a good hedge or screening plant. Manhattan spreading euonymus is also well suited to foundation plantings.

▬

False holly see *Osmanthus*

▬

Feijoa (fee-JO-a)
Guava

Shrub with striking foliage of dark bluish green upper surfaces and woolly white undersides; waxy white flowers tinged with red, and edible fruit. Zones 8-10.

Selected species and varieties. *F. sellowiana*, guava, pineapple guava: 10 to 15 feet tall and 10 feet or more wide with ascending branches. Oval leaves 2 inches long; 1½-inch-wide white flowers with red centers and long crimson stamens in late spring; 3-inch oval fruit that turns from reddish green to yellow when it matures in late summer or early fall. Flavor is reminiscent of pineapple.

Growing conditions. Plant in a light, well-drained soil rich in organic matter such as peat moss. Full sun is best, but guava also tolerates partial shade. It also tolerates salt spray. Guava can be kept small with pruning.

Landscape uses. Plant guava singly as an accent plant, in small groups as a screen or as a hedge.

▬

Fire thorn see *Pyracantha*

▬

Gardenia (gar-DEE-nee-a)

Rounded shrub with fragrant white flowers and lustrous dark green foliage. Zones 8-10.

Selected species and varieties. *G. jasminoides*, gardenia, Cape jasmine: 4 to 6 feet tall and wide; leathery leaves 2 to 4 inches; waxy flowers 2 to 3 inches across over a long period

in late spring and early summer, until night temperatures become warm. Along the West Coast, where nights remain cool, gardenias may bloom from spring until midfall.

Growing conditions. Plant in a moist, well-drained acid soil high in organic matter such as peat moss. Full sun or partial shade. In Zone 8 select a warm site sheltered from cold winter winds. Apply a mulch to keep soil moist.

Landscape uses. Gardenia can be used in a shrub border or as a hedge plant and can also be espaliered on a wall or fence. Choose a site near a terrace or a walk where its fragrance can be easily enjoyed.

▬

Grape holly see *Mahonia*
Guava see *Feijoa*
Hawthorn see *Raphiolepis*
Heath see *Erica*
Heather see *Calluna*
Heavenly bamboo see *Nandina*
Holly see *Ilex*
Holly grape see *Mahonia*
Holly osmanthus see *Osmanthus*

▬

Ilex (EYE-lex)
Holly

A varied group of shrubs with attractive foliage and, in some species, colorful winter fruit. Zones 4-9.

Selected species and varieties. *I. cornuta* 'Burfordii,' Burford holly: rounded shrub usually reaching 10 feet in height though it can grow to 20 feet or more. Lustrous, convex dark green 4-inch leaves with few or no spines. Large bright red berries produced without pollination. Zones 7-9. *I. cornuta* 'Rotunda,' dwarf Chinese holly: dense plant 3 to 4 feet tall spreading to 6 to 8 feet across. Lustrous, convex dark green leaves roughly rectangular in shape with very sharp spines. This cultivar bears no fruit. Zones 7-9. *I. crenata*, Japanese holly: 6 to 10 feet tall and wide; rounded form; ½- to 1-inch-long dark green oval leaves resembling boxwood foliage. Black berries on female plants only. Zones 6-8. There are many cultivars. *I. crenata* 'Convexa,' convexleaf holly: usually 4 to 6 feet tall with a width nearly twice the height. Dense branching and foliage. Half-inch-long dark green leaves are convex. Zones 5-8. *I. crenata* 'Helleri,' Heller Japanese holly: neat,

EUONYMUS KIAUTSCHOVICUS

FEIJOA SELLOWIANA

GARDENIA JASMINOIDES

ILEX CORNUTA 'BURFORDII'

129

LEUCOTHOE FONTANESIANA

LIGUSTRUM JAPONICUM

MAHONIA AQUIFOLIUM

compact, mounded dwarf 3 to 4 feet tall and wide. Zones 5-8. *I. crenata* 'Microphylla': 8 feet tall and wide. Small, narrow dark green leaves. Zones 5-8. *I. glabra,* inkberry: 6 to 8 feet tall and wide. Upright stems and rounded form. Small, lustrous dark green leaves. Black fruit on female plants only. May spread to form colonies. One of the hardiest broad-leaved evergreens. Zones 4-9. *I. glabra* 'Compacta,' compact inkberry: 3 to 4 feet tall; dense foliage and branches and globular form. Zones 4-9. *I.* × 'Nellie R. Stevens,' Nellie R. Stevens holly: large shrub 15 to 25 feet tall; pyramidal form. Large, lustrous dark green leaves with several spines. Profuse red berries. Zones 6-9

Growing conditions. These hollies all grow well in moist, well-drained slightly acid soil. Inkberry also grows well in damp to wet soils. Hollies produce the most berries in full sun but also grow well in partial shade. The Japanese hollies and inkberry withstand heavy pruning.

Landscape uses. Japanese hollies and inkberry are versatile. Use them for hedges, in masses or as accents. The smaller varieties are excellent foundation plants. Grow them informally or prune into formal shapes. Nellie R. Stevens makes a handsome specimen plant; it also works in a hedge. Grows fairly fast.

Leucothoe (loo-KOTH-o-ee)

Shrub with beautiful, glossy lance-shaped foliage arranged in an attractive zigzag pattern along gracefully arching stems. White flowers in spring. Zones 5-9.

Selected species and varieties. *L. fontanesiana,* drooping leucothoe, fountain leucothoe: 3 to 6 feet tall and wide. Spreading form with many slender, smooth shiny green stems; may sucker to form broad colonies. Leaves are 2 to 5 inches long, apple green in spring, dark green in summer and bronze to burgundy in winter. Waxy white bell-shaped flowers in clusters along undersides of the stems in mid- to late spring. Zones 5-9. *L. fontanesiana* 'Scarletta': foliage purplish in winter. *L. populifolia,* Florida leucothoe: 8 to 12 feet tall and wide with many arching stems. Spreads by suckers. Leaves up to 4 inches long. Clusters of small cream-colored flowers in mid- to late spring. Zones 7-9.

Growing conditions. Plant leucothoe in a moist, well-drained acid soil rich in organic matter such as peat moss. In Zone 5 plant drooping leucothoe in spring only. Florida leucothoe grows in partial to deep shade only; drooping leucothoe does best in shade but tolerates full sun if the soil is kept moist. Neither species tolerates drought or drying winds. Both leucothoes can be kept small by pruning.

Landscape uses. Drooping leucothoe can be placed in the front of taller shrubs in a shady border, planted in masses or used as a ground cover. Florida leucothoe is a handsome accent plant and adds interesting texture to a shrub border. Both species are well suited to naturalistic plantings.

Ligustrum (li-GUS-trum)
Privet

Dense, upright shrub with shiny dark green foliage. Very adaptable and has many landscape uses. Zones 7-10.

Selected species and varieties. *L. japonicum,* Japanese privet: usually 6 to 12 feet tall but can reach 15 feet or more. Width about two-thirds the height. Broad oval leaves up to 4 inches long. Pyramidal clusters of creamy flowers in late spring have a strong fragrance many find unpleasant. Small round black fruit attractive in fall and winter.

Growing conditions. Plant in virtually any type of well-drained soil. Full sun or partial shade. Withstands heavy pruning.

Landscape uses. Japanese privet is an excellent hedge or screen plant and is handsome enough to use as a specimen. It can be pruned to grow as a small tree with one or several trunks. Although hardy in Zone 7, Japanese privet may suffer severe leaf burn there in winter.

Mahonia (mah-HO-nee-a)
Holly grape, grape holly

Upright shrub with leathery, spiny leaves, clusters of decorative flower buds in winter, fragrant yellow flowers in winter or early spring, and grapelike fruit in summer and fall. Zones 5-9.

Selected species and varieties. *M. aquifolium,* Oregon holly grape: 3 to 6 feet tall and wide. Stems have few or no branches. Compound leaves have five or more pairs of shiny leaflets that are reddish when young, yellow-green to dark green in summer and bronze in winter. Flowers in early spring. Zones 5-9. *M. bealei*, leatherleaf holly grape: thick stems 8 to 12 feet tall. Few or no branches. Compound leaves up to 18 inches long with dark green or bluish green leaflets. Flowers fragrant, opening early to late winter, depending on the climate. Fruit bluish when young, maturing to black. Zones 6-10.

Growing conditions. Plant in moist, well-drained acid soil in a spot sheltered from wind. Partial shade is best, but the shrub will tolerate full sun if the soil is kept moist. Remove suckers to keep plants from spreading. Cut back stems to control height.

Landscape uses. Oregon holly grape is well suited to foundation planting or a shrub border and can also be used as an accent in a shady planting. The large, coarse-textured leatherleaf holly grape makes a bold specimen or accent plant. It looks better against a wall by itself than with other plants, since it tends to overwhelm them.

Mexican orange see *Choisya*

Myrtus (MERT-us)
Myrtle

Rounded shrub with glossy, aromatic leaves and sweetly fragrant creamy white flowers in summer. Zones 9 and 10.

Selected species and varieties. *M. communis*, myrtle: 5 to 8 feet tall and wide. Dark green leaves 2 inches long; ¾-inch flowers followed by blue-black fruit in fall.

Growing conditions. Myrtle adapts to many soils and grows well in hot, dry locations. Full sun or light shade. Withstands frequent shearing. Does not do well in Zone 10 in Florida.

Landscape uses. Use myrtle in shrub borders, in masses or in hedges, and place it where its fragrance can be easily enjoyed. Myrtle is a good subject for pruning into formal shapes.

Nandina (nan-DEE-na)
Nandina, heavenly bamboo

A graceful vase-shaped shrub with erect stems bearing finely divided blue-green compound leaves. Spikes of creamy white flowers and bright red berries that last through the winter. Zones 7-10.

Selected species and varieties. *N. domestica*, nandina, heavenly bamboo: 6 to 8 feet tall; width about half the height. Leaves up to 18 inches long with slender, pointed 2- to 4-inch leaflets that are bronze when young, blue-green in summer and red-tinged in winter. Flowers bloom in late spring or early summer, and round berries ripen in fall. *N. domestica* 'Harbor Dwarf': graceful mounded shrub 1 to 3 feet tall with dense foliage.

Growing conditions. Nandina will grow in almost any soil but does best in a moist, fertile one. It can adapt to conditions ranging from full sun to heavy shade but will have more flowers and fruit and brighter winter foliage color in a sunny location. Every spring remove a few old stems to promote new growth. Nandina can be grown in Zone 6 but is often killed to the ground in winter.

Landscape uses. Nandina makes a delicately textured hedge and is an excellent specimen for sun or shade. It is also attractive planted in drifts. It competes well with tree roots.

Nerium (NEE-ree-um)
Oleander

Rounded shrub with narrow, leathery leaves and showy clusters of flowers from early summer into fall. Zones 8-10.

Selected species and varieties. *N. oleander*, oleander, rosebay: height ranges from 6 to 20 feet; less where winter freezes kill or injure branches. Width is approximately equal to the height. Pointed, dark gray-green leaves 3 to 6 inches long; 1-inch flowers may be white, yellow, pink or red and either single or double, depending on the variety. Fairly fast-growing. All parts of this plant are highly poisonous if eaten, and some people develop a rash from touching it.

Growing conditions. Oleander grows best in a moist, well-drained soil, but it also adapts to gardens that are hot, dry, windy or subject to air pollution. Full sun or partial shade. Plant in a warm, sheltered spot in the colder parts of Zone 8. Can be heavily pruned to limit size.

Landscape uses. Plant oleander as a hedge or screen or incorporate it into a shrub border. In windswept gardens use it as a windbreak. Handsome anywhere, it is especially valuable for a desert or a seaside garden.

MYRTUS COMMUNIS

NANDINA DOMESTICA

NERIUM OLEANDER

OSMANTHUS HETEROPHYLLUS

PHOTINIA SERRULATA

PIERIS JAPONICA

PITTOSPORUM TOBIRA

Oleander see *Nerium*

Osmanthus (oz-MAN-thus)

Rounded shrub 8 to 15 feet or more in height and a little less in width, with spiny, holly-like leaves and wonderfully fragrant flowers in fall. Zones 7-10.

Selected species and varieties. *O. heterophyllus,* holly osmanthus, false holly: Glossy, dark green leaves about 2 inches long. On older plants leaves may have only one spine, at the tip. Tiny inconspicuous white flowers in early to middle fall. Zones 7-9. *O. × fortunei,* Fortune's osmanthus: leathery, dark green leaves 2 to 4 inches long, densely spined along the margins. Tiny flowers in midfall. Zones 8-10.

Growing conditions. Plant in a fertile, moist, well-drained soil in full sun or light shade. Osmanthus can be pruned heavily to control size.

Landscape uses. Plant holly osmanthus or Fortune's singly as a fragrant specimen or use several of them in shrub borders, as hedge plants or as screens.

Photinia (fo-TIN-ee-a)

Large, upright shrub with bold-textured shiny foliage that is a brilliant red or bronze when young. Profuse clusters of bright red fruit from late summer until the following spring. Zones 7-9.

Selected species and varieties. *P. × fraseri,* Fraser photinia: 8 to 15 feet tall and about half as wide. Three- to 5-inch leaves with toothed edges, red when young, maturing to dark green: 4- to 7-inch clusters of white flowers with a somewhat unpleasant scent in early spring. *P. serrulata,* Chinese photinia: large shrub growing to 20 feet or more; width is about two-thirds the height. Flowers and foliage are very similar to Fraser photinia's, but the leaves are larger, up to 8 inches in length. New foliage is bronze.

Growing conditions. Plant photinia in a well-drained fertile soil in full sun or partial shade. In desert gardens give the shrub protection from afternoon sun.

Landscape uses. Plant photinias as hedges, screens or specimens. Allow ample room, especially for the large and vigorous Chinese photinia. Light pruning during the growing season encourages the plant to produce more new shoots with brightly colored young foliage.

Pieris (PY-er-is)
Pieris, andromeda

Graceful tiers of branches bearing rosettes of glossy foliage. Drooping clusters of white or red flower buds throughout the winter, opening in early spring. Zones 5-8.

Selected species and varieties. *P. japonica,* Japanese pieris, Japanese andromeda: 7 to 10 feet high and about two-thirds as wide. Three-inch leaves that are reddish bronze when young, turning to dark green by summer. Small white flowers in clusters 3 to 6 inches long. Slow-growing. *P. japonica* 'Dorothy Wyckoff': compact shrub with deep red buds opening to deep pink flowers. *P. japonica* 'Mountain Fire': new growth is fiery red; white flowers. *P. japonica* 'Variegata': leaves have white margins; white flowers. More compact than other members of the species.

Growing conditions. Plant in moist, well-drained acid soil rich in organic matter such as peat moss or compost. Select a site sheltered from winter wind. Partial shade is preferable in the South, though pieris can tolerate full sun.

Landscape uses. Pieris makes a beautiful specimen plant. It is also handsome under deciduous trees, in masses or in combination with other broad-leaved evergreens in a shrub border.

Pittosporum (pit-o-SPOR-um)

Spreading shrub with glossy dark green leaves. Small clusters of white spring flowers scented like orange blossoms. Zones 8-10.

Selected species and varieties. *P. tobira,* Japanese pittosporum: 10 feet or more in height, sometimes spreading twice as wide. Leathery leaves 2 to 4 inches long with broad, blunt tips. Slow-growing. *P. tobira* 'Variegata' has gray-green leaves with white borders.

Growing conditions. Plant in almost any well-drained soil. Although pittosporum grows best in moist soil, established plants can tolerate dryness. Pittosporum also withstands hot locations, wind and seaside conditions. Full sun to heavy shade. Can be pruned heavily to limit size.

Landscape uses. With its dense

form and handsome foliage, pittosporum is an excellent hedge or screen plant and blends well with other evergreens in a foundation planting. It is a good choice for desert and seaside gardens. After many years, an unpruned pittosporum develops an open form with broadly spreading picturesque gray branches.

—

Privet see *Ligustrum*

—

Prunus (PROO-nus)
Cherry laurel

Very dense shrub with broadly spreading branches, lustrous dark green willow-like leaves and 4-inch clusters of white flowers in mid-spring. The genus also includes deciduous cherry trees. Zones 6-10.

Selected species and varieties. *P. laurocerasus* 'Otto Luyken,' Otto Luyken cherry laurel: 3 to 4 feet tall; width 6 feet or more. *P. laurocerasus* 'Schipkaensis,' Schipka cherry laurel: usually 4 to 6 feet tall but can reach 10 feet. *P. laurocerasus* 'Zabeliana,' Zabel cherry laurel: 3 feet tall with a width of 10 feet or more.

Growing conditions. Plant in moist, well-drained soil rich in organic matter such as peat moss. Full sun or partial shade. Tolerates salt spray. Can be pruned heavily.

Landscape uses. Use any of the cherry laurels as hedge plants or plant them in small groups for a strikingly broad low-growing mass. The height of Otto Luyken and Zabel cherry laurels makes them suitable for planting beneath windows.

—

Pyracantha (py-ra-CAN-tha)
Fire thorn

Thorny shrub with 2-inch clusters of white flowers in mid- to late spring followed by spectacular masses of small red, orange or yellow fruit in fall and winter. Lustrous dark green foliage. Zones 6-10.

Selected species and varieties. *P. coccinea* 'Lalandei,' Laland fire thorn: 6 to 9 feet tall and wide; stiff, upright branches. Orange-red fruit. *P.* × 'Mohave,' Mohave fire thorn: 6 to 10 feet tall; upright, densely branched form. Orange-red fruit ripens in late summer. *P.* × 'Navaho,' Navaho fire thorn: 6 feet tall and 7 to 8 feet wide; dense, mounded form. Orange-red fruit. *P.* × 'Teton,' Teton fire thorn: 15 feet tall

and 6 to 9 feet wide; strongly upright form. Yellow-orange fruit. Fire thorns are fairly fast-growing.

Growing conditions. Set out container plants in spring in almost any well-drained soil. More fruit is produced in full sun, but fire thorns will grow in light shade.

Landscape uses. Fire thorns are handsome espaliered on a wall or fence. Because of their thorns, they also make good barrier hedges.

—

Raphiolepis (ra-fee-OLL-ep-is)
Hawthorn

A neat, mounded shrub with clusters of fragrant pink or white flowers, glossy, leathery foliage and purplish black fruit in fall and winter. Zones 8-10.

Selected species and varieties. *R. indica,* Indian hawthorn: 3 to 5 feet tall and wide. Lance-shaped leaves 2 to 3 inches long with toothed edges; ¾-inch flowers in winter or early spring are white or pink, depending on the variety. *R. indica* 'Springtime' has pink flowers and bronze-tinged foliage. *R. umbellata,* yeddo hawthorn: 6 to 10 feet tall and wide. Oval leaves 2 to 3 inches long are dark green in summer and purple-tinged in winter. White flowers in early to middle spring.

Growing conditions. Raphiolepis grows best in moist, well-drained slightly acid soil. It will tolerate dry soil and salt spray. Prefers full sun or light shade.

Landscape uses. Use either of these species for an informal hedge, in a shrub border or in a foundation planting. Both grow well in containers.

—

Rhododendron
(ro-do-DEN-dron)
Azalea, rhododendron

Shrub prized for its clusters of spectacular spring flowers in white and shades of yellow, pink, red and purple. The genus contains hundreds of species and cultivars and is divided into two major categories, rhododendrons and azaleas. The flowers are similar: rhododendrons usually have bell-shaped flowers and azaleas have funnel-shaped flowers. Both groups include shrubs of varying sizes, flower color and hardiness. Zones 4-10.

Selected species and varieties. Rhododendrons. *R. carolinianum,*

PRUNUS LAUROCERASUS 'OTTO LUYKEN'

PYRACANTHA COCCINEA

RAPHIOLEPIS INDICA 'SPRINGTIME'

RHODODENDRON × 'PJM'

SKIMMIA JAPONICA

VIBURNUM × BURKWOODII

Carolina rhododendron: 3 to 5 feet tall and wide. Rounded shape. Shiny dark green leaves with rusty undersides. Rosy pink or rosy purple flowers in 3-inch clusters in late spring. Zones 4-8. *R. catawbiense*, Catawba rhododendron: 6 to 10 feet tall. Shape varies from compact to spreading. Dark green oval leaves up to 6 inches long. Lilac-purple, rose-purple or white flowers in 6-inch clusters in mid- to late spring. Zones 4-8. *R. catawbiense* 'Cunningham': compact variety 4 feet tall with white flowers blotched with greenish yellow in late spring. Zones 5-8. *R. catawbiense* 'Nova Zembla': dark red flowers; withstands cold winters especially well. Zones 4-8. *R. catawbiense* 'Roseum Elegans': rose-lilac flowers; withstands cold winters especially well. Zones 4-8. *R.* × 'PJM,' PJM rhododendron: rounded shrub 3 to 6 feet tall and wide; 2-inch dark green leaves turn mahogany or bronze in winter. Lavender-pink flowers in early spring. Tolerates direct sun unusually well. Zones 4-9. *R.* × 'Ramapo': dwarf shrub 2 feet tall with 1-inch gray-green leaves and pale violet flowers in midspring. Zones 5-8.

Azaleas. Most hybrid azaleas belong to one of the following groups. Gable azalea: 6 feet tall or less. Shiny 1-inch leaves; may lose some leaves in harsh winters. Flowers 1½-2 inches across. Zones 5-10. Glenn Dale azalea: size ranges from low compact forms to shrubs 5 feet or more in height. Flowers up to 3½ inches across. May lose some leaves in harsh winters. Zones 6-9. Indica azalea: large, spreading shrub 6 feet tall or more and 10 feet across. Flowers are large; many varieties have double flowers. Most Indicas are hardy in Zones 8-10; some are limited to Zones 9 and 10. Kaempferi azalea: height to 5 feet or more. Flowers 2 to 4 inches across. May lose leaves in harsh winters. Zones 5-9. Kurume azalea: dense, low-growing shrub up to 2½ feet tall. Small shiny leaves. Flowers 1 to 2 inches across, sometimes with stripes or flecks. Zones 7-9.

Growing conditions. Plant rhododendrons and azaleas in a constantly moist, loose, well-drained acid soil mixture that is at least 50 percent organic matter such as peat moss. All rhododendrons and azaleas grow well in light shade. Some, including the Carolina, PJM and Ramapo rhododendrons and the Indica azaleas, do well in full sun if the soil is kept moist. Protect from strong, drying winds. Near the

northern limit of hardiness, set out plants in spring; in other areas plant in spring or fall. Maintain a mulch 2 or 3 inches deep to keep roots moist. Prune only to remove dead, diseased or damaged branches.

Landscape uses. The enormous diversity in this genus is matched by diverse uses. Low-growing types are useful in rock gardens, massed as ground cover or as edgings. Plant larger azaleas in evergreen shrub borders, in masses, as hedges or as screens. All are ideal for planting in woodland gardens.

—

Rosebay see *Nerium*

—

Skimmia (SKIM-ee-a)

Low, dense, mounded shrub with white early-spring flowers and clusters of bright red berries through winter on female plants. Zones 7-9.

Selected species and varieties. *S. japonica*, Japanese skimmia: 3 to 4 feet tall and wide. Bright green oblong leaves 2 to 5 inches long. Male and female flowers are borne on separate plants in 3-inch upright clusters. Both sexes are required for fruit production. Male flowers are fragrant. Round, ⅓-inch berries ripen in fall. Slow-growing.

Growing conditions. Plant in moist, acid soil rich in organic matter such as peat moss. Partial to deep shade only; foliage discolors in full sun. Plant one male for every six to eight females.

Landscape uses. Mass skimmia in shaded beds or combine with other broad-leaved evergreens in shrub borders or foundation plantings. Its light foliage stands out against the darker shades that are more typical of broad-leaved evergreens. Skimmia can also be planted in shady perennial borders.

—

Viburnum (vy-BUR-num)

Upright multistemmed shrub with handsome dark green foliage and clusters of white flowers in spring. Zones 5-9.

Selected species and varieties. *V.* × *burkwoodii*, Burkwood viburnum: open shrub 6 to 8 feet tall and 4 to 6 feet wide; 4-inch shiny oval leaves with fuzzy brown undersides may turn purplish red in fall. In Zones 5-7 Burkwood viburnum may be either evergreen or deciduous. Pink flower buds open to form 2- or 3-inch rounded clusters of waxy white, intensely fragrant flowers in early spring. Slow-growing. *V. × rhytidophylloides,* lantanaphyllum viburnum: 8 to 10 feet tall and wide; rounded form with stout, slightly arching branches. Deeply veined leathery leaves up to 6 or 7 inches long are deciduous in northern zones. Flat 4-inch clusters of flowers in early to middle spring, followed by fruit that turns from reddish to black. The cultivar 'Alleghany' has very dark green foliage, a dense form and especially handsome fall fruit. *V. rhytidophyllum,* leatherleaf viburnum: 8 to 12 feet tall and wide. Shiny, leathery, deeply veined leaves 4 to 8 inches long with fuzzy gray or yellowish undersides. Numerous 4- to 8-inch clusters of creamy white flowers in midspring. Fruit changing from red to black as it matures in fall.

Growing conditions. Plant viburnums in a slightly moist, well-drained soil. They prefer one that is slightly acid but are adaptable to other soils. Select a spot sheltered from the wind to prevent damage to foliage. Full sun or partial shade.

Landscape uses. Their bold, coarse foliage and strong forms make lantanaphyllum and leatherleaf viburnums good specimen plants. All three species combine well with other broad-leaved evergreens in shrub borders. Plant Burkwood viburnum where its fragrance can be enjoyed.

NEEDLE-LEAVED EVERGREEN SHRUBS

Arborvitae see *Thuja*

—

Chamaecyparis
(kam-ee-SIP-ar-is)
False cypress

Slow-growing pyramidal or conical shrub with flat fans of dark green scalelike leaves streaked with white on their undersides. Zones 5-8.

Selected species and varieties. *C. obtusa* 'Nana,' dwarf Hinoki false cypress: a wide, bushy shrub under 2 or 3 feet tall at maturity. *C. obtusa* 'Nana Gracilis' grows up to 8 feet in the shape of a broad cone.

Growing conditions. Plant in a moist soil in full sun, in a site protected from winter winds. False cypress thrives in a cool, humid at-mosphere but will grow well under average conditions.

Landscape uses. Use dwarf Hinoki false cypress in a rock garden or as a dark green accent in a flower border. Because it grows so slowly, it is a useful shrub where long-range control of size is important. Choose carefully labeled nursery stock, however, as there are many tree and shrub varieties of false cypress, and they are often confused in the trade.

—

Dwarf pine see *Pinus*
Dwarf spruce see *Picea*
False cypress see *Chamaecyparis*
Hemlock see *Tsuga*
Juniper see *Juniperus*

—

Juniperus (joo-NIP-er-us)
Juniper

A group of shrubs in a broad range of greens. Adapts well to city conditions. Zones 2-9.

Selected species and varieties. *J. chinensis,* 'Hetzii,' Hetz Chinese juniper, rapidly grows to a height of 6 feet and 12- to 18-foot widths with silvery blue-green leaves; *J. chinensis* 'Keteleeri,' Keteleer juniper, with bright green foliage growing in a loose pyramidal form up to 20 feet tall; *J. chinensis* 'Mint Julep,' a compact spreading juniper with bright green leaves; *J. chinensis* 'Pfitzeriana,' Pfitzer juniper, a fast-growing spreading juniper with arching branches, grows up to 10 feet tall with golden, green or blue-green foliage; and *J. chinensis* 'San Jose,' a flat spreading juniper with drab green foliage that seldom grows more than 2 feet tall. All Chinese junipers are hardy in Zones 4-9. *J. communis depressa,* prostrate juniper: spreading shrub up to 4 feet tall with a width three or more times the height. Gray-green needles, sometimes turning brownish in winter. Slow-growing. Zones 2-7. *J. conferta,* shore juniper: slow-growing, an ideal seaside ground cover no more than 1 foot tall and up to 6 feet wide, with bright green leaves. Zones 6-9. Varieties include *J. conferta* 'Blue Pacific,' up to 6 inches tall, with blue-green foliage, and *J. conferta* 'Emerald Sea,' same height, with bright green foliage. *J. horizontalis,* creeping juniper: ground cover with trailing streamers that grow about 1 foot a year to reach an eventual spread of 10 feet. Zones 2-9. Varieties include *J. horizontalis*

CHAMAECYPARIS OBTUSA 'NANA'

JUNIPERUS COMMUNIS DEPRESSA

PICEA PUNGENS 'GLAUCA GLOBOSA'

PINUS MUGO MUGO

'Bar Harbor,' with deep blue foliage that turns purple in winter; *J. horizontalis* 'Turquoise Spreader,' which forms blankets of blue-green foliage no more than 10 inches tall; and *J. horizontalis* 'Wiltonii,' Wilton carpet juniper or blue rug juniper, a juniper so low-spreading that its shape shows the contours of the garden's surface. *J. procumbens,* Japanese garden juniper: a widely spreading shrub 6 to 24 inches tall and five times as wide, with sea green foliage. Slow-growing. Zones 2-9. The variety *J. procumbens* 'Nana' is seldom more than a foot tall, growing very slowly into a mat about 2 feet wide. *J. sabina,* savin juniper: a vase-shaped juniper with foliage ranging from yellow-green through deep green to blue-green. Some find the odor of its crushed needles unpleasant. Zones 3-8. Varieties include *J. sabina* 'Broadmoor,' a low-growing juniper with bright green needles that spreads about three times its height, and *J. sabina* 'Buffalo,' with bright green needles that form a blanket a foot high and up to 8 feet across.

Growing conditions. Junipers do best in full sun in any ordinary, well-drained soil. Pfitzer juniper tolerates light shade. Junipers can withstand heat and drought. Common juniper and shore juniper thrive under seashore conditions; savin juniper tolerates city pollution better than other species. Older plants can be difficult to establish. Plant balled-and-burlapped young shrubs for best results. Prune individual branches with hand clippers to shape plants.

Landscape uses. Plant all junipers with their mature size and shape in mind. This reduces the need to prune or remove overgrown shrubs. Spreading junipers look best planted at or below eye level and are often used in foundation plantings. Use creeping and prostrate forms as ground covers or to hold banks, or in rock gardens. Mass taller shrubs as background plantings for a flower border. Junipers are easily sheared into hedges.

—

Picea (PY-see-a)
Spruce

Slow-growing dwarf varieties of tall tree species. Diverse shapes and growth patterns. Soft or stiff needles in colors ranging from light through deep green to blue-green and bright blue. Zones 3-8.

Selected species and varieties. *P. abies* 'Maxwellii,' Maxwell spruce: dense, prickly cushion of stiff foliage up to 3 feet tall and spreading irregularly to about twice as wide. Zones 3-8. *P. abies* 'Nidiformis,' bird's nest spruce: branches curve upward and out. Depression in center of young plants. Up to 6 feet tall after many years. Zones 3-8. *P. glauca* 'Conica,' dwarf Alberta spruce: compact cone up to 10 feet tall. Branches tightly packed with ½-inch grass green needles. Zones 5-7. *P. pungens* 'Glauca Globosa': irregularly shaped globe dense with short gray-blue needles. Up to 3 feet tall and somewhat wider. Zones 3-7. *P. pungens* 'Montgomery': compact bush under 3 feet with pointed blue-gray needles. Zones 3-7.

Growing conditions. Grow dwarf spruce in full sun in a well-drained sandy soil. Protect from the drying effects of wind.

Landscape uses. Use dwarf spruce as foundation plants, border accents or rock garden specimens.

—

Pine see *Pinus*

—

Pinus (PY-nus)
Pine

Dwarf varieties of tree species. Slow-growing, with unique growth habits. Clusters of needles in varying shades of green. Zones 3-9.

Selected species and varieties. *P. densiflora* 'Pendula,' weeping Japanese pine: rich green trailing shrub up to 6 feet across. Zones 5-7. *P. densiflora* 'Prostrata': low, spreading form. Zones 5-7. *P. mugo mugo,* mugo pine: low mounds of stiff-needled medium green foliage. Develops into shrub with ascending branches up to 8 feet tall. Zones 3-7. *P. strobus* 'Nana,' dwarf white pine: compact, slow-growing blue-green shrub under 2 feet tall. Branches hidden by dense bundles of needles. Zones 3-9.

Growing conditions. Plant dwarf pines in full sun in a well-drained soil that is sandy or gravelly. Dwarf white pines tolerate light shade. Protect shrubs from winter winds.

Landscape uses. Use dwarf pines as rock garden specimens, foundation plantings or accents in a border.

—

Spruce see *Picea*

Taxus (TAX-us)
Yew

A shrub with rich, glossy, green foliage. Inch-long needles spiral around twigs and branches. Broad variety of forms includes prostrate, round, vase-shaped and columnar. Slow-growing. Zones 5-7.

Selected species and varieties. *T. baccata* 'Repandens', spreading English yew: most cold-hardy variety of English yew. Broad, flat-topped shrub 3 or more feet high and 9 feet across. *T.* × *media* 'Densiformis': a fast-growing, compact, round shrub that becomes pyramidal with age. *T.* × *media* 'Hatfieldii,' Hatfield yew: a nonfruiting yew with upright branches, columnar when young and growing into a pyramidal shrub up to 12 feet high and almost as wide when mature. *T.* × *media* 'Hicksii,' Hicks yew: a columnar yew that eventually reaches about 20 feet in height and 7 feet in width, with multiple stems and upright branches.

Growing conditions. Yews can thrive in full sun or light shade in any average soil with good drainage. Wet soil will inhibit the growth of young plants. Protect them from summer heat and winter winds. Careful site selection is the key to growing yews at the limits of their range.

Landscape uses. Plant yews as specimens or as background plants; mass them for screens. Many yews, especially Hatfield and Hicks yews, can be grown and sheared as hedges. The foliage and the fleshy red berries that appear on many yews in fall are poisonous to mammals.

Thuja (THOO-ya)
Arborvitae

Formal globes of foliage with flat sprays of scalelike leaves. Zones 3-7.

Selected species and varieties. *T. occidentalis* 'Globosa,' globe arborvitae, maintains its round shape as it grows slowly to 5 feet in height and width. *T. occidentalis* 'Hetz Midget': a dense, extremely slow-growing dwarf that generally reaches only 12 to 15 inches in height. *T. occidentalis* 'Woodwardii': a globe-shaped shrub that spreads with age, becoming about 8 feet high and twice as wide.

Growing conditions. Plant arborvitae in full sun or light shade in a moist location. It does best where humidity is high. Larger shrubs need to be protected from the weight of winter snow.

Landscape uses. Use arborvitaes as foundation plants or as accents in a rock garden.

Tsuga (TSOO-ga)
Hemlock

Flat, feathery sprays of foliage in drooping mounds up to 6 feet tall. Zones 3-8.

Selected species and varieties. *T. canadensis* 'Sargentii,' also called *T. pendula*, Sargent weeping hemlock: weeping branches on contorted trunk. Dense foliage. Grows twice as broad as high.

Growing conditions. Plant hemlocks in sites with moist but well-drained soil where they will receive full sun. Light shade is recommended in areas where summers are hot and dry. Protect hemlocks from drying winter winds.

Landscape uses. Use Sargent weeping hemlock as a rock garden specimen or in the back of a border or foundation planting.

Yew see *Taxus*

VINES

Akebia (a-KEE-bee-a)
Five-leaf akebia

Deciduous or evergreen vine with lacy blue-green leaves composed of 1½- to 2-inch oblong leaflets with notched tips arranged like the fingers on a hand. Clusters of dainty purple flowers in spring, fragrant but inconspicuous, followed by 2- to 4-inch purple pods. Zones 4-9.

Selected species and varieties. *A. quinata*, five-leaf akebia: climbs by twining its stems from left to right. Grows 3 to 15 feet annually, ultimately to 30 or 40 feet.

Growing conditions. Plant five-leaf akebia in sun or light shade in any moist but well-drained soil. Prune annually, cutting back to the ground if necessary, to restrain its aggressive growth. Five-leaf akebia holds its leaves throughout the winter at the southern end of its range. Zones 7-9.

Landscape uses. Provide a sturdy support for five-leaf akebia to climb as a screen or wall specimen. Let vines sprawl as ground covers or use them to hold the soil on steep banks.

TAXUS BACCATA 'REPANDENS'

THUJA OCCIDENTALIS 'HETZ MIDGET'

TSUGA CANADENSIS 'SARGENTII'

AKEBIA QUINATA

ANISOSTICHUS CAPREOLATA

ARISTOLOCHIA DURIOR

CAMPSIS RADICANS

CLEMATIS × 'HENRYI'

Anisostichus (an-is-o-STY-kuss)

Evergreen vine with leaves composed of pairs of pointed oval leaflets. Green summer foliage turns reddish purple in winter. Profuse 1½- to 2-inch yellow and red-brown flowers from early to late spring. Zones 6-10.

Selected species and varieties. *A. capreolata,* crossvine: very fast growth, 15 to 20 feet annually, up to 50 or 60 feet at maturity. Climbs by means of curling tendrils with sticky adhesive tips.

Growing conditions. Plant crossvine in a moist but well-drained soil. Although crossvine tolerates shade, foliage will be thicker and flowers will be more abundant in full sun. Prune after flowering to control the crossvine's aggressive growth. May be killed to the ground by cold at the northern end of its range but will regrow the following spring.

Landscape uses. Use crossvine as a wall covering, allow it to climb tree trunks or let vines sprawl as a ground cover. Grow crossvine on a trellis as a thick screen.

Aristolochia (a-ris-to-LO-kee-a)
Dutchman's pipe

Deciduous vine with enormous, overlapping heart-shaped leaves up to a foot long. Flowers like 3-inch pipes with curved yellow-green stems and a mahogany-purple bowl, hidden by the leaves and with an unpleasant odor. Zones 5-8.

Selected species and varieties. *A. durior,* Dutchman's pipe: very aggressive growth, 6 to 20 feet per year. Climbs by twining its stems from left to right.

Growing conditions. Plant Dutchman's pipe in full sun or partial shade in any moist but well-drained soil. Vines tolerate city pollution. Prune as necessary to control rampant growth.

Landscape uses. Train Dutchman's pipe to a sturdy trellis or arbor for a dense screen or shade.

Boston ivy see *Parthenocissus*

Campsis (CAMP-sis)
Trumpetcreeper

From middle through late summer, brightly colored flower trumpets flare in clusters at the tips of new stems on extremely fast-growing vines up to 30 or 40 feet long. It climbs by adhering to supports with rootlike holdfasts. Leaves up to 18 inches long composed of pairs of pointed oval leaflets. Foliage turns yellow-green in fall, dropping to expose 7-inch-long seed pods. Zones 4-9.

Selected species and varieties. *C. radicans,* common trumpetcreeper: clusters of up to 12 red to orange flower trumpets 2 or 3 inches long with outer lips flaring 1½ inches. *C. × tagliabuana* 'Madame Galen': slightly larger red-orange flowers flaring up to 2½ inches across but less hardy. Zones 5-9.

Growing conditions. Plant trumpetcreeper in full sun in any well-drained soil. In fertile soils kept moist with mulch, it grows vigorously. Massive older vines are heavy and require more support than their holdfasts alone provide. Sticky holdfasts may damage painted wooden surfaces. Regular, even severe, pruning is necessary to control its rampant growth. Flowers bloom on new shoots; prune in late winter or very early spring for most prolific blooming.

Landscape uses. Use trumpetcreeper as a wall covering or grow it on a support as a screening or specimen planting. Its coarse-textured foliage looks best in large-scale gardens, where its brilliant flowers lend a tropical air.

Carolina jessamine
see *Gelsemium*

China fleece vine see *Polygonum*

Clematis (KLEM-a-tis)

A diverse group of flowering vines that are either soft-stemmed perennials or thin, woody climbers. Hybrids generally deciduous but species sometimes evergreen depending on the climate. Heart-shaped foliage with twining leafstalks on slender, brittle stems from 4 to 30 feet long. Flowers single or in clusters, small bells or flat stars composed of petal-like sepals in a broad spectrum of colors appearing from spring through frost, depending on the species and the variety. Spidery green pods open to expose tan fluff and decorate vines into winter. Zones 4-8.

Selected species and varieties. *C. jackmanii:* deep violet, star-shaped blooms up to 6 inches across from summer through fall; flowers on current year's growth on vines up to 12 feet long. Zones 4-8. *C. montana,* anemone clematis: very fast-growing vine up to 25 feet long with clusters of 2-inch white to pink flowers in late spring blooming on the previous year's growth. Zones 6-8. *C. virginiana*, virgin's bower: delicate small white flowers in 6-inch clusters on new growth from summer through fall on vines up to 20 feet long. Zones 3-7. In general, clematis that produces flowers in spring and early summer blooms on the previous year's growth and is slightly less hardy than the hybrids that produce flowers from summer through fall on new growth.

Growing conditions. For best blooms, grow clematis in full sun in a constantly moist but well-drained soil that is enriched with organic matter and has a neutral to slightly alkaline pH. Grow on any light support of string, wire, netting or wood; use more permanent supports in areas where vines remain evergreen or partially so. Clematis that blooms in summer or fall on the current year's growth, such as *C. jackmanii* and virgin's bower, can be pruned in spring or early summer before flowering. Clematis that blooms on growth made the previous year, such as *C. montana*, should be pruned after flowering. At the northern end of its range, if clematis has been killed to the ground by cold, prune it to 6 inches or less; the plants will regenerate from the roots and bloom again within the year.

Landscape uses. Allow clematis to creep into bushes or through a ground cover. Use it to accent architectural details, or train vines on a wire-mesh frame in a perennial border. Plant clematis next to a trellis for an airy screen or let vines twine over an arbor for light shade.

—

Creeping fig see *Ficus*

Crossvine see *Anisostichus*

Dutchman's pipe see *Aristolochia*

—

Euonymus (yew-ON-i-mus)

Small evergreen vine with fine-textured, thick, leathery foliage on somewhat stiff stems. Pointed oval leaves ½ to 3 inches long, often with silvery or white veins. Sprawls or climbs using rootlike holdfasts. Older plants often develop mutant branches exhibiting variations in foliage size and color. Zones 5-9.

Selected species and varieties.

E. fortunei 'Minimus,' baby wintercreeper: ½-inch deep green leaves with silver veins on stems 1½ to 3 feet long. *E. fortunei* 'Sarcoxie': 1-inch leaves with white veins on upright stems up to 4 feet tall. *E. fortunei* 'Vegetus': thick, rounded 2-inch medium green leaves on erect plants up to 4 feet in height. Prolific orange-red fruits in fall, often lasting through winter.

Growing conditions. Wintercreeper may be planted in full sun or light shade in well-drained soil. At the northern end of its range, select sites that provide winter shade and protection from drying winter winds. Spray to control euonymus scale, which is a serious problem, especially at the southern end of the plant's range.

Landscape uses. Train wintercreeper against rocks and walls or allow it to climb against tree trunks. Without some support, baby wintercreeper will sprawl and trail, and 'Sarcoxie' and 'Vegetus' will develop as loose shrubs.

—

Ficus (FY-kus)
Fig

Dense flat mats of dark, leathery heart-shaped evergreen leaves on vines that grow up to 60 feet long and cling firmly to porous surfaces by aerial rootlets. Zones 8-10.

Selected species and varieties. *F. pumila*, creeping fig: 1-inch light green juvenile leaves on new growth contrast with 3- to 4-inch leaves on mature fruiting stems. Fruiting branches grow at angles to the stems and bear puffy inedible fruits.

Growing conditions. Creeping fig does best in full sun in a moist but well-drained soil. Southern exposure is best at the northern end of its range. For best appearance and vigor, prune creeping fig heavily every second or third year to encourage fine-textured juvenile foliage and delay fruiting, and remove any fruiting branches that appear.

Landscape uses. Use creeping fig as a decorative cover for masonry or wooden walls. Its aerial rootlets can damage some surfaces.

—

Five-leaf akebia see *Akebia*

—

Gelsemium (jel-SEEM-ee-um)
Carolina jessamine

Evergreen vine with pairs of slim, pointed 3- to 4-inch leaves that turn

EUONYMUS FORTUNEI 'MINIMUS'

FICUS PUMILA

GELSEMIUM SEMPERVIRENS

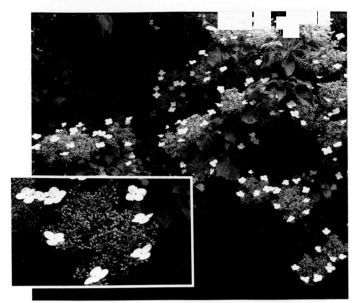

HYDRANGEA ANOMALA PETIOLARIS

LONICERA SEMPERVIRENS

PARTHENOCISSUS QUINQUEFOLIA

wine red in winter. Fragrant tubular yellow flowers grow where leaves join stems from early through late spring. Climbs up to 20 or 30 feet by twining stems. Zones 8 and 9.

Selected species and varieties. *G. sempervirens,* Carolina jessamine: golden 2-inch flower trumpets among lustrous leaves. *G. sempervirens* 'Pride of Augusta' is a double-flowered variety.

Growing conditions. Carolina jessamine may be planted in full sun or in shade in any well-drained soil. Vines that are grown in full sun and fertile soils will have more vigorous growth, denser foliage and more flowers than those grown in shade or poorer soils. Prune as necessary to control aggressive spread and to create fullness. Carolina jessamine may not always be fully evergreen at the northern end of its range.

Landscape uses. Train Carolina jessamine to a trellis or an arbor for a screen, or allow vines to twine decoratively around a mailbox, up a downspout or over a fence. All parts of this attractive vine are poisonous to both humans and livestock, a factor that should be taken into account when planting it on properties where small children, horses, sheep or cattle reside.

Honeysuckle see *Lonicera*

Hydrangea (hy-DRAN-jee-a)
Climbing hydrangea

A vigorous deciduous vine that climbs to 75 feet or more by means of rootlike holdfasts. Broad oval leaves lining branches are held on varying planes. Flat clusters of white flowers appear in the middle of summer. Shredding reddish bark on older stems. Zones 5-8.

Selected species and varieties. *H. anomala petiolaris,* climbing hydrangea: broad oval 4-inch leaves with toothed edges. Branches up to 3 feet long growing laterally from main stems. Flower clusters 6 inches or more across with inconspicuous fertile flowers surrounded by showier sterile ones.

Growing conditions. Climbing hydrangea will grow in full sun and in shade. It may be planted in any moist, but not wet, soil. Climbing hydrangea grows slowly for several years, but once the vine is well established, it grows rapidly. Prune as necessary to contain its spread.

Landscape uses. The coarse texture of climbing hydrangea looks best against the background of a large structure. Allow vines to climb into large trees or against rough masonry that can visually and physically support the massive weight of mature vines. The holdfasts can damage wood and painted surfaces. Climbing hydrangea can also be used as a ground cover.

Lonicera (lon-IS-er-a)
Honeysuckle

Twining deciduous or sometimes evergreen vine with wiry stems and glossy foliage. Noteworthy for its tubular summer blooms in shades of pink, red, orange and yellow. Red berries follow in fall. Zones 4-9.

Selected species and varieties. *L. sempervirens,* trumpet honeysuckle: oval blue-green leaves up to 3 inches long on stems up to 20 feet or more. Clusters of 2-inch flower tubes, red with yellow-orange throats, in early to late summer. The variety 'Sulphurea' has clear yellow flowers. *L. × heckrotti,* everblooming or goldflame honeysuckle: pink-purple 2-inch flowers with yellow throats in extremely large clusters from early summer through fall. Berries sparse on vines up to 10 feet long.

Growing conditions. Honeysuckle can flourish in full sun or light shade in any well-drained soil. Prune after flowering to encourage new shoots and increase the vine's density. Honeysuckle becomes partially or fully evergreen toward the southern end of its range.

Landscape uses. Plant honeysuckle against a trellis or other support as a screen or use it as decorative twining around posts or mailboxes, or over fences.

Parthenocissus
(par-thee-no-SIS-us)

Rapid-growing deciduous vine up to 50 feet or more with loose foliage that develops into thick, flat mats. Deep red to red-orange fall color. Inconspicuous flowers often hidden by leaves. Berries bluish black and showy against fall foliage and after leaves fall. Zones 3-9.

Selected species and varieties. *P. quinquefolia,* Virginia creeper: large leaves composed of 4-inch leaflets arranged like the fingers on a hand. Climbs using branched tendrils with sticky discs at the ends. Deep red autumn color. Zones 3-9. *P. tricuspidata,* Boston ivy: broad 8-inch deep green leaves with three pointed lobes. Clings using short tendrils with sticky tips. Red or red-orange fall color. Zones 4-8.

Growing conditions. Plant Virginia creeper and Boston ivy in full sun or partial shade in a moist but well-drained soil. Fall color will be best when the vines are grown in full sun. Prune as necessary to control and direct growth.

Landscape uses. Grow Virginia creeper and Boston ivy as covering for masonry structures. Allow the vines to climb the trunks of large trees or to ramble freely over fences and walls. The sticky ends of the tendrils may damage wooden and painted surfaces.

Polygonum (po-LIG-on-um)

Copious clusters of tiny flowers bloom along the tops of branches from midsummer through fall. Extremely rapid-growing deciduous vine, twining 15 to 30 feet or more, with handsome pointed oval leaves, reddish when young, unfurling to a bright green. Zones 4-8.

Selected species and varieties. *P. aubertii,* silver lace vine, silver fleece vine, China fleece vine: dainty, fragrant, ⅕-inch white to greenish white or sometimes faint pink flowers in billowy clusters up to 6 inches long. Grows up to 15 feet annually.

Growing conditions. Plant silver lace vine in full sun in any soil. It will grow in partial shade but will not flower abundantly. It tolerates dry growing conditions and city pollution. Silver lace vine blooms on new growth. Prune heavily in late fall or winter to encourage young shoots and to contain rampant growth.

Landscape uses. Use silver lace vine as a screening plant on wire fences where its vigorous stems will quickly grow to the top and cascade back to the ground. Allow vines to grow over walls or up tree trunks where they can provide late-summer flower interest.

Silver fleece vine see *Polygonum*
Silver lace vine see *Polygonum*
Trumpetcreeper see *Campsis*
Virginia creeper
see *Parthenocissus*

Wintercreeper see *Euonymus*

Wisteria (wis-TEE-ree-a)

Deciduous twining vine reaching lengths of 20 feet or more, ultimately developing twisted, woody trunks. Long leaves composed of pointed leaflets paired along a central rachis. Clusters of delicate white, pink or violet to blue flowers hang from the branches of vines 10 to 15 years old or older in spring. Long, velvet-covered seedpods remain on vines through winter. Zones 5-9.

Selected species and varieties. *W. floribunda,* Japanese wisteria: fragrant violet to violet-blue flowers appear in late spring. Clusters 8 to 20 or more inches long open progressively from top to bottom. Vines twine upward from right to left. Leaves dull yellow in fall before dropping. Zones 5-9. *W. floribunda* 'Rosea' has extremely fragrant light pink flowers. *W. sinensis,* Chinese wisteria: mildly fragrant violet-blue flowers opening all at once in clusters 6 to 12 inches long. Long-lasting blossoms appear in midspring. Climbs by twining from left to right. No autumn color. Zones 6-9. *W. sinensis* 'Alba' has white flowers.

Growing conditions. Plant wisteria in full sun in a moist but well-drained soil enriched with organic matter. Wisteria can be difficult to transplant. Select container-grown specimens and plant them about a foot away from their support. Select three or four stems to train and remove any suckers that appear. Vines often take years to produce their first blooms. To encourage early flowering, root-prune young plants, cut new shoots back to half their length in summer and winter, and avoid overwatering or fertilizing. Prune mature vines heavily in late summer to encourage blooms and to keep vines from becoming tangled mats. Avoid late-winter or early-spring pruning, since wisteria flowers on the previous year's growth.

Landscape uses. Wisteria's vigorous twining branches and bold flower clusters require ample room to develop and show at their best. Provide supports sturdy enough to hold the considerable weight of mature vines. Grow them on a heavy timber arbor or anchored against a masonry structure. Avoid planting wisteria against wooden walls; the strongly twining stems will quickly work their way into crevices and can literally pry boards apart.

POLYGONUM

WISTERIA SINENSIS

ARCTOSTAPHYLOS UVA-URSI

ASARUM EUROPAEUM

CONVALLARIA MAJALIS

COTONEASTER SALICIFOLIUS 'AUTUMN FIRE'

GROUND COVERS

Aaronsbeard St.-John's-wort
see *Hypericum*

—

Arctostaphylos
(ark-to-STAFF-il-os)
Bearberry

Fine-textured, creeping evergreen shrub growing slowly up to a foot tall and 2 to 4 feet wide. Lustrous dark green oval leaves, bronzy in fall. Zones 2-7.

Selected species and varieties. *A. uva-ursi,* bearberry: nodding white spring flowers touched with pink among ½- to ¾-inch leaves followed by red berries in summer.

Growing conditions. Plant bearberry in full sun in a well-drained, even dry, soil. While bearberry grows best in an acid soil, it will tolerate other soils. Protect from the drying effects of winter sun and wind. Purchase container-grown plants and space them 1½ to 3 feet apart. Bearberry seldom requires pruning, never needs fertilizer.

Landscape uses. Bearberry is a valuable low-maintenance evergreen ground cover in areas with cool summers. Use it on banks with poor, rocky soils or plant it in seaside areas with sandy, infertile soils.

—

Asarum (as-AR-um)
Wild ginger

Ground cover with glossy round evergreen leaves held aloft on slender 5- to 6-inch stalks. Spreads very slowly by creeping underground stems. Zones 4-8.

Selected species and varieties. *A. europaeum,* European wild ginger, has leaves up to 3 inches across. Inconspicuous juglike ½-inch green or brown flowers hidden by leaves.

Growing conditions. European wild ginger prefers light to deep shade and a moist but well-drained acid soil enriched with organic matter. Set young plants 12 inches or less apart for good coverage. Select a site that provides protection from winter as well as summer sun. At the northern end of its range, adequate winter snow cover or other protection is necessary for its survival.

Landscape uses. Wild ginger is unsurpassed as an evergreen ground cover for areas with deep shade.

It does best beneath other evergreens, which provide the winter shade it requires.

—

Barrenwort see *Epimedium*
Bearberry see *Arctostaphylos*
Candytuft see *Iberis*

—

Convallaria (kon-val-AIR-ee-a)
Lily of the valley

Ground cover of dense, fast-spreading mats of broad, pointed leaves that die to the gound in fall. Stems of waxy flower bells tucked among leaves from mid- to late spring. Zones 3-7.

Selected species and varieties. *C. majalis,* lily of the valley: pairs of 8-inch oval leaves up to 3 inches broad. Delicately fragrant ¼-inch bell-shaped flowers dangle along 6- to 8-inch flower stalks, occasionally followed by red-orange berries.

Growing conditions. Plant lily of the valley in partial to deep shade in a moist but well-drained soil. Set new plants 9 to 12 inches apart and mulch to conserve moisture until plants become established.

Landscape uses. Mass lily of the valley beneath trees and shrubs or use it to edge a border planted with spring bulbs. Small clumps are excellent in naturalized settings.

—

Cotoneaster (ko-TO-nee-as-ter)

Low-growing evergreen or almost evergreen creeping shrub up to 1½ feet tall. Spreads rapidly into a wide, dense mat. Dark green glossy foliage turns purplish in winter. Zones 5-9.

Selected species and varieties. *C. dammeri,* bearberry cotoneaster: has slender creeping stems that root where they arch to touch the ground. Oval leaves ½ to 1½ inches long. Half-inch white flowers in spring followed by sparse ¼-inch red berries. *C. dammeri* 'Skogholm': arching branches that can spread several feet per year; slightly more cold-tolerant than other varieties. *C. salicifolius* 'Autumn Fire,' Autumn Fire willowleaf cotoneaster: leaves have deeply incised veins. Small white flower clusters in Spring followed by red fruits that last into winter. *C. salicifolius* 'Repens,' spreading willowleaf cotoneaster: pointed oblong leaves 3½ inches long and ¾ inch wide with deeply incised veins.

Red berries in fall and winter. *C. salicifolius* 'Scarlet Leader': spreading branches form mats 6 to 12 inches high. New growth has reddish tinge.

Growing conditions. Plant in full sun in any well-drained soil. At the northern end of its range, cotoneaster may not retain its leaves through the winter, depending on the amount of protection it receives from snow cover. Provide ample space for this wide-spreading plant, setting new ones 3 or more feet apart.

Landscape uses. Use cotoneaster as a quick-spreading ground cover on banks or slopes or in rock gardens. Let it creep along the top of a retaining wall and tumble over the edge.

Dwarf lilyturf see *Ophiopogon*
English ivy see *Hedera*

Epimedium (ep-i-MEE-dee-um)
Epimedium, barrenwort

Ground cover with leaves composed of three heart-shaped leaflets dangling from 9- to 12-inch wiry leafstalks. Thin, lustrous, leathery foliage tinged red while unfolding, light green in summer, then turning bronze in fall. Flowers resemble a bishop's pointed hat when they first appear in small clusters among leaves. Epimedium spreads slowly by underground stems that send up stalks that eventually form dense mats of uniform height. Zones 3-8.

Selected species and varieties. *E. grandiflorum,* bishop's hat: early to middle spring, 1- to 2-inch flowers that are white or pink to lavender. *E. × rubrum,* red barrenwort: small red flowers in late spring. *E. × versicolor* 'Sulphureum,' Persian epimedium: yellow spring to summer flowers less than an inch across.

Growing conditions. Plant epimedium in light to deep shade in moist but well-drained soil enriched with organic matter. Leaves remain erect through winter unless crushed by snow. Clip dead and ragged foliage in spring before new growth begins. Space young plants 8 to 12 inches apart.

Landscape uses. Use epimedium as a ground cover in a shade garden with hostas and other shade plants or in combination with flowering and evergreen shrubs and trees.

Galium (GAL-ee-um)
Sweet woodruff

Whorls of sweetly fragrant foliage with a smell like new-mown hay when dried. Loose clusters of tiny white flowers raised above the leaves in mid- to late spring. Slowly forms dense mats that die back in autumn. Zones 5-9.

Selected species and varieties. *Galium odoratum,* sweet woodruff: pointed 1-inch leaves encircle sticky, square stems 4 to 6 inches tall. Dainty flowers ¼ inch or less in conspicuous clusters above the deep, rich green foliage.

Growing conditions. Sweet woodruff prefers light to deep shade and a moist but well-drained soil, preferably acid, enriched with organic matter. Tolerates dry soils. Space new plants 12 inches apart. Thin established plantings as necessary to control spread.

Landscape uses. Sweet woodruff is a versatile ground cover useful in moist, shady sites under evergreen shrubs such as rhododendrons or azaleas, and also in drier sites under deciduous trees such as maples.

Hedera (HED-er-a)
Ivy

Fast-spreading evergreen vine or ground cover with rootlike holdfasts that will cling to rocks or tree bark or quickly root in soil to enlarge the plant's spread. Forms dense carpet of foliage 6 to 8 inches tall. Zones 5-9.

Selected species and varieties. *H. helix,* English ivy: deep green leaves 2 to 4 inches long with lighter veins and pointed lobes. *H. helix* 'Baltica,' Baltic ivy, has smaller leaves only 1 to 2 inches long and is renowned for its hardiness. *H. helix* 'Minima' has rounded lobes and wavy leaf edges; *H. helix* 'Pedata,' bird's foot ivy, has leaves with narrow pointed lobes and white veins.

Growing conditions. Plant English ivy in full sun or partial to deep shade in a moist but well-drained soil enriched with organic matter. At the northern end of its range, English ivy grows best where it receives protection from drying winter sun and wind. Set new plants 12 to 18 inches apart. Prune any time to control rampant growth.

Landscape uses. English ivy will quickly creep across a garden, filling in areas underneath trees and shrubs and following uneven contours. Allow

EPIMEDIUM × VERSICOLOR 'SULPHUREUM'

GALIUM ODORATUM

HEDERA HELIX 'PEDATA'

143

HYPERICUM CALYCINUM

IBERIS SEMPERVIRENS

LIRIOPE MUSCARI 'VARIEGATA'

OPHIOPOGON JAPONICUS

it to climb up large tree trunks or onto walls for a multidimensional effect.

Hypericum (hy-PER-i-cum)
Aaronsbeard St.-John's-wort

Roots wherever its creeping stems touch the ground, rapidly forming 1-to 1½-foot-tall dense mounds of elliptical 2- to 4-inch leaves that are evergreen or semi-evergreen, depending on the climate. Long-lasting, bright yellow midsummer flowers. Zones 6-9.

Selected species and varieties. *H. calycinum,* Aaronsbeard St.-John's-wort: golden 3-inch flowers with a conspicuous froth of red-tipped stamens in their centers, blooming on the current season's new shoots.

Growing conditions. Aaronsbeard St.-John's-wort thrives in full sun or partial shade in a moist but well-drained soil. It also grows well in sandy soils. Set new plants 18 inches apart. Mow in spring as necessary to control growth and promote flowers. Aaronsbeard St.-John's-wort is evergreen in Zones 8 and 9; in Zones 6 and 7 it is evergreen but may die to the ground in fall.

Landscape uses. Use Aaronsbeard St.-John's-wort to cover large areas under tall shrubs and on sunny banks.

Iberis (eye-BEER-is)
Candytuft

Slowly sprawls into 6- to 12-inch-tall mats of evergreen foliage. Fine, narrow leathery leaves. Flat clusters of white flowers for several weeks in mid- to late spring. Zones 5-7.

Selected species and varieties. *I. sempervirens,* evergreen candytuft: narrow ½- to 2-inch deep green leaves almost hidden in spring by 1- to 2-inch clusters of tiny white flowers. Stems up to 2 feet long root where they touch soil. *I. sempervirens* 'Christmas Snow' blooms twice, first in spring, and again in fall.

Growing conditions. Plant evergreen candytuft in full sun or partial shade in a moist but well-drained soil enriched with organic matter. Set new plants 12 or more inches apart. Too much fertilization causes leggy growth. Clip after flowering to encourage new foliage.

Landscape uses. Use evergreen candytuft as a ground cover under shrubs, at the edge of a flower border, or along steps and walks.

Ivy see *Hedera*
Lily of the valley see *Convallaria*
Lilyturf see *Liriope*

Liriope (li-RY-o-pee)
Lilyturf

Spreading mounds of arching leaves. Evergreen or nearly so, depending on the climate. Flower spikes amid foliage from midsummer to fall. Zones 6-9.

Selected species and varieties. *L. muscari,* big blue lilyturf: tiny ¼-inch purple flowers clustered in spikes on stems 1 to 2 feet tall. The variety 'Majestic' has very dark green leaves and dense, compact flower spikes. 'Monroe's White' has white flowers. 'Variegata' has leaves streaked with white or yellow.

Growing conditions. Plant big blue lilyturf in full sun or shade in any well-drained soil. 'Monroe's White' does best in at least partial shade. Tolerates heat, poor or dry soil, and seaside growing conditions. Sometimes dies to the ground in fall in Zones 6 and 7. Space new plants 12 inches apart. Established beds can be mown in spring to renew straggly foliage.

Landscape uses. Use big blue lilyturf to edge flower borders, as a ground cover under large trees or shrubs, or on difficult slopes or soils.

Ophiopogon (of-fi-o-PO-gon)
Dwarf lilyturf

Slow-spreading 6- to 12-inch-tall mounds of grasslike evergreen foliage. Short spikes of early-summer flowers followed by clusters of blue berries. Zones 8-10.

Selected species and varieties. *O. japonicus,* dwarf lilyturf: arching 8- to 12-inch leaves only ¼ inch wide. Blue to violet flowers on short spikes among leaves.

Growing conditions. Dwarf lilyturf may be planted in full sun or in shade in a moist but well-drained soil enriched with organic matter. Set new plants 12 inches apart.

Landscape uses. Use dwarf lilyturf as a ground cover beneath low-branching trees and shrubs or to outline a flower border.

Pachysandra (pak-i-SAN-dra)
Pachysandra, spurge

Spreads slowly into dense mats 6 to 12 inches high of evergreen or deciduous foliage with toothed edges. Spikes of white or pink flowers borne above the leaves in early spring. Zones 5-7.

Selected species and varieties. *P. procumbens,* Alleghany pachysandra, Alleghany spurge: dull gray-green or blue-green wide, oval leaves up to 4 inches long, sometimes mottled. Showy 2- to 4-inch spikes of white or pink flowers. Deciduous at the northern end of its range, evergreen in warmer climates. *P. terminalis,* Japanese pachysandra, Japanese spurge: whorls of lustrous, narrow evergreen leaves on upright stems. White 2-inch flower spikes. Slower-growing *P. terminalis* 'Silver Edge' has leaves mottled white.

Growing conditions. Plant pachysandra in partial to full shade in a moist but well-drained acid soil enriched with organic matter. Pachysandra will yellow if grown in sun. It is able to compete with shallow tree roots. Set new plants 12 inches apart and mulch until established.

Landscape uses. Use pachysandra as a ground cover under trees and shrubs, especially those with shallow roots and dense shades such as maples and beeches. Alleghany pachysandra looks appropriate in naturalized settings.

■

Sarcococca (sar-ko-KOK-a)
Sweet box

Evergreen shrub, 1½ to 2 feet tall, with lustrous pointed oval leaves, that spreads by slender underground stems. Insignificant spring flowers followed by ¼-inch black berries. Zones 5-9.

Selected species and varieties. *S. hookerana humilis,* sweet box, Himalayan sarcococca: dense foliage on wide-spreading plants. Clusters of fragrant white flowers.

Growing conditions. Himalayan sarcococca prefers light to deep shade and a moist but well-drained soil, either acid or alkaline. Tolerates city growing conditions.

Landscape uses. Use Himalayan sarcococca as a ground cover in shaded sites where dense mass is needed or to integrate a flower border with trees behind it.

■

Spurge see *Pachysandra*
Sweet woodruff see *Galium*

PERENNIALS

Astilbe (a-STILL-bee)
Astilbe, garden spirea

Plumy spikes of white, pink or red flowers in late spring and summer rising above mounds of finely cut shiny leaves 12 to 18 inches tall. Zones 4-8.

Selected species and varieties. *A. × arendsii* 'Fanal': overall height 24 to 30 inches. Brilliant deep red flowers in spikes 1 foot or more in length early to middle summer. Young leaves are red-tinged, maturing to a dark coppery green. *A. × arendsii* 'Peach Blossom': overall height 18 to 26 inches. Light salmon pink flowers and deep green foliage. Blooms early to middle summer. *A. × arendsii* 'Snowdrift': overall height 30 inches. Pure white flowers in midsummer. *A. tacquetii* 'Superba': overall height 48 inches. Bright rosy purple flowers in conical spikes atop reddish stalks. Blooms middle to late summer.

Growing conditions. Astilbes can thrive in a constantly moist, well-drained fertile soil rich in organic matter such as peat moss. All astilbes grow best in light shade but tolerate full sun if the soil is mulched and kept moist. 'Superba' adapts to a sunny spot better than the other varieties described above. Fertilize annually in spring and divide clumps every two or three years in spring or fall.

Landscape uses. Plant astilbes in groups of three or more in a shaded border for splashes of summer color and attractive ferny foliage throughout the growing season. The height of 'Superba' makes it a good focal point. The broad solid leaves of hostas combine well with astilbes.

■

Baby's breath see *Gypsophila*

■

Bergenia (ber-JEN-ee-a)

Rosettes of large leathery evergreen leaves and clusters of pink flowers in early spring. Zones 4-9.

Selected species and varieties. *B. cordifolia,* heartleaf bergenia: 18 inches high; clumps 2 or more feet wide. Rounded, glossy cabbage-like leaves up to a foot across with wavy edges. In Zones 6-9 foliage remains attractive in winter, often in tones of red or bronze. Three- to 6-inch clusters of small waxy pink flowers in early spring. *B. cordifolia purpurea* has

PACHYSANDRA TERMINALIS 'SILVER EDGE'

SARCOCOCCA HOOKERANA HUMILIS

ASTILBE × ARENDSII 'FANAL'

BERGENIA

145

CERATOSTIGMA PLUMBAGINOIDES

CIMICIFUGA RACEMOSA

DIANTHUS PLUMARIUS

magenta flowers on red stalks and purple-tinged leaves. There are also several good bergenia hybrids.

Growing conditions. Bergenia grows best when planted in partial shade in moist, well-drained soil rich in organic matter such as peat moss. It tolerates full sun and some dryness but will not grow as large or as fast.

Landscape uses. Plant bergenia in the front of a perennial border, in bold drifts under trees or as an edging. Because it spreads slowly by underground stems, it can be used as a ground cover.

▬

Black snakeroot see *Cimicifuga*
Border pink see *Dianthus*
Bugbane see *Cimicifuga*
Butterfly lily see *Hedychium*

▬

Ceratostigma (ser-at-OS-tig-ma)
Plumbago

Cobalt blue flowers from late summer through midfall on neat, low-spreading plants. Zones 5-9.

Selected species and varieties. *C. plumbaginoides,* blue plumbago, leadwort: overall height 12 inches, spreading to 18 inches across. Small diamond-shaped leaves on reddish wiry stems. Foliage turns bronze in cool weather. Three-quarter-inch flowers in small clusters.

Growing conditions. Plant blue plumbago in full sun or light shade in light, well-drained soil supplemented with peat moss or other organic matter. Protect blue plumbago in Zone 5 with a winter mulch.

Landscape uses. Place blue plumbago in the front of a perennial border, where it will look especially good with yellow flowers, or use it as an edging or as a ground cover. Blue plumbago is late to emerge in spring.

▬

Christmas rose see *Helleborus*

▬

Cimicifuga (sim-i-SIFF-yew-ga)
Bugbane

Imposing plants with slender white flower spikes resembling bottle brushes in summer or fall. Handsome clumps of large ferny leaves. Zones 3-9.

Selected species and varieties. *C. racemosa,* cohosh bugbane, black snakeroot: overall height 4 to 8 feet;

clumps 2 feet across. Finely divided dark green compound leaves up to 2 feet long. Strongly scented tiny fuzzy flowers grouped in 1- to 3-foot erect spikes atop slender branching stems. Blooms for several weeks in midsummer. *C. simplex,* Kamchatka bugbane: similar to *C. racemosa* but smaller, with an overall height of 1 to 3 feet. Narrow flower spikes bloom in midfall.

Growing conditions. Plant bugbane in a moist, well-drained soil rich in organic matter such as peat moss or compost. Do not allow the soil to dry out. Bugbanes do best in partial shade but they will tolerate full sun and deep shade.

Landscape uses. Plant bugbanes at the rear of a perennial border or use them in drifts for a dramatic focus in a woodland garden.

▬

Coralbells see *Heuchera*
Daylily see *Hemerocallis*

▬

Dianthus (di-AN-thus)

Clove-scented flowers in white and various shades of pink and red. Narrow, arching silvery blue evergreen leaves form a neat, compact tuft. Zones 4-8.

Selected species and varieties. *D. plumarius,* border pink, cottage pink, grass pink, Scotch pink: overall height 12 to 15 inches; width is approximately 12 inches. Blooms late spring to early summer with two or three 1½-inch flowers on each stem. There are numerous named varieties. Flowers may be single or double, with fringed or toothed petals. Besides solid colors including salmon, rose, coral and deep red, flowers may have an eye of a contrasting color.

Growing conditions. Border pinks need a light, well-drained soil. They prefer one that is slightly alkaline but will also grow in slightly acid soil. Add lime to raise pH of more acid soils. Plant in full sun.

Landscape uses. Plant small groups of border pinks in a rock garden or the front of a perennial border or use them as an edging. In warmer zones their attractive foliage remains in good condition through the winter.

▬

Garden spirea see *Astilbe*
Ginger lily see *Hedychium*

Gypsophila (jip-SOFF-ill-a)
Baby's breath

Rounded lacy-looking plant with profuse tiny white or pink flowers borne on intricately branched wiry stems. Zones 4-9.

Selected species and varieties. *G. paniculata*, baby's breath: 3 to 4 feet tall and wide. Small, narrow leaves. Quarter-inch white flowers in early summer and midsummer. Shearing the plant back after it blooms stimulates a second blooming period lasting into fall. *G. paniculata* 'Bristol Fairy' has double white flowers. *G. paniculata* 'Perfecta' has double white flowers ½ inch or more across. *G. paniculata* 'Pink Fairy' grows 18 inches tall and wide and has light pink double flowers.

Growing conditions. Baby's breath requires full sun and a moist, alkaline soil with excellent drainage. To raise the pH, work one cup of lime per square yard into an acid soil. The taller-growing baby's breaths need staking. Baby's breath does well in Zone 9 only on the West Coast.

Landscape uses. Baby's breath is invaluable in a perennial border. Its airy form contrasts well with larger-flowered plants and spiky flowers and foliage. Use white-flowered baby's breath in all-white borders or beds. It makes an excellent cut flower and dries well for winter bouquets.

—

Hedychium (hed-IK-ee-um)
Ginger lily

Tall plant with striking-looking, intensely fragrant white flowers in summer and fall. Zones 9 and 10.

Selected species and varieties. *H. coronarium*, ginger lily, butterfly lily: overall height 5 to 7 feet; foliage clumps 2 feet or more in width. Broad, straplike leaves up to 2 feet long. Three-inch flowers have large petals resembling butterfly wings and antenna-like stamens. Flowers are borne in 1-foot spikes atop a tall stem.

Growing conditions. Plant ginger lily in a moist to damp fertile soil and keep it well watered during the growing season. Full sun to light shade. In Zone 9 and the colder part of Zone 10 protect the roots in winter with a mulch.

Landscape uses. Plant a large group of ginger lilies for a bold tropical look. A single clump provides a strong vertical accent. Even at night ginger lily is attractive, when its sweet fragrance is most pervasive.

Hellebore see *Helleborus*

—

Helleborus (hell-e-BOR-us)
Hellebore

Five-petaled roselike flowers blooming over a long period in late fall, winter or early spring. Colors include white, pale green and plum. Leathery evergreen compound leaves. Zones 3-9.

Selected species and varieties. *H. lividus corsicus*, Corsican hellebore: overall height 1½ to 3 feet. Shrubby mounds of spiny-edged leaves marbled with pale green or gray. Clusters of 2-inch pale green flowers, sometimes tinged with purple, in early spring. Zones 7-9. *H. niger*, Christmas rose: overall height 9 to 12 inches; broad, low-growing dark green notched foliage. Three-inch white flowers with prominent yellow stamens are borne one per stem and stand well above the foliage. Blooms appear between late fall and late winter. Zones 3-8. *H. orientalis*, Lenten rose: 18 inches tall. Shiny lobed leaflets in a clump 1 foot or more in width. Each flower stem bears several 2- to 3-inch flowers. The range of colors includes cream, green, pink, rose and purple; petals are often spotted or streaked with maroon and tinged with green. Blooms in early spring. Zones 4-9. All hellebores are poisonous.

Growing conditions. Plant hellebores in partial shade in a constantly moist but well-drained fertile soil rich in organic matter such as peat moss. Corsican hellebore tolerates somewhat drier soil than the other two species. It is rarely necessary to divide hellebores.

Landscape uses. Plant hellebores in woodland gardens under deciduous shrubs and trees for flowers when few other plants are in bloom and for handsome foliage throughout the year. A warm, sheltered spot next to a building encourages early blooming. Individual blossoms are remarkably weather-resistant, sometimes remaining in good condition for two months or more.

—

Hemerocallis
(hem-er-o-KAL-us)
Daylily

Profusely flowering perennial with trumpet-shaped blossoms borne on branching stems above decorative clumps of arching bright green foliage. Each flower lasts just one

GYPSOPHILA PANICULATA

HEDYCHIUM CORONARIUM

HELLEBORUS ORIENTALIS

HEMEROCALLIS × 'HYPERION'

HEUCHERA SANGUINEA 'CHATTERBOX'

HOSTA UNDULATA

day, but a single plant can produce hundreds of flowers in a season. Zones 3-10.

Selected species and varieties. *H.* hybrids: the old-fashioned species are overshadowed by thousands of hybrid forms, which come in a wide range of sizes, colors, flower forms and blooming times. The average overall height is about 3 feet, but sizes range from less than a foot to over 6 feet. Flowers measure from less than 2 inches across to 7 inches or more. Colors include cream, yellow, apricot, orange, pink, rose, red and purple; many hybrids are bicolored. Petals may be broad, narrow, heavily overlapping, ruffled or sharply curved. Some daylilies are fragrant. Blooming times range from early spring to frost. Hybrids vary in their hardiness and are not all reliable throughout Zones 3-10. Ask a local nurseryman to recommend daylilies suited to your area.

Growing conditions. Daylilies are among the easiest to grow of all perennials and adapt to a wide range of conditions. Growth is best in a moist, well-drained, fairly fertile soil that contains peat moss or some other organic matter. Blooming is most profuse in full sun, but daylilies tolerate light shade well. Plant or divide in spring or fall.

Landscape uses. In a perennial border daylilies are valuable not only for their flowers but for their appealing foliage, which is a good foil for other plants. They are also attractive planted in masses and as a ground cover. For these purposes, space them about a foot apart so their foliage will inhibit weeds and minimize maintenance.

Heuchera (hew-KAIR-a)

Low-growing plant with rounded evergreen leaves and clusters of ¼-inch white, pink or red bell-shaped flowers on tall wiry stems. Zones 4-9.

Selected species and varieties. *H. sanguinea,* coralbells: overall height 12 to 24 inches. Two-inch scalloped leaves sometimes marbled with gray. Flowers most numerous in late spring and early summer, but blooming continues into fall. There are many hybrids, including 'June Bride,' with white flowers; 'Chatterbox,' with pink flowers; and 'Pluie de Feu,' with bright red flowers.

Growing conditions. Plant in moist, well-drained soil enriched with organic matter such as peat moss. Good drainage is essential in winter. Full sun or light shade. To encourage blooming, cut fading flower stems. Divide clumps every three years.

Landscape uses. With their pretty evergreen leaves, coralbells are valuable in the garden in and out of flower. Plant them in groups of three or more in the front of a perennial border or use them as an edging. Coralbells are also well suited to a rock garden. They can be used as a ground cover and they make good cut flowers.

Hosta (HOS-ta)
Hosta, plantain lily

Perennials prized for their broad, neat clumps of handsome foliage in various shades of green. Spikes of lily-like 1- to 2-inch flowers in late spring or summer. Zones 3-9.

Selected species and varieties. *H. fortunei,* Fortune's hosta: overall height 2½ feet; foliage forms a clump 3 feet or more across. Pale green oval leaves 5 inches long and 3 inches wide with wavy edges. Pale lavender flowers in midsummer. *H. fortunei* 'Aureo-marginata': dark green leaves with a yellow border. Lilac flowers in late summer. *H. sieboldiana,* Siebold's hosta: overall height 2 to 3 feet; foliage forms a clump 3 feet or more across. Blue-green deeply veined leaves up to 12 inches wide and 15 inches long. White flowers in early summer, often hidden by the leaves. *H. sieboldiana* 'Frances Williams': leaves edged with yellow. *H. undulata,* wavy-leaved hosta: overall height 2 feet or more. Shiny green leaves with cream or white markings; leaves undulating or spirally twisted. Lavender flowers in midsummer. *H. ventricosa,* blue hosta: overall height 3 feet. Glossy heart-shaped dark green leaves 8 inches long with wavy edges. Dark violet flowers in late summer. *H. ventricosa* 'Aureo-marginata': leaves edged with yellow.

Growing conditions. Hostas grow best in light shade and a moist, well-drained soil rich in organic matter such as peat moss. They will also grow in deep shade or in full sun, where they must be kept well watered. Division is rarely necessary. Slugs and snails can be a serious problem.

Landscape uses. Plant hostas in masses in shady gardens, where they can compete well with tree roots. Their lush, bold leaves make an interesting contrast with ferns and with narrow-leaved plants such as liriope. A single clump of the large-leaved Siebold's hosta makes a dramatic focus in a shady border. Hostas can be grown in containers if they are kept well watered.

Iris (EYE-ris)

Perennial with orchid-like six-petaled flowers in almost every color imaginable in spring and early summer. The genus includes thousands of hybrids. All have upright sword-shaped foliage. Zones 3-10.

Selected species and varieties. Bearded iris: hybrid named for the fuzzy strip of hairs on three of its petals. Bearded irises are categorized by size: dwarf bearded irises range up to 16 inches in height with 1½- to 2½-inch flowers in midspring; intermediate bearded irises are 16 to 28 inches tall with 2- to 4-inch flowers in midspring; miniature tall bearded irises are 18 to 26 inches tall with 2-inch flowers in late spring and early summer; border bearded irises are 16 to 28 inches tall with 3- to 4-inch flowers in late spring and early summer; tall bearded irises are 28 inches or more in height with 4- to 8-inch flowers in late spring and early summer. Some bloom a second time, in fall. Colors of bearded irises range from white through the softest of pastels to rich deep shades of brown and purple. Flowers may be solid or have a combination of colors, depending on the variety. Zones 3-10 except in Florida and along the Gulf Coast. *I. ensata,* also called *I. kaempferi,* Japanese iris cultivars: heights range from 2 to 4 feet. Flat, crepelike flowers range up to 10 inches or more across. Colors include white, blue, purple, pink and red; there are sometimes marks or veins of a second color. Flowers appear in summer. Zones 5-9. *I. sibirica,* Siberian iris cultivars: heights range from 1 to 4 feet. Slender, grasslike leaves. Two- to 5-inch flowers in white and shades of blue, pink, purple and wine red. Late spring to early summer. Zones 3-9.

Growing conditions. Bearded irises require soil with very good drainage and full sun. Plant from midsummer to early fall with the tops of their rhizomes, or underground stems, just even with the level of the soil. The flower stems of tall bearded irises may require staking. Plant Japanese irises in constantly moist to well-drained acid soil rich in organic matter such as peat moss. Full sun or light shade. Siberian irises grow best in moist, slightly acid soil rich in organic matter but will adapt to other soils. Full sun.

Landscape uses. The dwarf bearded iris hybrids are well suited to rock gardens and other small-scale sites. Plant small clumps of the larger types of bearded irises, Japanese irises and Siberian irises in perennial borders, where they contrast well with rounded plants. Siberian irises also blend well with shrubs and can be massed on steep banks where their deep roots will help control erosion. Use Siberian and Japanese irises beside streams and ponds. Plant a bed of tall bearded irises in front of a dense hedge, a wall or a fence.

Leadwort see *Ceratostigma*
Lenten rose see *Helleborus*
Lily see *Hedychium*

Macleaya (mak-LAY-a)
Plume poppy

Stately perennial with large rounded gray-green leaves and plumy clusters of ivory or pinkish flowers in summer. Zones 3-9.

Selected species and varieties. *M. cordata,* plume poppy: overall height 6 to 8 feet. Deeply lobed leaves with whitish undersides; leaves are up to 1 foot across near the base of the stem and become progressively smaller toward the top of the plant. Small flowers in branching clusters up to 12 inches long in mid- to late summer.

Growing conditions. Plant plume poppy in any well-drained soil in full sun. Staking is unnecessary.

Landscape uses. Plume poppy is best used as a specimen plant where its beautiful foliage can be seen from the ground up. The cool blue-green foliage is a nice counterpoint to perennials with hot-colored flowers.

Paeonia (pee-O-nee-a)
Peony

Long-lived dependable perennial with spectacular flowers and neat glossy foliage that is attractive from spring until frost. Many hybrids exist in a great variety of forms, colors and blooming periods. Zones 3-10.

Selected species and varieties. *P.* hybrids: overall height is usually between 2 and 4 feet; the deeply lobed leaves, often reddish when

IRIS SIBIRICA 'DEWFUL'

MACLEAYA CORDATA

PAEONIA 'KRINKLED WHITE'

PHLOX PANICULATA 'BRIGHT EYES'

POLYGONATUM ODORATUM THUNBERGII 'VARIEGATUM'

SEDUM × 'AUTUMN JOY'

young, form a bushy clump 2 to 3 feet across. Flowers, which are often fragrant, range from 3 to 6 inches across and are available in white, light yellow and shades from pale pink to deep red. There are five basic flower forms: single, with five or more large petals arranged around a center of prominent yellow stamens; Japanese and anemone, two similar forms with one or more rows of petals arranged around a fluffy center of enlarged stamens that look like small, finely cut petals; semidouble, with a large number of petals; double, with even more petals and stamens. Blooming time varies from late spring to early summer.

Growing conditions. Plant peonies in well-drained soil rich in organic matter such as peat moss. Full sun or light shade. Container-grown peonies may be planted whenever the ground is not frozen; bare-root peonies are planted any time from late August until the ground freezes. Allow 3 to 4 feet of space for each peony. Position the peony in the planting hole so the tips of its eyes, or buds, are no more than 2 inches below the soil surface. Mulch the first winter. Staking is often required for the large-flowered hybrids. Peonies need never be divided and can live for half a century or more. In Zones 9 and 10 they grow only on the West Coast.

Landscape uses. Peonies are among the most beautiful, versatile and carefree of perennials. Plant them singly or in groups of three or more in a perennial border. Their bushy shape and substantial-looking leaves suit them to planting in the foreground of a shrub border, and a long row of peonies makes an excellent low hedge.

Peony see *Paeonia*

Phlox (flox)

Large pyramidal clusters of sweetly fragrant 1-inch flowers from summer into fall. Many cultivars available in a spectrum of colors. Zones 4-9.

Selected species and varieties. *P. paniculata,* garden phlox, summer phlox: overall height 18 inches to 4 feet; width of clump about 2 feet. Flower clusters up to 1 foot tall. Colors include white and shades of pink, salmon, orange, red, lavender and purple. Many cultivars have an eye of a contrasting color. Some cultivars begin to bloom in early summer, and others not until early fall.

Growing conditions. Plant in moist soil rich in organic matter such as peat moss. Choose a spot in full sun or light shade that is protected from the wind. Allow 2 feet between plants for good air circulation. Keep well watered in summer and remove fading flower clusters to prolong blooming. Divide clumps every three or four years.

Landscape uses. Plant garden phlox in groups of three or more in the front, middle or rear of a perennial border, depending on the height of the cultivar. If both early- and late-flowering cultivars are planted, their combined blooming periods will extend over three months or more. In warmer zones, plants bloom for a shorter period than in cool climates. In Zone 3 phlox can be grown in protected places.

Pink see *Dianthus*
Plumbago see *Ceratostigma*
Plume poppy see *Macleaya*

Polygonatum (po-lig-o-NAY-tum)
Solomon's seal

Shade-loving perennial valued for the broad leaves that extend horizontally from arching stems and for its bell-shaped spring flowers. Zones 4-9.

Selected species and varieties. *P. odoratum thunbergii* 'Variegatum,' variegated Japanese Solomon's seal: overall height 2 to 3 feet. Clear green leaves 4 inches long edged with white or light yellow. Fragrant greenish white flowers up to 1 inch long along the underside of each stem, followed by blue-black berries.

Growing conditions. Plant in moist acid soil rich in organic matter such as peat moss. Solomon's seal is partial to deep shade.

Landscape uses. Use Japanese Solomon's seal for its dainty flowers and beautiful foliage in woodland gardens or in the shadow of a building. It combines well with hostas, ferns and azaleas and is excellent for cutting.

Rose see *Helleborus*

Sedum (SEE-dum)
Stonecrop

Low-maintenance perennial with year-round appeal. Small starry flowers in summer dry to an attractive russet brown and can be left standing throughout the winter. Zones 3-10.

Selected species and varieties. *S.* × 'Autumn Joy': overall height and width 2 feet. Fleshy, toothed gray-green leaves. Small flowers in 4-inch heads turn from pink in summer to coppery red in fall and finally to russet brown. *S. spectabile,* showy stonecrop: overall height and width 18 inches. Very similar to 'Autumn Joy' stonecrop but with mauve-pink flowers. *S. spectabile* 'Brilliant' has raspberry red flowers.

Growing conditions. Stonecrops adapt to almost any well-drained soil and will grow in sun or light shade. They are drought-resistant, will grow in poor soils and rarely require division. Cut the dead flower stems to the ground in early spring before new growth begins.

Landscape uses. Plant showy stonecrops in small groups in a perennial border or use them in masses where their dried stems will provide winter interest. Their flowers will attract butterflies and bees.

GRASSES

Calamagrostis
(kal-a-ma-GROS-tis)
Reed grass

Dense clump of narrow, arching leaves and bristly flower spikes on tall stems in summer. Turns golden tan in late fall and can be left standing to provide winter interest. Zones 6-9.

Selected species and varieties. *C. acutiflora stricta,* feather reed grass: overall height 5 to 7 feet; clump width 2 feet or more, increasing slowly by underground stems. Slender buff flower spikes on strong straight stems rise about 2 feet above the foliage.

Growing conditions. Plant feather reed grass in well-drained soil in full sun or light shade. Cut the clump to within 6 inches of the ground before new spring growth appears.

Landscape uses. The narrow, erect form of feather reed grass provides an interesting contrast with rounded shrubs, and its dense growth of slender leaves and stems is a nice foil for large-leaved plants such as Macleayas. Its winter color is handsomely displayed against an evergreen background.

Cortaderia (kor-ta-DEE-ree-a)
Pampas grass

Large luxuriant mound of graceful foliage and numerous long plumy flower clusters in late summer and fall. Attractive through the winter. Zones 8-10.

Selected species and varieties. *C. selloana,* pampas grass: overall height 10 feet or more. Arching ¾-inch-wide leaves with sharp edges turn beige in winter. Silky flower clusters 2 to 3 feet long and 6 inches or more in width are silvery white, cream or pinkish and are held above the leaves on erect stems.

Growing conditions. Plant pampas grass in well-drained soil in full sun. It thrives in hot locations and tolerates fairly dry soil. Cut dead foliage to the ground in late winter before new growth appears.

Landscape uses. Plant a single clump of pampas grass as a specimen in an expanse of lawn or in front of a solid evergreen background. Pampas grass makes a magnificent screen or hedge for a large sunny garden.

—

Eulalia grass see *Miscanthus*
Fountain grass see *Pennisetum*
Japanese silver grass
see *Miscanthus*
Maiden grass see *Miscanthus*

—

Miscanthus (mis-KAN-thus)

Tall, fine-textured grass with long, narrow, gracefully arching leaves and feathery flower clusters on erect stems opening in late summer or early fall. Clump turns golden tan in winter. Zones 5-9.

Selected species and varieties. *M. sinensis,* eulalia grass, Japanese silver grass: overall height 6 to 8 feet; width of clump 3 feet or more. Fawn-colored flower clusters up to 8 inches long, followed by seed heads that persist through winter if the clump is left standing. Zones 5-9. *M. sinensis* 'Gracillimus,' maiden grass: overall height 4 to 5 feet. Silvery green leaves ¼ inch wide. Silvery white flowers. Zones 5-9. *M. sinensis* 'Purpurascens': overall height 3 to 4 feet. Foliage turns purplish red in late summer. Reddish flowers. Zones 5-9. *M. sinensis* 'Silberfeder,' silver-feather miscanthus: overall height 6 to 8 feet. Silky pale brownish pink flower clusters. Zones 6-9. *M. sinensis* 'Zebrinus,' zebra grass:

CALAMAGROSTIS ACUTIFLORA STRICTA

CORTADERIA SELLOANA

MISCANTHUS SINENSIS 'ZEBRINUS'

PENNISETUM ALOPECUROIDES

overall height 5 to 6 feet; yellow stripes across the leaves. Pinkish brown flower clusters. Zones 6-9.

Growing conditions. Plant these grasses in well-drained soil. They all grow best in full sun but will tolerate light shade. Cut clumps to within 2 to 6 inches of the ground before new spring growth appears.

Landscape uses. All of these grasses are good additions to the rear of a border, where they form a fine-textured green backdrop for the flowers of lower-growing perennials as well as providing late-season bloom and winter interest if left standing after frost. They can be grouped with contrasting coarse-leaved foliage plants or, in the case of the taller varieties, used as specimens or screens.

—

Pampas grass see *Cortaderia*

—

Pennisetum (pen-i-SEE-tum)

Graceful clumps of narrow, arching foliage and bristly flower clusters on long slender stems in summer and fall. Clumps turn tan in fall and can be left standing through winter. Zones 6-9.

Selected species and varieties. *P. alopecuroides,* Chinese pennisetum, fountain grass: overall height 3 to 4 feet. Small silvery rose flowers in cylindrical clusters up to 6 inches long, followed by seed heads that persist into winter if the clump is left standing. *P. caudatum,* white-flowering fountain grass: overall height 4 to 5 feet. Similar to Chinese pennisetum but flowers are white.

Growing conditions. Plant in well-drained soil in full sun. Cut to within 2 to 6 inches of the ground before new growth appears in spring.

Landscape uses. Use fountain grass as a dense, fine-textured backdrop for lower-growing perennials in a border or group it with plants with contrasting coarse-textured foliage. Fountain grass is especially effective in winter when it is planted in masses.

—

Reed grass see *Calamagrostis*
Zebra grass see *Miscanthus*

FURTHER READING

American Horticultural Society, *Fundamentals of Gardening.* Mount Vernon, Virginia: American Horticultural Society, 1982.

Bailey, Liberty Hyde, and Ethel Zoe Bailey, *Hortus Third: A Concise Dictionary of Plants Cultivated in the United States and Canada.* New York: Macmillan, 1976.

Better Homes and Gardens, Step-by-Step Successful Gardening. Des Moines: Meredith, 1987.

Better Homes and Gardens, Your Yard. Des Moines: Meredith, 1984.

Brookes, John, *The Garden Book.* New York: Crown, 1984.

Brookes, John, *The Small Garden.* New York: Macmillan, 1978.

Burke, Ken, ed., *All about Ground Covers.* San Francisco: Ortho Books/Chevron Chemical Company, 1982.

Bush-Brown, James, and Louise Bush-Brown, *America's Garden Book.* New York: Charles Scribner's Sons, 1980.

Calkins, Carroll, ed., *Illustrated Guide to Gardening.* Pleasantville, New York: Reader's Digest Association, 1978.

Carpenter, Philip L., Theodore D. Walker, Frederick O. Lanphear, *Plants in the Landscape.* San Francisco: W. H. Freeman, 1975.

Dietz, Marjorie J., ed., *10,000 Garden Questions: Answered by 20 Experts.* Garden City, New York: Doubleday, 1982.

Dirr, Michael, *Manual of Woody Landscape Plants.* Champaign, Illinois: Stipes Publishing, 1983.

Ferguson, Barbara, ed., *All about Trees.* San Francisco: Ortho Books/Chevron Chemical Company, 1982.

Ferguson, Barbara, eds., *Ortho's Complete Guide to Successful Gardening.* San Francisco: Ortho Books/Chevron Chemical Company, 1983.

Ferguson, Nicola, *Right Plant, Right Place.* New York: Summit Books, 1984.

Harper, Pamela, and Frederick McCourty, *Perennials.* Tucson, Arizona: HP Books, 1985.

Hill, Lewis, *Pruning Simplified.* Pownal, Vermont: Storey Communications, 1986.

The Hillier Colour Dictionary of Trees and Shrubs. London: David & Charles, 1984.

Hobhouse, Penelope, *Color in Your Garden.* Boston: Little, Brown, 1985.

Johnson, Hugh, *The Principles of Gardening.* London: Mitchell Beazley, 1979.

Loewer, Peter, *Gardens by Design.* Emmaus, Pennsylvania: Rodale, 1986.

MacCaskey, Michael, ed., *Complete Guide to Basic Gardening.* Tucson, Arizona, 1986.

Reader's Digest Editors, *Reader's Digest Practical Guide to Home Landscaping.* Pleasantville, New York: Reader's Digest Association, 1986.

Rose, Graham, *The Low Maintenance Garden.* New York: Viking, 1983.

Schenk, George, *The Complete Shade Gardener.* Boston: Houghton Mifflin, 1984.

Sinnes, A. Cort, *How to Select & Care for Shrubs & Hedges.* San Francisco: Ortho Books/Chevron Chemical Company, 1980.

Smith, Michael D., ed., *The Ortho Problem Solver.* San Francisco: Ortho Books/Chevron Chemical Company, 1984.

Strong, Roy, *Creating Small Gardens.* New York: Villard, 1987.

Sunset Editors, *Basic Gardening Illustrated.* Menlo Park, California: Lane Publishing, 1976.

Sunset Editors, *Bulbs for all Seasons.* Menlo Park, California: Lane Publishing, 1985.

Sunset Editors, *Garden Color: Annuals & Perennials.* Menlo Park, California: Lane Publishing, 1981.

Sunset Editors, *Landscaping Illustrated.* Menlo Park, California: Lane Publishing, 1984.

Taylor, Norman, *Taylor's Guide to Bulbs.* Boston: Houghton Mifflin, 1986.

Taylor, Norman, *Taylor's Guide to Ground Covers, Vines & Grasses.* Boston: Houghton Mifflin, 1987.

Taylor, Norman, *Taylor's Guide to Perennials.* Boston: Houghton Mifflin, 1986.

Taylor, Norman, *Taylor's Guide to Shrubs.* Boston: Houghton Mifflin, 1987.

Thomas, Graham Stuart, *The Art of Planting: The Planter's Handbook.* Boston: David R. Godine, 1984.

Weber, Nelva M., *How to Plan Your Own Home Landscape.* Indianapolis: Bobbs-Merrill, 1976.

Wilson, Charles L., *The Gardener's Hint Book.* Middle Village, New York: Jonathan David Publishers, 1978.

Wirth, Thomas, *The Victory Garden Landscape Guide.* Boston: Little, Brown, 1984.

Wyman, Donald, *Wyman's Gardening Encyclopedia.* New York: Macmillan, 1986.

PICTURE CREDITS

The sources for the illustrations in this book are listed below. Cover photograph by Larry Lefever/Grant Heilman Photography. Watercolor paintings by Nicholas Fasciano except pages 72, 73, 92, 93, 94, 95: Lorraine Moseley Epstein. 75: Sanford Kossin. Maps on pages 86, 87, 89, 91: digitized by Richard Furno, inked by John Drummond.

Frontispiece paintings listed by page number: 6: *Forsythia and Pear in Bloom* by Fairfield Porter, courtesy the National Museum of American Art, Smithsonian Institution; gift of the Woodward Foundation. 22: *Woman Seated in a Garden* by Frederick Carl Frieseke, courtesy Henry E. Huntington Library & Art Gallery. 46: *Flower Garden* by Emil Nolde, courtesy Thyssen—Bornemisza Collection, Lugano, Switzerland. 64: *Garden, Camp Highwall, Lake Placid, N.Y.* by Julian Levi, courtesy the Metropolitan Museum of Art, Bequest of Julian Clarence Levi, 1971 (1971.200.6). Photography by Bob Hansson.

Photographs in Chapters 1 through 4 from the following sources, listed by page number: 8: Pamela Harper. 10: Horticultural Photography, Corvallis, OR. 14, 16: Renée Comet. 18, 20: Horticultural Photography, Corvallis, OR. 24: Pamela Harper. 26: Michael Selig. 30: Renée Comet. 34: Horticultural Photography, Corvallis, OR. 40: John Shaw/Bruce Coleman Inc. 42: Laurie Black. 48: Ken Druse. 50: Margaret Bowditch. 52: Steven Still. 54: S. L. Craig Jr./Bruce Coleman Inc. 56: Rosalind Creasy. 58: Bob Grant. 62: Jerry Howard/Photo—Nats. 66: Nelson Groffman. 72: Hollen Johnson. 74: Joanne Pavia. 76: Michael Selig. 80: Hollen Johnson.

Photographs in the Dictionary of Plants by Pamela Harper, except where listed by page and numbered from top to bottom. Details in the dictionary designated as *A*. Page 98, 2, 2A: Horticultural Photography, Corvallis, OR. 99, 3: Horticultural Photography, Corvallis, OR. 100, 4, 4A: U.S. National Arboretum. 103, 17: Derek Fell, 17A: Al Bussewitz/Photo—Nats. 106, 1: Horticultural Photography, Corvallis, OR. 107, 1, 1A: Michael Dirr: 2, 2A: Steven Still, 3A: U.S. National Arboretum. 108, 2, 2A: Horticultural Photography, Corvallis, OR; 3, 3A: Harrison L. Flint: 4, 4A: Derek Fell. 109, 1, 1A: Horticultural Photography, Corvallis, OR; 2, 2A: William Aplin, 4, 4A: Horticultural Photography, Corvallis, OR. 110, 2: Horticultural Photography, Corvallis, OR; 2A: Eugene Memmler; 3, 3A: Horticultural Photography, Corvallis, OR. 111, 2, 2A: Paul Kingsley. 112, 2, 2A: 3, 3A: Renée Comet. 115, 1, 1A: Bob Grant; 4: U.S. National Arboretum. 116, 2, 2A: Al Bussewitz/Photo—Nats, 3, 3A: Paul Kingsley. 118, 2, 2A: Horticultural Photography, Corvallis, OR; 3: Renée Comet; 3A: Cole Burrell. 119, 1, 1A: Grant Heilman Photography. 120, 1, 1A: Grant Heilman Photography: 3: Derek Fell; 3A: Al Bussewitz/Photo—Nats. 121, 1, 1A: Paul Kingsley; 3, 3A: Michael Dirr. 122, 2, 2A: Bob Grant. 126, 4, 4A: Bob Grant. 127, 1, 1A: Bill Ross/Westlight. 128, 1, 1A: Horticultural Photography, Corvallis, OR; 2, 2A: Michael Dirr. 129, 1, 1A: Ann Reilly; 2, 2A: Eugene Memmler; 3: Horticultural Photography, Corvallis, OR. 130, 2: Steven Still; 3: Horticultural Photography, Corvallis, OR; 3A: Grant Heilman Photography. 131, 1: Michael Dirr; 3, 3A: William Allen Jr. 132, 3, 3A: Horticultural Photography, Corvallis, OR. 134, 1: Horticultural Photography, Corvallis OR. 135, 2, 2A: Steven Still. 136, 1: Barry L. Ruck/Grant Heilman Photography. 138, 2: Bill Thomas/Longwood Gardens; 3: Steven Still. 143, 2: Steven Still. 146, 1: Robert Lyons/Color Advantage. 147, 1: Steven Still. 150, 2: Paul Kingsley. 151, 1: Bob Grant.

ACKNOWLEDGMENTS

The index for this book was prepared by Lynne R. Hobbs. The editors also wish to thank: David Anderson, Park Seed Company, Greenwood, South Carolina; Marty Baldessari, Washington, D.C.; Jeff Burns, Robbinsdale Farm and Garden, Robbinsdale, Minnesota; Eugenia Dixon, Cheverly, Maryland; James Duke, U.S. Department of Agriculture, Beltsville, Maryland; Catriona Erler, Reston, Virginia; Mark Fasciano, East Norwich, New York; Paulette Fralick, California Redwood Association, Mill Valley, California; Betsy Frankel, Alexandria, Virginia; Karen Franklin, Alexandria, Virginia; Lloyd Greenberg, Studio Group, Washington, D.C.; Barbara Guarino, Lilypons Water Gardens, Lilypons, Maryland; Chris Tucker Haggerty, Alexandria, Virginia; Kenneth E. Hancock, Annandale, Virginia; Edward Hasselfkus, Department of Horticulture, University of Wisconsin, Madison, Wisconsin; Jerry Hill, Hill's Nursery and Camellia Gardens, Arlington, Virginia; Gary Island, I and E, Philo, California; Roland Jefferson, National Arboretum, Washington, D.C.; Keith Kersell, Pacific Lumber Company, Mill Valley, California; The Honorable and Mrs. Meldon Levine, Washington, D.C.; James McDonald, Alexandria, Virginia; Steven L. Mackler, The Landscape Group, Washington, D.C.; Dave Marselas, Rockville, Maryland; Bernie Mihm, Fine Earth Landscaping, Poolesville, Maryland; Annie Palson, National Wildlife Research Center, Austin, Virginia; Peter Rinek, EDAW, Inc., Alexandria, Virginia; Barbara Sause, Arlington, Virginia; Carol Schaffer, Hoboken, New Jersey; Henry Steffes, Washington, D.C.; Brooke Stoddard, Alexandria, Virginia; Scott Terrell, Annandale, Virginia; Mr. and Mrs. David Thomson, Alexandria, Virginia; Barbara Tufty, Washington, D.C.; Randy Werts, Potomac Fences, Rockville, Maryland; Rebecca Zastrow, Brookside Gardens, Wheaton, Maryland.

INDEX

Trees, characteristic shapes of, *11;* planting of, 10, *11-13. See also* Broad-leaved evergreen trees; Deciduous trees; Needle-leaved evergreen trees

Trenches, for double digging, *56-57;* for edgings, *58-61*

Trumpetcreeper. *See Campsis*

Tsuga, needle-leaved evergreen shrub, *137;* needle-leaved evergreen tree, *115*

Tulip tree. *See Liriodendron*

Tulips, *16, 17;* to deter animals, 93

Tupelo. *See Nyssa*

U

Ulmus, 108

Uplighting, *45*

V

Viburnum, broad-leaved evergreen shrub, *134-135;* cross-pollination of, 93; deciduous shrub, *124-*125; for fragrance garden, 94

Vines, 65, *137-141;* planting of, *72-73;* supports for, *73;* types of, 72

Virginia creeper. *See Parthenocissus*

Vitex, 125

W

Walkways, construction of, *14-15*

Water lily, for garden pools, 80, 83

Wattle. *See Acacia*

Weeping cherry, for winter gardens, 94

Weeping crabapple, *50*

Weigela, 125

Wildflower meadows, planting of, *40-41*

Willow, for polluted areas, 92; for winter gardens, 94. *See also Salix*

Willow oak, for polluted areas, 92

Windbreaks, *95*

Winter gardens, 94

Winter hazel. *See Corylopsis*

Winterberry. *See Ilex*

Wintersweet. *See Chimonanthus*

Wisteria, 141; for fragrance garden, 94

Witch hazel. *See Hamamelis*

Woodwaxen. *See Genista*

Y

Yaupon. *See Ilex*

Yellow corydalis, for planting in stone walls, 79

Yellowwood. *See Cladrastis*

Yew, 8; cross-pollination of, 93; for espaliers, 74; for polluted areas, 92. *See also Taxus*

Z

Zelkova, 108; for winter gardens, 94

Zinnia, *18;* to deter animals, 93

Zone map, *86-87*

159

THE CONSULTANTS

C. Colston Burrell is Curator of Plant Collections at the Minnesota Landscape Arboretum, part of the University of Minnesota, where he oversees the arboretum's collections and develops regional interest in the horticulture of the upper Midwest. He was formerly Curator of Native Plant Collections at the National Arboretum in Washington, D.C. He is the author of publications about ferns and wildflowers.

Sarah E. Broley is a landscape designer in Washington, D.C. She has redesigned the grounds for a number of public and private historic properties in Virginia and Kentucky. She has taught garden design at George Washington University.

Library of Congress Cataloging-in-Publication Data
Designing your garden.
   (The Time-Life gardener's guide)
   Bibliography: p.
   Includes index.
   1. Landscape gardening. 2. Gardens—Design.
I. Time-Life Books. II. Series.
SB473.D44 1988   712'.6   87-17989
ISBN 0-8094-6600-7
ISBN 0-8094-6601-5 (lsb)

Time-Life Books Inc. offers a wide range of fine recordings, including a *Rock 'n' Roll Era* series. For subscription information, call 1-800-621-7026, or write TIME-LIFE MUSIC, P.O. Box C-32068, Richmond, Virginia 23261-20680.